The Iliad of the Odd D.C.

The Experiences, Recollections, Rantings and

Epiphanies of an Everyday

Traumatic Brain Injury Survivor Victor

by

David Cole

Mother's House Publishing
Colorado Springs CO

"The Hammond Song" sung by the Roches, Maggie, Terre and Suze, at the Boulder Theatre in 1978 or 1979. Words on page 5. Used with permission

Published by
Mother's House Publishing
2814 East Woodmen Road
Colorado Springs, CO 80920
719-266-0437 / 800-266-0999
mothershouse@earthlink.net
www.mothershousepublishing.com

Cover design and interior layout by Jacqueline Haag
Printed and bound in Colorado Springs, CO

Made in the United States of America
ISBN 0-9797144-2-7

David's victory over traumatic brain injury (TBI) is a story that needs to be heard by every victim, every family of a victim, every neighbor of a victim, and every person that will ever come in contact with such a victim, because it will open their eyes to the quality and fullness of the victim's life rather than the things which put unyielding limits upon it.

David receives nearly 100% of profits from the sale of his book, a compassionate choice the publisher made to help assure that David can support his family by the proceeds. Know that each purchase is an affirmation of David's ability as survivor of TBI.

Karen E.

I met David Cole today – what a fascinating, interesting person with such a delightful sense of humor. Wow! I had to buy his book, am reading it (starting with the forward and the introduction :-)) and I have no doubt this will be the book I read in the morning and evening each day until I am done. So eloquent, humorous, thoughtful... a serendipitous meeting today . I will come back and comment further when I am done – but already I would recommend this book.

Holly

Thriving, not just living life - I TOO PLAN to read David's book after meeting him on the metro bus in Seattle this week... as he was returning to Vashon Island. He certainly had no problem with the memory of what good manners are as he offered to move from his bus seat to allow me to sit with my disabled husband. In so doing, we struck up a conversation where he shared something of himself and passed along his CARD and showed us a copy of his book... which he signed and handed to another passenger. We will read for our own understanding of this and the great human experience and a lack of bitterness allows the human spirit to thrive. Will be checking on borrowing or purchasing book since the author is so personal to this stranger on the bus.

Kathryn A

A fascinating and raw look into the mind of a traumatic brain injury.

Carl

This book is literally written by a person with a traumatic brain injury, recounting his own experiences in a manner that only someone who has experienced such a thing can do. The book sometimes wanders along with the author's beautiful but injured mind. Within the writing style itself are hints to the very nature of the injury and its effects on the brain, and the editor chose to keep it this way. This is a fascinating read for those wanting to understand traumatic brain injury – whether to understand a loved one who has such a condition, or the psychologist looking for deeper insights, or for folks like myself attempting to dig deeper into the nature of consciousness and what makes us who we are.

In my attempts to satisfy the dedicatory aspect of my previous 25 years... that's the last quarter of a century of my writing, researching, rewriting, rehabilitating, and just plain learning how to adjust to this new society in which I found myself thrust after my crash course in romancing the asphalt... I write this Dedication. By the grace of God I was kept alive that I might write this book.

Dedication

First: for my mom, Wendy Wharton. "Whoa, there, Nelly!" You've had more than your fair-share of me. That's right; you've had to sustain my "unique" personality (hah)... twice! Your stellar performance could almost be equated with your having raised 13 sons and daughters. You've even been able to withstand all of my tantrums, and each of my less seemly moments of behavior without so much as a Tommy gun or club.

Not really. No assault weaponry! What had required 18 years investment, initially, would become obliterated without anyone even blinking their eyes. You then managed my 2nd try, post humorously, in an abbreviated 2 years. THANKS!

#1-A: for my dad, Fred Cole, to whom I owe my life. I owe my masculinity, each of my physical, intellectual, and psychological strengths, in part my blue eyes, and also my appreciation for the fair sex! Thanks also for your wisdom, for your having had the ability to provide for the more fiscal aspects of my Odyssey!!

And for Barb Richards, for having been so stalwart. I hope I didn't give you any... warts. Your having kept a journal was good; it became a significant portion of my book. There'll be royalties, if anyone picks up a copy!

On to you, Gena R. Cole. You may not have been there while I was really, really down n out, but you showed up just in the nick-of-time. Thank you for guiding my prodigy to earth: our daughter, Aberdine Gena-C, our son, Malachi David... then finally our second daughter, Sariah Rose. You assist me while perched there in the director's chair. I do so love you! The kids are beautiful! You've sustained our family even while withstanding me in my crafting, the smithing, of my memoirs. You have done all of this in spite of your having sustained a Traumatic Brain Injury (TBI), as well as a Cerebral Vascular Accident (CVA, a stroke) before I even met you. Your having accomplished all that you have as Mrs. David Cole only serves to humble me further. Sure, I was there, but you, you did the really difficult stuff. I've had to struggle and work, once maybe twice, but you've labored… and done so thrice!

For Francis Ritts, "Aunt Francis!" I tear up at the thought of my book never seeing the light of day. If you hadn't appeared on the scene, this entire book, all my notes, would still be hastily stacked somewhere. I would never have found them until we moved again!

"Aunt Francis" served as Gena's PCP (personal care provider) 3 times a week during daylight hours for several years, and then on her own time and out of love, she would transcribe a quarter century of my notes into a single document, far into each corresponding night.

For Betsy Buck, for so much roast beef via Arby's® and so many rides to so much therapy. You get an entire chapter, so I'll stop here.

For Bryan Thompson, for all the cardiovascular conditioning, the 3:2 libations, and M&Ms® on the eastern summit of Flagstaff Mountain (by bicycle) for Fourth of July nocturnal festivities in the year 1977, 1978, and 1979. Gosh, were we ever stooopid! We could have been taken out, in the darkness, without anybody even realizing!

Ken Mann for being my high school locker partner junior and senior years and for having had a beautiful girlfriend named Becky Adams with whom I conversed daily in Ken's absence.

For Brandon, my closest in age brother. Thanks for so much selfless concern. I hope that your strength, your humble

ii

masculinity, and so much silliness will surface now that I have concluded with the assembly of my life's calling, my book. I also wish to thank your former wife, Jill, for such generous Canadian accommodations.

For JB, Jamie Bruce. I know where you are! Having a wife sort of makes you a dichotomy: more apparent as well as more a parent! My best to Melody and your children Oliver and Brianna.

For Spring. I wish the 3 of you hugely well! My best to your new husband and your daughter, Chelsea, who was so named long before the Clintons had even been inaugurated.

For Morgan. I'd always needed an older sister, but I'll settle for an eldest one. But it almost didn't happen. Until my mauling, our parents had only known each other as fellow Unitarian Universalist parishioners.

For Kendal. I love your haberdashery tact as well as your trait of always entering any room you go into voice first! I'll go malling with you whenever.

For my friends Barb Pinson (Lucas), and Margerate Pinson, and Brian and Becky Cabral (Lucas), Don, and Dan(ny) Lucas. I really want to extend an enormous handshake\hug of gratitude to all of you. Especially to you Pat Lucas- the Mom, for the financial sponsorship to start this project off! I'm really so very sorry it has required as long a time as it has for me to make good on your investment, but here it is! Also to the late Don Lucas, for your daughter, Barb, my girlfriend at the time of the accident. Each of you had been up to your eyelids in tears making sure I would never be termed a slacker. (Now that's up to my wife.)

For my Recovery Specialists. Mr. Brian Cabral, for all the muscular and neuromuscular assistance you saw fit to give me as you assisted Janice Tomita, Physical Therapy Specialist, and Emiko Hyashida as they taught me how to walk again. Barb (Meyers) Claus, Occupational Therapist, and Linda Rozek, Social Readjustment Specialist, and Carol Roth, Speech Pathologist. Dr. Scaer, Dr. Smith, Neurologists, and Dr.

Rebecca Hutchins, Optometrist, and Dr. Marci Rose, Opthoptist, and Linda, and Gus, secretaries for Dr. Scaer's Physical Rehabilitation Clinic under the auspices of Boulder Memorial Hospital, known now as the Mapleton Rehabilitation Center!

For Debbie, whom neither my wife nor I can remember the last name, for having chaperoned my courtship of Ms. Gena Choate while she resided at The Brighton House, Brighton Colorado, 1995.

For "Jimmy" Noland for having joined me on our bicycle-trip-of-a-life-time that very summer, 5-maybe 6 weeks prior to the accident, dubbed BT-80!

For Terry Shantz for having chaperoned the excursion, thus permitting the trip to have occurred, and for having kept pace for the portion of the trip you rode with us.

As crafted at the Circle 9 Wordsmithery

For the late David Bailey Wharton, my matriarchal grandfather, my namesake, my muse.

Foreword

Please allow me introduce you to David F. Cole, a 44 year old with a youthful vigor and a twinkle in his eye, a husband of 12 years to his wife Gena and the father of three bright and beautiful children, Aberdine, Malachi and Sariah.

David was just 18 years old and a brand new freshman at CU in his hometown of Boulder, CO, when an unthinkable accident happened. Nervous before his first exam scheduled in an engineering class the next day, but fully prepared, he decided to take a quick spin up Boulder Canyon on his bicycle to shake it off. David was an avid cyclist. After picking up an inexpensive pair of sunglasses he had left behind from a dinner shared a few weeks earlier at the home of a friend, he started down the hill, eager to make it to the food service on campus before it closed.

Things were looking pretty good for this handsome young honor student; college was just beginning to open horizons about which he had only dreamt. There were so many choices, so many opportunities! His classes were challenging and the campus atmosphere was intoxicating with friendships and excitement and the hormones of youth. David reminded himself that he only had a week left of the 30-day window before he needed to register with Selective Service; he would have to make a trip to the Post Office next week. Next month he was eager to vote for the first time. On October 2, 1980, David Cole was standing on the threshold of adulthood, filled with possibility and absolutely void of a sense of his own mortality.

He had just emerged from the twists and curves of the downhill Boulder Canyon route, speeding along on his Univega® road bike, head down, feet pedaling furiously to enjoy the thrill of ramping his speed beyond capacity by the addition of the downhill gravity. Along this straightaway, in the still warm, early evening setting of the fall sun bursting through the trees, a car slowed down to make a perpendicular turn into the Eben G. Fine Park, away from David's direction of travel. Behind the car making the turn was another car, a Volvo®, one with a driver who chose to deal with his impatience by hitting the accelerator and swerving to the left, around the car that was slowing down.

He did not see David speeding down the straightaway on his bicycle. He didn't see the handsome young honor student with a life full of promise; he didn't see the young man racing to the food service before it closed, squarely in his own lane of travel, harming no one.

He hit David head on. 1.4 tons of steel ramming head-on into a skinny-tire road bike with an aluminum frame that weighed 37 lbs. David was instantly propelled forward over the handlebars of his bike, his body rotating in a tight forward circle. When he slammed into the windshield, his left kidney took the brunt of the collision, instantly lacerating and bleeding profusely internally. After another hit by the roof of the car, his body was then thrown sideways to the hard packed gravel driveway of a residence, where he landed on his shoulder and head. In this instant of time, David Cole suffered such horrendous injuries that he could not be expected to survive. And the driver of the Volvo®, the one who did all the damage from a thoughtless moment of impatience, was only just beginning to realize that he had hit something. His mind was just beginning to comprehend what he had done.

The minutes that followed were drenched in grace. A Sherriff's deputy was in the park, witnessed the accident, and called for an ambulance on the car radio. An ambulance was 4 blocks away, on its way back, empty, from a call. The ambulance carried a brand new technology for victims of internal bleeding – an air-pressure suit. The community hospital was less than a mile away. These elements worked together to sustain David's life as he lay helpless on the hard packed gravel, his life's blood flooding inside his body, his brain already swelling from the trauma of the landing.

David was in a coma for 6 months in a total of two hospitals. His first test in his engineering class went untaken. He didn't make it to the Post Office to register with Selective

Service and he wasn't present to vote in the November election where the late president Ronald Regan was elected. He slept through the assassination of John Lennon on December 8. He couldn't be in the courthouse where the man who hit him with his car had his court date (though his father was). Halloween, Thanksgiving and Christmas passed that year without him; he was busy fighting for his life and for consciousness.

David didn't see the tears on the faces of his loved ones, his family, friends and girlfriend. David didn't see the anguish of his younger brother Brandon, who at sixteen was sitting cross-legged and with his face in his hands in the waiting room of the hospital, day after day. He didn't have to witness the shock on the faces of the other students at CU in Boulder, or the teachers and kids at Fairview High School from which he had graduated only four months earlier. He didn't see the reaction of his former band companions to the news or the reaction of his best buddy from across the street; he was busy fighting for his life and for consciousness.

David didn't get to see the lines of CU young people who rushed to the blood drive to make their contribution – to do anything they could to help one of their own who had been so badly injured. He didn't get to see his father's employer, through the actions of his manager at IBM, dismiss the co-pays needed to make the medical bills that were mounting higher and higher by the day. He didn't get to see the parents, relatives, friends and others who prayed for his recovery; he was busy fighting for his life and for consciousness.

Then one day in the new year, David began to awaken. His body had healed as best it could and the swelling in his brain had subsided. Slowly, slowly, slowly, he regained consciousness. But who was this new man? Where was the David Cole that had been slammed into a windshield and jammed on his head into the hard-packed gravel just six months ago?

Who David was before the accident wasn't coming back. The doctors, nurses, therapists and specialists did all they could, but medical science cannot fully fathom the workings of the mind, and to date there is no full restoration for the kind of injury David's brain sustained. To be sure, David entered into grueling therapy upon grueling therapy to try and recall or reinstate former skills and to resume his autonomy. He went back to school, first his old high school (where he quite miraculously remembered his old locker combination!) and then to college. But every path contained adjustments, revisions, and reworked goals, loss after loss after loss. In the glow of gratitude for his life, in the pride of each accomplishment of rehabilitation, a bitter reality had to be faced. David Cole, the young man on the magnificent brink of his manhood, the muscular and strong young man with a future in engineering and an unlimited optimism for life, the one who had bicycled over 200 miles down the West Coast the summer he graduated from high school, was not coming back.

But parts of David Cole were coming back. The friendly, funny, outgoing, upright young man with a twinkle in his eye and music in his heart was slowly coming back. His rehabilitation was a terrible teeter-totter ride. Angry outbursts were sprinkled throughout his days. He had to relearn certain boundaries of human behavior, to restore helpful inhibitions that permit us to interact healthily with one another. One moment the "new" David would be present, one moment a glimpse of the "old," but with the tragic and unspoken difference. It was a difficult route of constant attentiveness for those who loved him. David could handle math without effort before the injury; afterwards, he could not handle the basics of keeping track of his checkbook figures.

How high can he go with his rehabilitation? After all, he was only 18 at the time of the accident. The best answer for anyone experiencing a brain injury is "no one knows." At the time of this writing, David no longer takes specific therapies, although he does attend some of the conventions and programs for Traumatic Brain Injured (TBI) persons. In fact, at one such gathering he met the beautiful woman who was to become his wife, Gena, who had suffered a TBI in a car accident at 16 years of age and then a stroke five years later. The important thing to remember is that in this regard, a TBI person is no different from any person without a TBI. No one knows how far anyone can go – and to help remove any unnecessary obstacles to their success may be the best therapy ever.

This brings us back to the purpose for which this foreword has been written - introducing David Cole, the author. David toyed with the idea of writing his book from the very beginning, and indeed, he began journaling as soon as he was conscious after the accident. After twenty-five years post accident, he decided to get to work and put it all together. He created the **Circle 9 Wordsmithery** (as in the craftsman smithy, a worker of iron), put on his green workmen's apron, and wrote until he had a finished book. He wanted to answer the top two questions he is constantly asked: what was it like, and can you remember anything? With determination and purpose, David finished his book and he now offers it to you.

In order to read a book written by a person with a profound TBI, you will have to make some adjustments to your way of reading. For starters, from time to time, David gets his facts scrambled. You may notice that the story doesn't always sound the same, despite his best intentions. For example, he notes that he "totaled' the Volvo® that hit him. The reality is that he did considerable damage to the center of the windshield, but did not actually total the car. Digging deeper into his meaning, however, one can note that David is declaring his triumph over the car that damaged him so severely. In other words, the Volvo® didn't total him – he totaled (triumphed over) the Volvo®!

Another element of his writing to note that will make your reading experience better is to understand the nature of, and need for, repetition in David's brain. To see the benefit, it may help to imagine a cotton candy machine. After you start it up and the cotton candy gossamer begins to form on the inside of the tub, you take a long paper cone and begin to whisk it around and around. Each time you circumnavigate the tub, the cotton candy on the cone becomes pinker and thicker, fluffier and bigger. In a way, that is how David's brain functions for him post-TBI – he needs to think and speak or write over and over to capture all that his brain will reveal about a subject. Perhaps for you and me, the repetition is unnecessary, but for David, it is essential, and for the reader, immeasurably rewarding to uncover David's own unaltered communication.

You may legitimately ask why this publisher didn't simply edit his work to avoid the repetition and to "fix" his story. The answer is simple: David is seeking to answer the question, what was it like? You will be experiencing the answer first hand, and, as David says, at a savings of nearly a million 1980 dollars. That is what it cost to bring him through his TBI. In fact, David is fond of offering not just anybody, but every body still in possession of a head the opportunity to have a TBI, by proxy! Afterwards, he wryly states, you can go back to the way you were. Heck of a deal!

But of course, David cannot go back. And, I honestly believe he doesn't want to. He is very happy with his life overall, and the loss of the memory of who he was assists him in accepting the now of who he is. We at Mother's House Publishing adore him for his humor, his tact, his full-throated laughter, his enthusiasm, his love for his wife and children, his kindness, his honesty, his drive to accomplish his dream, and his skill with words. May you enjoy your sojourn into his world.

Jacqueline Haag
Publisher

Table of Contents

You may already know about
The *Iliad* and The *Odyssey*

by Homer
(*Iliad* means epic journey, narrative, spiritual
wandering)

Now you will know about
The Iliad of the Odd D.C.

by David Cole

Introduction

The content of this book is meant to be more than just a guide, a map. My own rehabilitation would have benefited enormously from my having had available a resource book such as this. My hope is that my message, my personal, experiential learning will be of benefit to you, or someone you know.

At the time of my own incarceration, it was true; I was entirely without a clue. I didn't even know what I didn't know. I intend on writing this book from the first person and to create a "trail map," a sort of guidebook depicting my unique methods for rehabilitating myself beyond the confines afforded by institutional rehabilitation.

I have met many traumatically brain injured persons, but no one who has exceeded a prognosis made by their own personal, conventional doctor. Why? Well, the new life, post trauma, has no baseline. There is no Dr. Spock who has written a book on the stages of life after having, for all intent and purposes, died. I want to help others, despite and in spite of, the throes of their living an impacted life.

I have put myself through the university system, carrying on with my life; however, I am still not well versed on Einstein's Theory of Relativity or the practice of neurosurgery. I have had to work the salt mines, the veritable smithies of this life, and maybe this is good. It may be good that I have seen over Pink Floyd's proverbial "Wall," and because I have been "down to Hammond*," maybe this is what I needed. It may also be a very good thing that I can appreciate the musical arts.

The hospitals with all their cutting edge technologies are hugely important. All the doctors and specialists are needed as well. Their bedside manners are probably quite smart. What they are missing is the first person classical

---

* "The Hammond Song" sung by the Roches, Maggie, Terre and Suze, at the Boulder Theatre in 1978 or 1979. Words on page 5. Used with permission.

1

learning, their empathy.

This is my story.

It is about me, yes, but not just a recreation of the horror, the bloody result of a head-on collision between a 3-ton vehicle and a 32-pound bicycle at the cumulative velocity I conservatively guesstimate had been between 95 and 100 m.p.h.

It is my story mostly as documented by myself, as well as gleaned from my journaling and the journaling of others.

My memory was compromised. In all actuality, what I had for dinner last night isn't that clear. I'm more than certain it was quite tasty, though. My wife, Gena-C, truly has the gift! There really isn't anything in my head to retain much of anything, except for locker combinations, phone numbers, and faces. I would put the remnants of my "grey matter" through a colander. This is what I've been able to retrieve. This book may twist and bend the way you look at, and otherwise deal with, the world in which we all live; like looking through a broken prism that's been glued back together again.... probably by all the King's horses and all the King's men. The actual purpose behind trying to create such a novel document, to create any more cat litterature,[*] is that I want to inform the entire world of the entirely unsanctioned series of nontraditional steps I'd taken in my rehabilitation, and to then examine where I've since taken my brain-injured body.

What I want to do is show people how life is with a traumatic brain injury, but then, for them, to be able to get up on the morrow still able to work, still able to speak, still able to tie their shoe laces, to love their children and to be able to love their husband, their wife.

I don't wish to cut anybody's vacation short, or to have them schedule a stepped up series of physical therapy exercises while visiting relatives. I don't want them to give up their

---

[*] Editor's note: this is an example of David's creative word composition; note litter as in kitty litter, and then enjoy the way your mind begins to understand his meaning.

education or whatever activity they are invested in. I don't want to injure the world; I'm just trying to "give" the world an education, to try to answer the big question – "What was it like?"

Clinically, I had not died. Physically, I don't think my heart ever stopped. Beginning soon after I was awake enough to actually write legibly, I'd been presented with a journal: a book of pretty much nothing, and a pen. I've thus kept journals, notebooks, and many other, less appealing forms of documentation: a blood and urine stained garment I'd worn while becoming comatose, a few pictures, mostly of old girl friends, my high school graduation celebratory excursion, a bike trip "down" the West coast, from Seattle, WA to Santa Barbara, CA.

Once discharged from the chronic care environment, the hospital, but not completely secure on my physical as well as metaphorical "own two feet," I returned to high school in order to stimulate the remnants of my grey matter to get it going again. Then I began to have strong thoughts of my going back to the university, back to the collegiate structure of education.

Who was there (at the college) to care that I could not walk? Who would care that my speech patterning sounded like I was drunk? Who would care that I could not drive? I was driven! (No, I wasn't a frequent customer of Yellow Cab®.)

1983, Fall Quarter, Winter Semester, and I'm back at it, plugging away! On my first try, I had room #109, and I was a strong, adventuresome, full of youthful exuberance and testosterone, "prime candidate as a date," student. On my second try, I am on the second floor. My room is down a long hall, around the corner, and just a couple rooms further. I am a weakened, jaded, older, disabled, still full of testosterone, "much less encouraging to future prospective dates," student.

Upon graduation, from the College of Therapeutic Recreation, I was very soon to discover the enormity of such an unforgiving society that we all live in. I would then discover that my services in my major were not in as great a demand as I had been led to believe; that my having volumes of experiential learning in the capacity as a patient was not as singularly sought after as I had been led to believe! I had so much empirical understanding to offer my clients, my patients. I hadn't realized that my experience would be as much a liability as a blessing. Would you want someone who had a severe stroke as the physician performing a brain procedure on you or your children? I know I sure wouldn't.

The Hammond Song

Words and music by Margaret Roche
Printed with permission

If you go down to Hammond, you'll never come back.
In my opinion you're on the wrong track
We'll always love you, but that's not the point.
Ooh. Ooh. If you go with that fella, forget about us.

As far as I'm concerned, that would be just throwing yourself
away, not even trying,
Come on, you're only in to me.
Ooh, ooh, Well, I went down to Hammond,
I did as I pleased.
I ain't the only one who got this disease.
Why don't you face the facts, you old upstart? We fall apart.

You'd be O.K. if you'd just stay in school.
Don't be a fool.
If your eyes have an answer, to this song of mine
They say we meet again on down the line.
Where is on down the line? How far away?
Tell me I'm O.K.
If you go down to Hammond, you'll never come back.

As far as I'm concerned, that would be just throwing yourself
away, not even trying,
Come on, you're only in to me.
Ooh, ooh, Well, I went down to Hammond,
I did as I pleased.
I ain't the only one who got this disease.
Why don't you face the facts, you old upstart? We fall apart.

The Major Events

Let me take you back. We're going to embark on this hiatus in late September, 1980.

Sometime in August, three, maybe four weeks previously, I had completed a bicycle tour of the Pacific coast from Vashon Island, Washington (in the Peugeot Sound, just off the pier from Seattle) to Santa Barbara, California.

I was a student, having enrolled as a civil engineering candidate, at the University of Colorado in Boulder. Before the 2nd of October, I had been very much like every other high school graduate-newly enrolled college freshman. I had my course for life all planned out. Surely, I knew what I wanted to accomplish with my life! I had already picked out a major; I even knew where I wanted to go to school: CU, Boulder, and yes, I was registered!

So much research, so many computer bubbles to be filled in with name, date of birth, and social security number. So many applications, so many possible schools, but I already knew where I was going to go! Would all of this monkey work conclude with my finally having been accepted to attend a most prestigious university, necessarily an institution offering my chosen major? My choice of schools, maybe just beautiful, maybe just a little more economical: a little less pricey, was in state, just across town even!

So, had all of this tedium reached a conclusion? Why yes, yes it had! Even the conclusion I'd been looking for! In another 4 years time I would graduate from CU as a civil engineer and go build bridges spanning both the physical and the more psychological, even metaphorical, spaces in civilized society!

Or, so I thought.

I'm more than certain that that's what a significantly large number of the other members of the 1980 CU, Boulder campus, freshmen student body, residing in Hallett Hall, were thinking. It's what we had all been seeking. I'm sure we'd all been even expecting life to lie down, prostrate before us. However, at the last moment my curriculum would take on a significantly more morbid luster! Not only would I no longer be expected to attend every lecture, participate in every recitation, even conduct each laboratory experiment; I was no longer expected over at Nancy's Restaurant by 6:30 a.m. Sunday, to make Eggs Benedict. (I made several dozen orders of Eggs Benedict each Sunday to hold down my position as the "Bene Chef!") I wasn't even expected to sit the Friday exam in expository writing.

I think that had been one of my classes.

I would now be expected to thread needles blindfolded, both hands tied behind my back, with only my tongue and cheek (tongue in cheek?). What must have been listed in the Fall-Term Course Offerings, as an afternoon seminar had become a crash course: section 009: Romancing the Asphalt by Bicycle 101.

Now, I would be challenged to resurrect my own allotment of humanity up off the asphalt and give it a really severe tweaking!

So, by the grace of God, I've survived and not only been allowed, but expected, to attend to the myriad of duties associated with my being thus "traumatically specialized!"

"Change for a Buck, Betsy?"

Betsy is one of my former neighbors off McSorely (Road) in Boulder, a friend who spanned the generations and who took me to doctor appointments and who frequently gave me a free lunch. I would like to thank her for her perseverance and friendship.

So Betsy, you co-conspirator, you! I've got such warm feelings about the eventual end result of the collaboration we've formulated this morning, the celebration of my birthday, the 31st, the beginning of my 32nd year aboard this spaceship, earth!

So let's begin with an outline: As a newly injured person, what do I need? What are my needs to help me as I come back?

What do I need? I need to regain my independence. I need to fight. I need to establish my own sense of individuality. I need my dignity. I need my pride. I am coming from a point zero, from rock bottom. I need confidence, the kind I have often seen spoken out by teenagers all over the world by their rebelling, by their seeming to defy other people's wishes. I need to regain a sense of trust, which is often spoken as a sense of love. I need to know that this world will offer a first, and a second, even a third chance, if need be. I think it was Ernest Hemmingway who said it best when he wrote so eloquently,

> The world breaks everyone and afterward many are strong in the broken places. But those that will not break it kills. It kills the very good and the very gentle and the very brave impartially. If you are none of these you can be sure it will kill you too but there will be no special hurry.[*]

---

[*]Ernest Hemingway, "A Farewell to Arms," 1929

9

There are so few who are curious in these times of striving for the bigger, larger slice of the pie. Even if you haven't had any stymied indoctrination, like I have, into the western American ideologies of that apple pie mentality, you've still got to struggle with this world, in this universe.

One of the issues surrounding my injury is the hugely thwarted capacity of initiating such a magnanimous project as this book. The norm following trauma is fear. You become frightened that there is so much out there that will get you if you are no longer able to protect yourself, creating the inspiration for such television documentaries as "911," "True stories," or "America's Most Wanted." Many persons are fascinated by the stories of people who can die from a traumatic experience; that can be so fun to observe. There's even the sense of wonder elicited when someone does not succumb to their injuries; however, afterward, society (generic) becomes closed to this new breed of people, these freaks, these people who become, through no fault of their own, disenfranchised from their own lives.

My own experience was that the people who knew me before the accident, for the most part, became better afterwards. In other words, they knew me before and they knew me after, and we remained friends. My accident was the pivoting point, allowing people to let go of their prejudices toward brain injury. I was a fulcrum for change within them, a fulcrum for adapting their own lives. My need to adapt became the stimulus for their adaptations. However, the larger community, the people who never knew me, don't always act like that. They are the ones who regard people like me as freaks.

We need this book to speak to persons who are not so fortunate, who, for convenience, are sequestered to the nursing home, the institution. I am talking about traumatized people... I am writing this book as a text for the Harvard-bound medical student. I am writing this book for the parents and caregivers of the 1st, the 2nd and 3rd grader at their local elementary school. I want to spread a sense of compassion and empathy; I want to become contagious with love.

I want to show the world that there is life beyond "death;" however, not as a means of encouraging death, but for those who've "died without dying," to show them there is still an enormous universe out there in which their soul needs to satisfy its need to learn, and to experience what it must.

I want to put an end to the need of so many souls, like myself, who are forced to go back and begin at point zero, before being able to learn what they need to have learned. Kids already are pre-programmed to achieve this, but then they become stultified; they lose their ability to learn what their soul had come to learn.

Psych professionals will need to read this book and understand empirically the experience of brain injury, from which they can draw more effective and affective conclusions. Psych professionals need my testimony to show people that they do actually have an ability to "get back to where they (sic) once belonged!"[*] No connection need be made with "all the King's men," of Humpty Dumpty fame, but to instead be an inspiration for people, all people, to wake up and smell the coffee! To get the benefits of my experience, they need to abandon their proclivity for playing the "patient," the "client," the "beggar-man," the "thief."

I am alive, and not entirely of my own accord! I had been chosen to land here on this earth in order that I might learn how to do something. For the longest time, I had no notion of what it was; however, I think I may now have an inkling of a clue. After your having imbibed of my text, you, too, could honestly proclaim that you have seen the other side of Pink Floyd's "Wall," and proudly proclaim that you've been down to the Roche's "Hammond," that you've been, traumatically brain injured - by proxy!

Car care professionals can find and piece together the bits and pieces of a broken carburetor, they can even replace a broken windshield and hammer out dents in the hood and on

---

[*] from the Beatles tune, written by Paul McCartney, "Get Back"

the roof of a car, but this book is not that kind of an owner's manual.

My mission to write this guidebook came either during the coma or as I was awakening. It came to me as a message, an internal message that my life was meant for more than canyon road kill. The mission of my life was to be a messenger, a carrier pigeon, a St. Bernard with a whiskey flask!

Like a Dream…NOT

I was in a wheel chair, surrounded by nurses and therapists and doctors. They had set my chair. I was in a wheel chair, on a hill, not with the brakes on but with the wheels parallel to the horizon. I assumed this was so that I wouldn't immediately roll down the hill the instant they let me out of their clutches. (A very appropriate method of instilling self-help skills?) Then everyone left. Leaving me there in that field, on that hill, they walked away and said, "Okay buddy, we've gotten you this far. The rest of the journey is up to you!" And now I am trying to eek-out as comfortable a route as possible to the end of this journey.

I was born on the 9th day of the 9th month. I weighed in at 9lbs. and 9 oz. It took me 9 years to complete my collegiate undergraduate education; however, I had to continue the process, despite, in spite of, having entertained a Volvo® face first. I was down, but I wasn't out. I had things to accomplish, and I'd be damned if I'd let anything as innocuous as being killed get in the way. I had begun my elementary education early, graduating from high school at age 17. I spent more than the usual 9 months in gestation. Instead, I spent 10 months so warm and snuggly. Having gotten beyond age 9, I did not expect to live beyond age 99. I have very little expectation of my living to become a centenarian!

The automobile, a.k.a. the car, was never intended to get around, to mobilate* without the auto, the self. Neither was a bicycle meant to operate without someone, a self, balancing on the rear wheel, right there behind the front wheel.

The medical profession is only here as mechanics; they haven't a clue how to process that spiritual piece of apparatus, the auto. Don't even hope to be able to look to these "professional Ps," these physicians, these psychiatrists, these psychologists, these psychoanalysts, *et.al.* to fix you after you've broken your "auto," or after someone else has thrown a

---

*Ed. note: created word

13

monkey's wrench into the gears making your life run. The mechanics of the "mobile" are extremely and easily damaged!

Do I make issue with the fact that my life was short-changed before it even began? Sometimes I like to think about all the great things that might have been, if only...

Had I missed something while I was primarily "dead?" While I was incommunicado with the world, had there been some major or even a minor slip in the historical continuum? So, is there anyone to whom I can turn? Who is there who can help me make amends with the degree of potential I'd been blessed with, the opportunity to have chanced? I think that maybe my wife and the children we have spawned. No, that's what fish do. Birthed, that's what people do... The children we have birthed! Who is there to assist me in making amends with the potential I had at my beckoning October 1st, 1980?

That brings me to the state of the globe, of the earth. What is it that fools us into thinking that we can cause the extinction of a species? Were we actually responsible for the demise of the carrier pigeon? Or were we maybe just the agents to have manifested their extinction? Instead of man's ever having seen about implementing any change in how we go about our existence, we just sit back reveling, reproducing and relying on someone else to see about implementing any, if there are any, changes. Instead, we have fallen back on that age-old process of procreation to foster propagation; and then, we grow old, and just like our fathers before us, we all die.

But do we really? With my story, not wanting to act as an ontological forum, I wish instead to inform everyone who has chosen to listen, a story about how I have superseded these processes.

When a man is born, he is birthed into this hugely beautiful world as a package, a package neither fully assembled, not entirely complete either. In the package, there are hints, potentials, and possibilities that we are capable of using. There are still all those classes that must be taken; there are still so many, many experiences yet to be had.

This might just be why we have put in place the institution we often refer to as childhood and why the CEOs of this institution, our parents, have been embodied as creatures so strange, so mystifying, that scream and cry as we might, we seem entirely unable to get rid of them. This might just be one of our greatest fortunes too.

In my speaking to you, I am assuming that by this time you've already been indoctrinated with the basics, those rudimentary abilities to develop a cognitively composite picture of what I am actually saying; however, that is also taking for granted the assumption that you are also able to see with Maslow's advanced level of cognition.

You see, I never got past first base! And I'm no longer willing to trust that anyone is on deck to come to bat behind me and help me to 2nd if I ever do make it on base. I've basically given up. You see, I've tried a couple times to succeed with this western mentality, but why? Why do I struggle? Why do I need to bother with having to struggle? I don't have to anymore! Now, I'm all alone in this world. I've no one to play ball with. Everyone turns their back and says, "That's all just silly kid's stuff." And I missed something. I was "dead" for a major shift in the historical continuum.

But would anything have been better? Would anything really have turned out more to my liking? And that is just another one of those questions best asked as a rhetorical question.

Dave's New Bike

My letter to the editor of the local paper, The Camera, after my bicycle was stolen while I lived on campus (the second time around).

Sunday Camera
February 27, 1983

Editor:

I wish to extend my extreme gratitude to both Barb Cole and Bob Gould, who responded to my dilemma when my Beach Cruiser was stolen. On Jan.27, I was in a hurry to get to my class at the University of Colorado, Boulder, and I was thinking I would have a nice refreshing ride.

I discovered where my bike had been locked, not a bicycle, but a lock with the shackles clipped and a chain lying destroyed. How can someone take, by force, a means of getting around on campus from someone whose gait is as slow as mine?

However, not two days after getting the tragedy publicized, I received separate calls, one from Bob Gould and another from Barb Cole (no relation of mine).

Bob was calling to express his concern and a truly empathetic desire of the Red Lacquer Room, a local body shop, to help make amends to my predicament. Bob offered, no strings attached, his services by purchasing another bike to take the place of my stolen one...and a huge lock.

Barb, in a truly commendable gesture, called relating to me that both her husband and she, also bike enthusiasts, were hurt to see a bicycle rider with no bike, like a runner with no legs. She spoke of her husband and herself and a visit they took in France. While over there they met a first-class bicycle racer, Jacque Boyer, who received many awards for his frequent victories racing, both at his home in France and in America. *Monsieur* Boyer, in a diplomatic gesture, bestowed upon Barb his bike racing jersey, which she in turn gave to me.

17

To the one who now owns my Beach Cruiser, I would like to extend my huge, "No thank you and please return the bike."

I now, thanks to these two extremely generous people, have in my possession a means of transportation about the campus at the University of Colorado, and an article of apparel no cyclist would have reason to trifle with!

It just goes to show how really nice people can be! Does it have to take the severity of such criminal behavior to expose the wealth of love and compassion of many?

Dave Cole
211 Hallett

Traumatic Brain Injury... by Proxy!

How would you like to save $999,980.20?

Back towards the beginning of my researching avenues to bring forth my book from the obscurity upon which it was founded, to a degree of clarity by which it could prove beneficial to persons reading it, I had whimsical visions of my being able to embroil my audience in the experience of having a closed head injury, otherwise known as being "Traumatically Brain Injured."

When first I was trying to write this book, I thought I could actually show people what it was like to have a Traumatic Brain Injury, the wholesale price as a subtle way of beginning their experience, and as indication that they had enrolled in the course for the long haul! (I also thought I could try and have insurance companies sponsor the purchase price of one million dollars).

Then I reconciled the state of the economy and the fact that I didn't want to exclude entire factions of humanity from their having the opportunity to read my book/ to have their own traumatic brain injury; therefore, the significantly adjusted price closer to $20. Now, I've only got my writing as a fallback in my trying to enable humanity to have a TBI without their needing insurance to offset the financial aspect of the injury.

The good fortune, which you may or may not have quite unwittingly, without any malice or forethought, just bestowed upon yourself, is probably not entirely evident at this point. The benefits are manifest either directly, there being activities, which I probably should not have been involved in, or conversely, there being programs I had not been involved in, which I probably should have investigated a little further.

One such program was wearing a helmet whenever I rode my bicycle, whether on campus or off. However, it was the late 70s and early 80s, 1980 to be precise. The nautilistic[*] design of the bicycle helmet had resembled that of a motorcycle helmet, which I declared "too hot, too bulky, it impedes my vision." For many of these very same reasons, I had never even owned one. Now I can only wish that maybe I had invested in one of those hot, clumsy, miserably distracting appliances.

Thursday, October 2nd, 1980, that's less than a month since I had been obligated to register for the draft...I hadn't yet obliged. That's when something else entered the picture. It was bigger than me, bigger than the draft! It might have even resembled an article in tomorrow's *Wall Street Journal*, but no one could see it or could have heard the impact of a young cyclist, head-on with an errant automobile, or read that he could now be reached in the Boulder Community Hospital's ICU.

Now that one's funny! This being less than 30 days since my becoming eligible to vote and legally obligated to register for the draft, and already I was a casualty. Without even being inducted... no draft, no boot camp, and already I was a "corpse." I could have used an honorable discharge, but no! None of this was on Uncle Sam's ticket. I had to foot the bill alone. Actually, my insurance had to, but I would have had to have it. Quite fortunately, my dad did!

Friday morning, October 3, 1980: Expository Writing 101, and there I am, missing the morning's exam. Darn, I may need to see what I should do about that one.

Let's go back a day, okay? It's a Thursday, I'm in my dormitory, the clock on the wall reads just about noon, and I am more than a little anxious about the next day's exam. The Hallett Hall communal telephone ring breaks through the institutional "silence." The call is for me; my hopes soar. Would it be my instructor calling to announce the cancellation of tomorrow's examination? Ha, I think not.

It's Gail Lurie. She called to ask if I wanted her to

---

[*]see Ed. note about created words

bring my "shades" with her when she came down to Boulder in the morning on her way to work. It seems I had left them at her house at the recent celebration of my 18th birthday. I hesitated; that would be easier, but I was sure my butt would enjoy the bicycle ride. "No, Gail, I'll try and pick them up later this afternoon."

Having never lived outside the United States, or Colorado, in Boulder since the age of 3, I was entirely unfamiliar with the Olde English ritual of jousting. It had not been among my more noble afternoon sports. Besides, jousting was not being offered that semester; it wasn't in the engineering curriculum, and I don't think I would have voluntarily chosen to duel with an opponent weighing easily 2700% as much as me.

I may have just been a freshman, still wet behind the ears, and plain ignorant; however, I doubt much I would have voluntarily chosen to wager my masculinity, my ability to play the piano, to ride a bicycle, or to love. My not being a gaming man, I don't think I would have risked my life, either. (The *Colorado Lottery* had not yet been instituted.)

The "suggested retail price" you've been asked to afford, the $19.80, besides 1980 being the beginning year of my Iliad, it is my attempt to immerse you in the experience without your actually having to go and put your ability to dance, to love and to be lovable right back on the line; to wager it all on the spin of life's bicycle-like roulette wheel, the roll of the dice. I hope that by my having done this, I've also done you even a small favor.

In this era of professionalism, with all the issues of liability and the need to find a specialist to pull all the thorns-of-life from all the pauses I've taken in my day, I sense that I have, quite unintentionally, become traumatically specialized. How about you?

As I glance back over my shoulder at this period in my life, the date 1980... so forth and so on, I often refer to this epoch as my "down-time" as if it's being nostalgically analogous to the holiday I'd only penciled in, the vacation I'd missed and should have taken prior to my embarking on the rest of my life.

If this was to be my big chance, my gilded introduction to the latter throes of the 20th century, why was there no map? Why hadn't I even been allowed to see and approve of the itinerary? I probably should have called my reservation in eons ago. Instead, I would be rushed to the emergency room – they always have a vacancy!

Maggie, Terre, and Suze Roche, better known as "The Roches" had been in my life, but only for musical entertainment. I was still a virgin. Following the percussive contact between me and my fate, I had begun to hear them with a new ear. Maybe they had heard of my injury while they were just passin' through… Boulder? Maybe they had borrowed on my inspiration for a couple of their yet to be written songs?

They saw the way to give a clean, artistic notoriety to the unkempt, notoriously deadening state of mind, which I had been experiencing, and for such a long time: six months comatose. My experience can best be related to the song entitled, "The Hammond Song." And yes, I have been "down to Hammond," and no, I will "never come back!"

Re-initiating me once again into the 20th century has not been without its own list of difficulties; however, I cannot say that my Heavenly Father had in any way seen it necessary to saddle me with more than anyone else has been expected to bear. The trials of steel, shatterproof glass and rubber tires, however, seem to have added a little zip and a whole lot more, to my otherwise scholastic life.

There I was, just trying to live life, my life, as an average 18-year-old Claude-on-the-street, which most assuredly, I must have been. Then, there was I, discovering the disparity between my having an 18 year old, hugely compromised, male body now at the mercy of a mind jumbled and stilted by what it had\had not already seen through my youthful experiences. I had no muscular control, but, in all humility, a moderately well accomplished physical appearance, necessary to appease an 18 year surfeit of raging, masculine hormones. My level of spasticity equaled that of hammering nails. Let me just say, very little of my new life existence seemed real encouraging. Besides, my personal, my more civil growth had been so hugely in sync with my already flagging social graces.

Society though, to keep me honest, had taken that "let the torpedoes be damned" type of attitude as they quickly flicked the remote to a better channel.

I still had the capacity to internalize the more subtle innuendos implied through the use of the word "inappropriate," although I lacked the physical ability to change any of my more aberrant behavior. I had been stuck screaming to be heard in a body without the control of even its nighttime bladder. I was still wetting my bed-sheets.

Speaking now, 25 years after the collision, and having learned the more clinical use of the word inappropriate, I can use it without any moral implication. All it means is that an activity or a motion needs to be conducted relative to the purpose or need, e.g. no silliness. You don't shower with your clothes on unless you're washing your hair with Tide™, Cheer ™, or Ultra™. My therapeutic studies have also identified a reality that a brain, the brain stem, and the human spinal column, the Autonomic Nervous System, do not function "appropriately" under duress: e.g., you don't hammer nails with only a clenched fist, and you won't become sunburned sunbathing under the illumination of the full moon.

I think I was stuck in some of Sigmund Freud's earlier stages of cognitive development. I began my post-mortem-mortal existence, once again, struggling at the oral stage of psychological growth. I was hungry. I was starving and not just for the metaphorical business of life. I ate everything in sight; I needed to chew, (an oral fixation). However, so entirely unlike your more bovine personalities, I had not been regurgitating my cud as food moved from stomach to stomach. Instead, I had been lining up a new set of calories in my only stomach. I had even begun to resemble that very same big fat cow.

Predictably, the next stage of cognitive development arrived: the anal stage. For me, it came on with a vengeance. All the complications extending from so much bruising on my brain stem, and a perforated colon, gave me an astronomical case of constipation.

All of the (hospital) staff, and all of the (hospital) dieticians couldn't put Humpty back together again, not even to go to the bathroom. The hospital in all of their noble efforts to remedy my situation did what every hospital is in place to do; they plied me with drugs *ad nauseum*. This eliminatory therapy, E. T., developed into a physiological dependency, which took 15 years to overcome.

This story is not meant to frighten people. I do not intend for my storytelling to scare people. I simply mean to identify some of the more personal, embarrassing tribulations as a way of engaging anyone new to the throes of an impacted life, and to tell them that someone has already been along the path, which they may now occupy, and to outline my hugely successful rebellion.

Besides my injury having been epitomized by the songs of the Roches, my revival had been predicted, if not glamorized, in the quote by Ernest Hemmingway on page 9. I wonder, am I indeed stronger about the broken place, e.g., my head? If so, and maybe even if not, are my messages meant to remain with me and continue no further, or will this map of my injury help others get over the pass of rehabilitation?

Life, though, is meant for the living! While there is always that extremely tender period when an injured person, the patient, commands so much freely given attention, there is also the time for the living to keep their own lives in order and to let a person die if necessary. This could be the time when an injured person's pre-mortal existence needs to be allowed to move on to other things.

Cover Letter: Part One[*]

This book was not the result of an inspiration, unless, of course, you consider my rehabilitation to be inspirational. Instead, I would consider my being able to pen these words a calling, just another darn good reason to be bothered writing about myself.

I want to offer others some security. I wish to alleviate many of the fears and insecurities that go along with another one of life's major transitions, analogous to going to college or giving yourself a hair cut with your eyes closed. I want to reach people who are new to the throes of an impacted life. I want to bring a sense of familiarity to those who are new to a life, which has been profoundly altered by injury. I want to show men and women, girls and boys that someone else has already been there. I want to show them that someone sees the futility of "ever coming back," and just maybe I have seen over Pink Floyd's' proverbial wall.

I want to give rehabilitation some of that grass-roots appeal. I want to provide a newly injured person with an alternative way of mastering all the softer, more emotional aspects, which accompany all of those very important physical, occupational, speech, psychological, and psychosocial therapies.

The technicians: the doctors, the neurosurgeons, the therapists, are all quite familiar with what it is they are supposed to be "practicing." What they are missing, however, is a level of empathy, and this is possibly good, too. I wouldn't want to be operated on by a physician who's been through my level of Traumatic Brain Injury.

I'm not fixated on talking to the technicians; my background is not in medicine! The technicians have already employed so much of the tried, tested, medically researched,

---

[*] Ed. Note: David writes a total of three Cover Letters to an unknown publisher. I allow all three so that the reader can evaluate for himself the increase in thought process by the author.

and scientifically validated methods of rehabilitation. However, most of them are without the touchy-feely contact; their bedside manners may be great, and this is hugely important too, but what they lack, or I hope they are lacking, is that first person experiential empathy.

My schooling, while in a helping field, wasn't as intensive as neurosurgery, but I have been there. I have been down in the coal (salt) mines, the veritable smithies of life. My observations with regard to the human condition may be *avant-garde*, veritably raw around the edges, and just a little too ripe; still they smack of this life. I hope my observations are able to help others with all of their personal, innovative attempts in mastering this satellite, earth.

Cover Letter: Part Two

This book is meant to be more than inspirational. It is meant to show people, brand-new to the throes of an impacted life, an alternative mode of thought. I want to give rehabilitation a grass-roots appeal. I want to show that others have been there/here, and that there are vastly alternative methods of mastering the softer, the more emotional aspects which accompany all those physical, occupational, speech, psychological, and psychosocial therapies. I want to share my alternative, *avant-garde* methods of rehabilitation, which has been enormously beneficial, an almost palpable succor for myself.

All those technicians: the doctors, the neurosurgeons, all the therapists, they are only allowed to utilize the tested and scientifically examined methods. Classical rehabilitation is necessary. I shudder imagining doctors with my degree of injury, attending to my health.

I have been there. I have been down in the salt mines, the veritable smithies of life. My observations with regard to this human condition: TBI, while maybe just a little ripe, *avant-garde*, and virtually raw around the edges, smack of this life. Even though each of these stories are indicative of my studies alone, I hope they will provide other "thu-rivors"- survivors with an innovative way to master this earth.

It seems I have been entrusted with this incredibly powerful, dynamic story so that I can include it among my gifts to the world. This story is more than a novel, more than fiction, and it has been wrought from entries in journals kept while I was comatose, and then by myself while I was deeply involved in my own recovery.

The calendar reads: Thursday, 10/02/80, and there I am, a newly enrolled freshman engineering candidate at the University of Colorado, Boulder; and so soon I was to experience my introduction to the latter throws of the 20th century and my life at the cumulative velocity of about 100

M.P.H. This is more than the mire of my injury. It is a story of process, an epic, a tale of how I've chosen to go on with my life, in spite of/despite a calamity of this magnitude. Nor am I so spiteful, either.

"I've got to go, 'cause they close the doors to the dinner line precisely at 7:00." These were, as best recalled, the final words, I, as the "idiot..." Dave Cole (I'd lost my "id") had spoken. I have since evolved; up from hard, blackened asphalt of that canyon boulevard, as an "odd D.C," my "id" having since been regained, is now fine and intact. I had figured that my life was about to deliver, that I had finally gotten that bull (life) by the b– (the horns). I think it was Ernest Hemingway who said, "This world breaks everyone while there are those who continue on stronger at the broken places."

Am I stronger about the broken place, e.g., my head? Have I may be seen over Pink Floyd's proverbial wall? Why yes, yes I have. Maybe I've already "been down to Hammond," and many thanks to the Roche sisters, I'll "never come back!" In the age of King Arthur and Camelot, knights would joust one another to establish supremacy. In the tournament before us today, the combatants had not only unintentionally taken the field of different armor; they had been aboard vastly differing steeds as well.

There I was wearing a pair a bicycle shorts, a t-shirt, and a leg-light. I do so hope my adversary had been wearing something. My mount: a white Univega® bicycle weighing just about 30 lbs without any touring gear and without books. My opponent's mount: a silver grey Volvo® automobile easily weighing in at 2,000 lbs with or without any books.

The politics had been quite severe as well. It had been the beginning of the tumultuous economic upheaval levied at the people of the United States by the soon-to-be-elected Ronald Reagan. And John Lennon was to be martyred. Four terms since the first edition of Reagan, we find our hero, David Cole, doing well: married, a BS, full of it, and now quite ready to share.

The content of this book is meant to be more than just a guide, a map. Even if my own rehabilitation would have benefited enormously from my having had available a resource book such as this, I hope that my message, my personal, experiential learning has not yet lost its credibility.

At the time of my own incarceration, it was true. I was entirely without a clue. I didn't even know what I didn't know. I intend to write this book from the first person to create a "trail map," a sort of guidebook depicting my unique if only *avant-garde* methods for rehabilitating myself beyond the confines afforded by institutional rehabilitation.

I have met many, but no one who has exceeded a prognosis made by their own, personal, and necessarily conventional doctors. Why? Well, my new life, post trauma had no baseline. There was no Dr. Spock who had written a book on the stages of life after having, for all intent and purposes, died. I want to help others live their lives despite and in spite of the throes of their living an impacted life.

I may have put myself through the university system, carrying on with my life; however, I am still not well versed on Einstein's Theory of Relativity or the practice of neurosurgery. But I have had to work the salt mines, the veritable smithies of this life, and maybe this is what I needed. It may also be a very good thing that I can appreciate the arts.

The hospitals with all their cutting edge technologies are hugely important. All the doctors and specialists are needed as well. Their bedside manners are probably quite smart. What they are missing is their first person, orienteered learning, and their empathy. This is very important too. I would probably blanch at the thought of someone with my degree of experience operating on me! My words may seem crude, veritably raw around the edges, maybe even a little too ripe. Still, they surely smack of this life! Don't you think?

My Own Bio: an Abstract

Born on the 9th day of the 9th month, in 1962, David Cole hadn't had a chance to really know about life, his life, until after he had died. He had never had an accurate feel for the pace of society until given the chance to experience, first hand, just how unforgiving his society really was.

Here is his bio, his abstract.

September 9, 1962: Wendy Cole gives birth. The child is named David Fredrick. He weighed in at 9 pounds 9 ounces.

High school graduation: 1980, GPA 3.65

College: enrolled as a civil engineering candidate at CU Boulder

First dormitory room: Hallett Hall 109 (his later, post mortem residency involved steps)

Roommate: Paul Harris, but he would spend the lion's share of his time with Kelsey Harvey and Eileen Powell, in their room

October 2, 1980: he "died"... was "killed" upon his encountering an automobile, head on! Dave Cole, for all intents and affective purposes, became "deceased." (He had the "id"[*] knocked out of him... some ego, and super-ego as well, and a whole lot of blood!)

1981: 5 or 6 months post mortem, and only a couple of months into the next year, Dave Cole emerged from his traumatically induced coma. Later that fall he was to go on a voyage with some schoolmates, Cathy Carefrae and Marylynn Davies, on their return to classes at the University of Peugeot Sound.

Friday, August 13, 1982: Dave Cole is finally able to reboard a "bi"cycle.

Fall 1982: he returns to the high school from which he

---

[*] from David as well as the psychological term, id

31

graduated two years earlier in order to jumpstart his cognitive abilities. He still cannot walk at all well, even with a cane.

Fall Quarter, 1983: UNC Greeley, under the tutelage of Psychology 101 Teaching Assistant Jerrie Chance; "Dave" rediscovers his "id."

1986: David rides in that year's Hardscrabble Century ride out of and back to Canyon City.

1987: David rides his bicycle over Loveland Pass… Actually, not 'over.' He just rode to the summit and then back down the same way he rode up. The car was parked on the shoulder of I-70, at the entrance to the Eisenhower tunnel, at the bottom of the Pass.

Spring 1989: Dav "id" successfully graduates with a BS as a Therapeutic Recreation Specialist.

1990: With the help of his mother, David buys and moves into his own town home in Louisville CO. He takes on co/editing of the Boulder Head Injured Group, the BHIG Newsletter, (where, quite sadly, the mailing list is getting bigger).

1994: Working as a counselor for the Easter Seals' Handicamp in Empire, CO. David meets Gena Choate.

June 12, 1995: David marries Gena ... she becomes "Gena-C" Cole. They move into David's town home. She, too, is living an impacted life.

1996: David and Gena-C relocate to Loveland, CO. David is hired as a dishwasher for sub-contractor Marriott at the Loveland campus of Hewlett Packard. He was a successful employee for 365+ days. Upon the discovery that there would be no chance of his ever moving upwards, downwards (he was already at the bottom), or laterally into a different type of employ, he subconsciously, or perhaps unconscionably, masterminds his dismissal. He is "terminated."

1997: following the Denver Broncos'®Super Bowl® win, he originates a Super Bowl® Pizza Hut® commercial. He is still yet to sell it to the Pepsico® Corporation,

May 15, 1998: May 15, Aberdine Gena-C is born. David names her and she is promptly nicknamed "Abby."

February 4, 2000: Malachi David is born. Gena-C names him and he is promptly nicknamed "Doc," after his initials.

2001: David and Gena-C decide to relocate closer to Gena-C's parents, and, more importantly, onto more land. They exchanged 1/6th of an acre in Loveland for 5.25 acres in Calhan, CO.

2003: David finally has the time and space to compile his manuscript, the title for which he composed in 1992 in Boulder while in conversation with Char Ann, "CAP'n" Porter.

April 19, 2006: Sariah Rose Cole is born, bringing the number of children in excess of the number of parents. Sariah spent her first month of life in the NICU.

2007: ***The Iliad of the Odd D.C. transitions*** from a dream into reality, and David's career is born.

Can You Hear Me Now?

I need to send out letters and e-missives. I need to establish a web site, and to otherwise advertise across the entire nation, the entire globe, searching for abstracts, essays, pictures, stories, and bios. All tales from the experiences of others. I need to get a feel for the different levels of ability reached after a person's visit DOWN TO HAMMOND. I need these manuscripts to be an indication of all the opportunities to see over PINK FLOYDS'S WALL. Not as a catharsis for myself, and not just as an affirmation to family and friends keeping vigil at all the hospital bedsides around the world, but as a tour guide – a map for everyone who reads this book or has it read/ shown to them.

I am not going to try and design a better toothbrush or reinvent the wheel, first hand. Then again, maybe I should. However, my wheel wouldn't travel up and down along all the avenues, the streets of pavement, concrete, or cobblestone, dirt, or bricks; nor will I need people to follow road signs for direction. Actually, there won't be any!

There isn't actually a single person who has been everywhere anyone-everyone has already been, or will be going. There are few road signs, fewer maps and probably no experienced Sherpas either... yet.

As a recreation specialist, I've always wanted to be a cruise director, a travel agent for those with TBI. I dreamed it was possible while it may have been only uninviting. I want to take them where they have never ever been able to go before; somewhere not included in their vacation itinerary. There will be little chance for calling ahead, and no need to make reservations.

I know it sounds pretty grim, but I want to give everyone a "TBI" a Traumatic Brain Injury, by proxy, and to manage all of this for them without needing massive doses of medical insurance, to impact upon the United States' Gross National Product, or the economy of other nations! There will hopefully be no need to take any time off from work. There'll be no need to miss their child's next birthday or to forget the last one! Or to forget when their spouse or their children were born, or even that they have a birthday.

If you'd like for me to say that this is a purpose, my purpose, my calling, then that is precisely what I'm doing. I'm calling: for abstracts, essays, pictures, stories, bios. I want my knowledge and understanding for who's out there to increase immeasurably. I don't want to continue without having a concrete feel for the many, widely divergent circumstances which accompany a person's entry and residency in this new society, one that is tangental to the more common, familiar society – the one which I, too, had once called home. I, too, was cloaked behind that blissful shroud of ignorance. That is to say, as of October1, 1980, I hadn't had any association with the members, the individuals collectively referred to as the Traumatically Brain Injured.

Then on October 2nd of that same year... wham! Some 6 months later, I would awake to an entirely different universe. I don't think I'd ever even applied to belong to such an exclusive, members-only society.

My being entrusted with the "gift-of-gab," and the ability to express myself was maybe one of my Heavenly Fathers' biggest goofs. I hope to succeed in applying my MO (my *modus operendi*)! I'd also like to put my university time to use, and as a recreation specialist, maybe now I will be recognized as the cruise director, or the travel agent. Maybe I'll finally be able to take people to that remote get-away, to visit that exclusive ranch, and then be able to return to the former, the unimpinged life. I would like to entreat people to a visit down to The Roches' "Hammond." I would like to give people that glimpse over Pink Floyd's' Wall. I'd like to find a use for so much cat litterature collecting in my head and piling up on my desk.

Surely, if all of this is beginning to sound pretty grim, then I've accomplished a small portion of what I intended to. This is my feeble attempt to "give" everyone a TBI: a

Traumatic Brain Injury; thereby, leaving them with a bold understanding of the gross need to educate the automobile population that without the presence of so many bicycles, the availability of petrol would significantly be challenged. However, it is also my intention to manage such an intrepid voyage without the reader missing their child's or their Mom's, their Dad's, their brother's, their sister's, their wife's, their husband's next birthday or to even forget that they, too, have a birthday!

In terms of my recovery, I had been counseled not to expect the miraculous. Much of the implication behind this has been not to expect any sort of return to a life similar to the one I had left there on the boulevard down from the canyon. I do not want to go on record that I even sympathize, much less support, such a pessimistic, though entirely safe, form of bedside manner of post mortem counsel. This applies to all physicians, nurses, therapists, the traumatized patient, and even their family.

Family is, after all, pretty much the only reason, the primary purpose for life on earth as we've come know it. I invite you to offer a logical disputation for this sociological argument!

Even though I cannot support the idea of establishing a false sense of security, or to set someone up for the major let-down of drawing only pictures of roses, it seems to me that if you don't aim for all the strengths you once enjoyed as well as those not even a part of your *repertoire*, there is no chance of reaching a level of health any further along than the one to which you've "awoken."

It may be more accurate to remember that I had only wished to manage a return to everything I had neatly tucked away in the normalcy that I had at my control on October 1st. My sense of grandeur, at that time, had been extremely miniscule. I could only see what the four walls, the ceiling and floor of my hospital room had within them. My room even had a window. I could gaze out at the beveled facial expanses of the Flatirons, four of which I had climbed, but they seemed so far away, so unattainable. It is true that, initially, I had only wished to return to the familiar confines of my own comfort zone; however, that had been while I was restrained by a posey! A posey is the strap that binds a patient into their wheelchair, presumably to prevent further injury.

When I finally moseyed around to documenting my story, I was told that I should write weight bearing information; I was also told that I need to stay focused on me. I was told that I needed to assure my readers that all is well at the helm. Well, all is not well at the helm- my helm, my head! I am getting pretty much done, all through this chaotic route, which I seem to have chosen to get through life.

Hello, glad to introduce myself. My name is David Cole. Get it right! That's David, not Dave, not Davie... or Davinial. Ihave found my 'id'. Someone taped it, along with the ego and the super-ego, to the back of the seat in front of me. That seat is the second seat in, third row from the bottom of the Mckee Lecture Hall at UNC, Greeley. "Hor(rors)ace Greeley," was someone "cheating" on his, on her exam? The classand the exam was my mid-term for Psyche 101. There must have been an examination. I just left the lecture hall; it was, after all, halfway through the quarter.

As a result of the accident, where I was the only person to receive physical injuries, I became an example. However, I would not encourage you to schedule this experience into your next weekend or vacation plans.

What I mean is life is not meant to be a torture, a struggle, nor is it in place to be a time of embarrassment. I am working from the idea that life is meant to be (at least when you are 18, the age I was at the time of my accident) a time to have fun, to be enjoyed, and to explore the universe. "Universe" defined as being everything, the gestalt of your existence. The accident changed the chapters in my own gestalt.

I was told that I should write weight-bearing information; I was told that I need to stay focused on me and

38

my experience. Then I was told I need to assure my readers that all is well at the helm. Well, all is not well at the helm!

Should I write historical fiction? Is that just another one of life's more effective oxymorons? Or does it apply to great writers everywhere, like Ernest Hemmingway or James Michener?

Hello, glad to meet you; my name is David Cole. Get it right! That's David; not Dave or Davie... or Davinial. I found my 'id'. Someone taped it to the back of the seat; second seat in, third row from the bottom at the Mckee LectureHall. The class, Psych 101, must have had an exam, it was, after all, finals week.

Anyway, this is a tangential outline of how I've been educated. Ooooh, and I must tell you that it's only been since I graduated. Soona gonna Cum Louda from UNC, that I've also become a Philanthropic Upthemallogist! I got my phd (post humeral diplodocus), or the last laugh. I don't want anyone to waste their time learning lessons the way I did, grinding through all the muck-n-mire that has limited me. I only wish to share my life's learning, so that someone else can take off from where I've left off. Who knows where I might be if I had a manual of this caliber.

The Great Fall!

Boy did I ever want to scream! Everyone is working so bleeding hard watching out for everyone else's back. It's really a shame that we spend so much time in the bathroom in the morning, washing our faces. Faces have really become obsolete; they are only as important as they are flawed.

Promises are only made to be broken! That's the only way you know how good they are in the first place. And because promises are no-good at that point, why does anyone bother to promise anything to anyone? Why?

The next time you find yourself in a predicament where you're looking for a promise, or a guarantee, don't bother with it. If it wasn't made with quality in the first place, what makes them think they can have it stand for more than it is by "guaranteeing it from failure?"

Do they guarantee a cut of the meat? Was it ever guaranteed that this life would get you what you've always wanted? Like there was ever something in this life that we had anything to do with its creation. Wake up and smell that proverbial cup of coffee! Get a grip! There is not a h– of a lot out there that is any different from what you expected in the first place!

Do I make an issue about the fact that my life was short-changed at the very beginning? Sometimes I like to think about all the great things that might have been, if...

There's not a whole hill of beans to fuss over, except I would like to choose if those beans are Arabica, or "coker?" I went to the university with the innocent intent of emerging from an academic institution so full of it that I would be lusted after by all the major conglomerate industries. Those were my intentions, and they were probably not too far off the mark, but I will never know.

You see, I never got past first base! And I'm no longer willing to trust that anyone is on deck to come to bat behind me to help me get to 2nd base. I've basically given up. You see,

I've tried a couple of times to succeed. But with this western mentality, why try?

I struggle. Why should I have to struggle? I don't have to, not anymore! Now, I'm all alone in this world. I have no one to play ball with. Everyone turns their back and says, "That's all just silly kid's stuff." I missed something. I was "dead" for a major shift in the historical continuum.

For example, I missed Lennon getting shot! I was entirely unable to make my selection for Carter or Reagan in the 1980 presidential election. I'm sorry! The burden of mistakes for all of society rests on my shoulders, but I can't help you with your finger pointing. I can't help you place any blame.

Who can I turn to now? Who is out there who can help me make amends with the degree of potential I was blessed with? With my opportunity? My chance?

Would anything be better? Would anything really have turned out more to my liking? These questions are best asked rhetorically.

This brings me to the state of the globe, of the earth. What is it that fools us into thinking that we can cause the extinction of a species?

So tell me, why are you here? Here is the quintessential question that has plagued the questioning mind ever since minds could question. Man has already subjected this query to the process of elimination, to the process of scientific examination and is still trying to verify all the discoveries he's already made over and over *ad nauseum*. Instead of implementing changes in how we go about our existence, we just sit back reveling, reproducing and relying on someone else to implement the changes, if any, which need to take place. Instead, we fall back into the age old process of propagation. Then we grow old, and just like our fathers before us, we all die.

But do we really? My story, not wanting to act as an ontological forum, wishes instead to enlighten everyone who has chosen to listen. My story is a story about how I have superseded these processes.

When a man is born, he is birthed into this hugely beautiful world as a package, a package that is neither fully assembled nor complete. There are still classes that must be taken, and many experiences still to be had. This might be why we have put in place the institution we often refer to as childhood, and why the CEOs of this institution have been embodied so strangely. So mystifying is the concept that scream and cry as we might, we seem unable to change the institution. And this is probably one of our greatest fortunes.

In speaking to you, I am assuming that by the time you've chosen to read such a boring manuscript, you have already been indoctrinated with the basics, those rudimentary abilities to be able to develop a cognitively composite picture of what I am actually saying. However, that is also taking for granted the assumption that you are also able to see with (Freud's-Maslow's) advanced level of cognition.

I do not mean to imply that only persons with a 6th grade level of education are susceptible to injury to the head. Only that it seems that before the age of 17 or 18, a person - albeit a young person - is so overly well protected, there is typically little importance for frightening, for exposing, a matter of life which can actually be even worse than death.

So, why do I even hope to somehow get beyond what anybody's been able to accomplish since the beginning of accomplishments? Why indeed!

To answer this question, you see, I've got these little cheat sheets taped to the back of the desk in front of me. I want only to help you get it, that this life does not come with anything that even remotely resembles a guarantee.

At this point in our history there are those seeking vast sums of financial wealth to give the illusion that they expect to survive well into infinity, while they still have tenancy in a finite set of carbon blocks. Maybe they think that by receiving such lucrative settlements, they might somehow "get even."

43

The one problem I can see with this statement is that there is never a justified, *bona fide* validation for getting even with another human being. This would entail some malicious intent by the accused human being. The entire issue, therefore, deserves to be seen by a criminal magistrate, not a civil lawyer. Just think title. The lawyer, being someone well versed in the different aspects of the law, eliminates, desecrates, the sanctity, and any unviable integrity their "profession" may have once held.

Do You Remember Anything?
What was It Like?

Dear Maximus, my name is David Cole. I've been given the chance of identifying, maybe even correcting, the errant driving behaviors of one Joe Lynn. At the time, I was a freshman Civil Engineering candidate.

I was also returning to the Nichol's Dining Hall at the University of Colorado, Boulder campus, on my bicycle. Joe was driving his Volvo® up the same canyon I was coming down.

When Joe rushed to pull around the slower moving vehicle in front of him, after presumably checking the road for any oncoming traffic, my bicycle and I were there to greet him... and his car.

For the remainder of 1980, and the first two or three months of 1981, I could be reached in the intensive care unit of the Boulder Community Hospital in a traumatically induced coma. I was later moved to the therapeutic ward of the Boulder Memorial Hospital. I was enrolled, post mortem, in a stepped up (?) regimen of Physical Therapy, Occupational Therapy, Speech and some Psychosocial counseling... "to build me back together again." Faster, stronger..? Nah, nothing of the sort. I was stapled back together again. I was slower and a heck of a lot weaker.

For the last 23-24 odd years, I've been attempting, albeit struggling, to write and publish a book. The book is a result of my journalings, my memoirs. It is a first person attempt to document the thrills of having a vast portion of youth erased or at least muddied, to illustrate my latent bounce-back abilities and society's acceptance. It shows people's willingness to embrace this new, horrifically ambulating "creature" back amongst the general populace, severely curtailed! Then to identify my being able to have gone into a university setting, graduate Soona Gonna Cum Louda, get married, become a father (the specifics will be left to the reader's imagination), and how it is to raise a child not only living your own Traumatically Specialized Life, and to do so on only one income. There's no "blood money."

My motives, my MO, part of my mission statement, is to shed some light on the frequently asked question, "Do you remember anything, what was it like?" The other question I am often asked is, "How was I able to return to the university, the collision having been on the eve of President Reagan's Americans with Disabilities Act? I have since discovered the speed of society exceeding my own ability to adjust to and accommodate.

I am trying to raise my family (of 4) on the annuity I was able to have an attorney set up with the monies I received as a cash settlement. For the last 9 years, I have been quite successful, too.

I tried to manage the funds, just as best I could; however, I've recently been able to identify the futility of the concept of "money management." There is not enough money to be managed.

My wife had also been receiving benefits due to her own disability. She lost her benefits when she married me. She's still disabled...I mean I'm good, but there has only been one redeemer, one Jesus Christ!

Currently, I'm seeking to have my wife's benefits reinstated, the backlog of her benefits reimbursed, and my book published. I may be a candidate for the "Ticket to Work and Self-Sufficiency" program, but first I want *The Iliad of the Odd D.C.* on bookstore shelves!

The book may be my own ticket to work, my own program for study. My target audience is not just anyone with a head, no, but more specifically, everyone with a head. It may also be the needed forum on which to base a web site, and\or a scientific journal. I'd like *The Iliad of the Odd D.C.* to be appropriate and worthy of a Library of Congress catalog number; however, I am entirely unfamiliar with the parameters for such an accomplishment.

If you want me to say, "This has purpose, this is my purpose, my calling," then that is precisely what I'm doing! I want my knowledge and collective understanding for this new society, and for what's out there in terms of Traumatic Brain Injury, to increase by an immeasurable degree. I also want my own understanding to increase

There was, of course, a time when I, too, was cloaked behind the blissful shroud of ignorance. Up through October 1 and most of October 2, 1980, I didn't have any association with members of this new society of individuals; individuals who are both shunned and pitied because of their medical categorization which is Traumatic Brain Injury!

Fall,1980. I was an honorary high school graduate, living both the life of a full time scholar and a bachelor! I had just recently concluded a tour of the West Coast by bicycle. I was beginning my introduction into society in quite the usual, the acceptable manner. I was enrolled as a freshman at a university, and an engineering candidate to boot. I was at the University of Colorado, Boulder campus. I had it made! There I was soaking up the myriad of possibilities, the ledgers of technical information, so much suntanned skin and Lycra.^{TM}

Then, wham, it hit me!

Some 6 months plus later, I would emerge from my traumatically induced coma to a new and very different world. This world, while not completely unfamiliar, belonged to an entirely unforgiving universe...with my being enlisted as a survivor. My name I still owned. I hadn't yet registered for military draft, and by now I could empathize with all those listed as wartime casualties. I don't think I ever filled out an application or even sought to belong to such an exclusive, "members-only" society.

Am I, bridging the chasm to\from infinity? While I'm here, I want to put my university tenure to some viable, constructive use. And as a recreation specialist, I want to be recognized as the cruise director or a travel agent. I want to treat people to a visit down to The Roches' "Hammond," quite possibly giving them a glimpse over Pink Floyd's "Wall." I want to find a use for all the cat litterature I've been collecting in my head and piling up on my desk for some 23-24 odd years.

Surely, if all of this is beginning to sound confusing, maybe even pretty grim, then I've accomplished much of what I've interpreted as the reason for my having lived; however, it is also my intention to manage such an intrepid voyage without everyone needing massive dosages of medical insurance. I don't want people to miss their child's, their mom's, their dad's, their wife's, their husband's, their brother's, their sister's next birthday or even to forget that they, too, have a birthday! I want to turn The Circle 9, my home, into a veritable repository.

To Get Right Back...For Life

Generally, to structure a book, and especially my book, around the premise of giving anyone who buys the book a head injury would be consistent with delinquency, a liability, or just plain curious. Surely, a perspective reader wouldn't rush right out and buy a copy of the book as a Christmas gift, in their spare time, or on their lunch break, would they?

I don't have any homicidal desire, or even the physical ability, to strike everyone in the world "about the head."

With this book, however, I might have a chance to impact everyone... with a head.

The year was 1980. What a year! It was my year, too. I had recently graduated from high school (not a big feat, no paws either), and the brother of my prom date and I rode our bicycles down the West Coast from Seattle, WA to Santa Barbara, CA (quite the feat, still no paws). On a less narcissistic, somewhat political scale, Ronald Reagan would become our president, and a couple months later, on a more global-nay, universal - scale, John Lennon would be assassinated. Surely, such a moment must have given most of my friends and family, all of society, a pause.

I was a 60s child. Shall I point out that everyone born before they grow up fits into such a notorious, curious category (of being a child)?

It was also getting dangerously close to the end of my 30-day grace period. Me? I still hadn't registered for the draft.

Then, before I would/could take advantage of all the benefits that I, as an American citizen, had at my fingertips, before I would have a chance to make my impression on the social fabric of the world, that is, before I took the opportunity to stretch my fiscal finger tips, I would become just another roadside casualty.

What I did was to identify, maybe even become, a statistic... I didn't die, but then this book doesn't focus

49

exclusively on my injury.

What I am trying to do is provide an alternative medium, a much different and less impacting way of enjoying a Traumatic Brain Injury (a TBI) without taking any time away from your family, or your place of employment. There is no need to schedule the TBI into your next vacation. No need to put your education and the training of paramedics and neurosurgeons to task.

I want to put my education as a therapeutic recreation specialist to use. Graduate from the ICU, move through the chronic therapy schedules, and then get right back at it!

I wantto identify an aspect of rehabilitation, which is quite readily available in the ER, though far too often overlooked beyond the ER.

Mission Statement

It is my dream to witness the eradication of Traumatic Brain Injury (TBI) here in the Western hemisphere, the Eastern hemisphere... in the Northern and Southern hemispheres, too. I am seeking to eliminate the generic (while not necessarily the geriatric) head injury and not just for anyone, more specifically for everyone who still has a head!

If you would like to hear me say, "This has a purpose," my calling, that then is precisely what I am seeking to accomplish. I'll be calling for: abstracts, essays, stories, pictures, bios. I want everyone with a head to "sit this exam!" I want my knowledge and collective understanding of, for and with this new society to benefit enormously from my intimate association; and then to discover what all is out there in terms of Traumatic Brain Injury. I want this knowledge to increase by and to an immeasurable degree, to a veritable Avogadro's number, and for me to be the conduit, able to share so much knowledge!

There was, of course, the time when I, too, had enjoyed this life entirely cloaked behind that blissful shroud of ignorance. That is, up through October 1st and much of the 2nd, 1980, I hadn't had any association with members of this new society... who without any prejudgment or bias are both shunned and pitied; their medical categorization: Traumatically Brain Injured!

Fall, 1980 an honorary graduate from Fairview High School living both the life of a full time scholar and bachelor, my having only recently concluded my tour of the Pacific coast by bicycle. I could now be found across town enrolled as a freshmen civil engineering candidate at the University of Colorado, Boulder. I had it made! There I was, soaking up the myriad of possibilities, the ledgers of so much technical information, so much suntanned skin and Lycra.

Then, wham, something hit me!

It would be some 5-6 months, give or take, before I

51

would "wake up," my having sustained a traumatically induced coma. The new reality I found myself confronted with wasn't completely unfamiliar; however, it had belonged to an entirely unforgiving universe, and now I was enrolled as a survivor. My name, David Cole, I still owned. I hadn't yet registered for the military draft. My dormitory roommate, Paul Harris, had financed his tuition by registering ROTC, and by now, I could empathize with all those listed as wartime casualties. I hadn't even filled out an application or sought to belong to such a "members only" society.

Am I maybe bridging the chasm between here and infinity? Anyhoo, while here, I'd like to put my university tenure to some viable, constructive use, and as a recreation specialist, I would enjoy being both the travel agent or recognized as the cruise director.

I would like to entreat people with their visit down to The Roches "Hammond," quite possibly giving them a glimpse over Pink Floyd's "Wall." I'd also like to find a way of utilizing all the kitty litterature which I've had collecting on my desk and muddying my brain now for the last 23-4 odd years.

If all this is seeming awfully confusing to you, maybe even grim, I've then accomplished much of what I've interpreted as the reason for my having lived! It is my intention to manage such an intrepid voyage for everyone without their needing to have a massive dosage of catastrophic medical insurance. I don't want my readers to miss their mom's, dad's, wife's, husband's, sister's, or brother's next birthday, or even to forget that they, too, in fact have a birthday. I want to witness the Circle 9, my home, becoming a veritable repository for this book...

Dear Editor

Dear Universe and Editor,

I grew up in Boulder; I became educated, at least began my collegiate career in Boulder, and I died there in Boulder.

Maybe died is too strong a word. I was subject to a Traumatic Brain Injury down there on Arapahoe. I've since relocated to 6,500 feet.

Without guidance, I'm directionless. Without a mentor, I am at a standstill. I don't know what style, what language, what format I need to prepare and/or address the manuscript to fit.

I am ready. It is my 2004 Resolution! Not that it hasn't always been my resolve, I just want 2004 to see *The Iliad of the Odd D.C.* on bookstore shelves, on coffee tables, in the library, stuck in the web, headlining *The Boulder Sunday Camera*...and many other similar periodicals all across the state, across the nation, all over the world!

Because Traumatic Brain Injury isn't exclusive to the United States, but endemic to humanity, I would seriously like to work with translators from Germany, France, Czechoslovakia, the former USSR, Mexico, Spain, Switzerland, Austria, Italy...anywhere where there are people... with a head...

In order to be counted, you've got to have a head. I think this is called a "head count!" I want to go overseas as an ambassador, almost as an ambassador in search of a country, in search of survivors in each of the different governing states. I want to encourage these people to represent themselves, their country, to document, collect, and compile similar manuscripts, to spiritually, intellectually, maybe even financially embolden this new society, this army of Traumatically Specialized Persons!

Your comrade about the head, David Cole.

If there is another person who has survived or has

witnessed a life completed by having survived a TBI, please, please speak up. It is you who I'm trying to reach!

I am not seeking a conversation with all the Headless Horsemen, the Rip Van Winkles of the world, because they still exist primarily in myth. I am seeking to compile a document that will answer questions and provide information for all the patients who find themselves in reality struggling to make sense of what has happened to them.

Because they are already witnessing the basis of this book, I have written the book for everyone on the sidelines, too... For everyone waiting at hospital bedsides, and maybe as my answer to the oft asked, "What was it like, do you remember anything?"

I don't really have recollection about those 6 months I was pretty much unconscious. Maybe I should be glad that I was "dead" to the world? After all it relieved me of blame for either Ronald Reagan's being elected to our presidency, or for the resulting assassination of John Lennon. Any connection is metaphysical at best.

The Iliad of the Odd D.C., while of a timeless nature, is begging to be on bookstore shelves for Christmas 2004. My target audience is anyone with a head; however, I don't know if such a timeline is realistic.

Attention: Potential Publishing Agent

Dear PPA,

How many "auto" biographical queries do you receive annually? Each week? Every day? By the hour? How many have, in fact, been written by a car?

I don't lay claim to writing an autobiography, either...I wasn't the car!

However, ***The Iliad of the Odd D.C.***, while not entirely an autobiography, has been gleaned from the journalings completed while I was deep in the throes of rehabilitation. Rehabilitation, which I consider to have ended, finally, upon the birth of my daughter, Aberdine Gena-C, and my son, Malachi David! My rehabilitation has identified and may be even corrected the errant driving behaviors of just another "Joe" out there on the streets.

If you would actually like to "see" some of my initial entries, I'll have to trim the sketchpads so they'll fit into my fax machine. Either that or you'll need to pay a visit to The Circle 9, my home. I'm not mailing my entries anywhere. They are far too valuable! Besides, at this juncture, I'm far too poor to be able to Fed Ex® them, either, even though that is an option I'd be willing to investigate! Not the only option, I'm sure.

That Oft Asked Question

This story, while not necessarily rife with inspiration, not unless you consider my route towards becoming rehabilitated, the story, and the legend of my having been stuck by an errant automobile head-on, to be inspirational.

That part was easy!

I am not seeking notoriety for having identified the folly of just another driver "Joe" out there on the streets. I am instead attempting to offer an outline on my methodology for my relearning how to walk, to use my innate dexterity, to be able to master my disarthria to a level at which I could be understood, all the while having to master the level of my own psychosis, so I could function in society.

That is how I was able to resurrect my own allotment of humanity. To pick myself up off the asphalt and get immediately out of the canyon and return to the bicycle, complete my university education, get married, make several attempts at employment, while raising the family I.... okay, "we" created.

These are words transcribed from all the journaling I was able to complete, as well as several of the stories used in my attempts to answer, and document, the prevailing question, "What was it like, do you remember anything?"

You may be tempted to call my being able to record these thoughts a calling. Or you might consider me, writing about myself, almost a narcissist.

Are you tempted to shelve this book among the novels? I actually haven't heard of another man or woman who has successfully conducted my level of research.

A pretty novel undertaking, don't you think?

Smithies of Life

The content of this book is meant to be more than just a guide, a map. My own rehabilitation would have benefitted enormously from having a resource book like this available. I hope that my message, my personal, experiential learning has not lost much, if any, of its credibility.

At the time of my own incarceration, it was true. I was entirely without a clue. I didn't even know that I didn't know. I intend to write this book from the first person and to create a "trail map," a sort of guidebook depicting my unique if only *avant-garde* methods for rehabilitating myself beyond the confines afforded by institutional rehabilitation. I have met many, but no one, who has exceeded a prognosis made by their own, personal, and necessarily allelopathic doctors. Why? Well, the new life, post trauma, has no baseline. There was no Dr. Spock. No one has written a book on the stages of life after having, for all intent and purposes, died. I want to help others despite and in spite of the throws of their living an impacted life.

I may have put myself through the university system, carrying on with my life: however, I am still not well versed on Einstein's Theory of Relativity, or the practice of neurosurgery. But I have had to work the salt mines, the veritable smithies of this life, and maybe this is good. It may be good that I have seen over Pink Floyd's proverbial "Wall," and because I have been "down to Hammond," maybe this is what I needed. It may also be a very good thing that I can appreciate the arts.

The hospitals with all their cutting edge technologies are hugely important. All the doctors and specialists are needed as well. Their bedside manners are probably quite smart. What they are missing is their first person oriented learning, their empathy. This is very important too. I would probably blanch at the thought of someone with my degree of experience operating on me!

My words may seem crude, veritably raw around the

edges, maybe even a little too ripe. Surely though, they smack of this life. Don't you think?

Me down there, I need to love that too! So, by injury I would heal myself. I was never more alive than when I was dead. There was more love, more support shown when I was "dead" than when I was "up" and "whole."

My moments of greatest healing would happen not in spite of a subsequent injury, but because of the injury. Second, my body would bleed and I knew that I was alive, and because my body would bleed, that particular spot on my leg-or hand-or arm was alive and needed to be loved.

A pretty pathetic way of learning to love all over I know, but isn't the means irrespective of the results, does not the end make the means? I didn't see but this was my indication, this was my cell. The perfection of the universe is embodied in such innocuous activities. My perfection was that I needed to die in order really to appreciate this life!

On Inventing Reality

I suppose I was really kind of "out-there" when I shared in the whimsical development of the title.

This book is going to be my reality fabricated. Not historical fiction, that department has been cornered by the likes of James A. Michener, who had a library named after him at the University of Northern Colorado - UNC, where I spent seven years after taking a 2 year hiatus. Hiatus, a sabbatical leave, a leave of absence, death and re-birth whatever you want to call it. I decided to take two years to reprogram all the "hardware," machinery, it had taken 18 years to accomplish the same task in my first life. O.K., I'll grant you the fact that my body had already been in the growing phase of human maturation. I hadn't needed to wait for Mother Nature to implement the different stages of bodily evolution. I hadn't needed to suffer through the usual phases, which accompany the pre-operational, operational, childhood, adolescence, and puberty phases.

Attention: Potential Publishing Agent

Dear PPA,

How many "auto" biographical queries do you receive annually, each week, every day, by the hour, which in fact, have been written by a car?

I don't lay claim to have written an autobiography either... I wasn't the car!

However, ***The Iliad of the Odd D.C***, while not entirely, has been gleaned from the journalings I completed while deep in the throes of rehabilitation, which I consider to have ended, finally upon the birth of my daughter, Aberdine Gena-C and, soon to follow, my son, Malachi David! I had identified, maybe even corrected, the errant driving behaviors of just another "Joe" out there on the streets.

If you would actually like to "see" some of my initial entries, I'll have to trim the sketchpad so they'll fit into my fax machine, either that, or you'll need to pay a visit to The Circle 9, my home. I'm not mailing them anywhere!

They are far too valuable! Besides, at this juncture, I'm far too poor to be able to Fed Ex® them either, even though that is an option I'd be willing to investigate! Not the only one, I'm sure.

This book is not necessarily rife with inspiration, not unless of course you consider my route towards rehabilitation to be inspirational. Instead, my being able to "pen" these few words is, I guess, a calling. Maybe just another "darn good reason" to be bothered writing about oneself, me!

I want to offer sanctity, to provide some sanity, or at least a sense of security. I want to alleviate so many of the fears, the insecurities which go along with another one of life's major transitions analogous maybe with going to college, or getting a hair cut with your eyes closed. I want to show people who are new to the throes of leading an impacted life, the opportunities which may lie in wait, and to those who are brand new to life profoundly altered by injury, their friends, and their families a sense of familiarity. I want to show men, women, girls, and boys, that there is someone else who has already been there. Not as a sacrifice of their own bravado, but maybe to introduce them to the veritable Lewis and Clark of traumatic Brain Injury. I want to be the one to take you down to The Roches' Hammond to see the utter futility of ever "coming back," or maybe the first person to have seen over Pink Floyds' proverbial Wall. That Humpty Dumpty is through masquerading as a simpleton egg, that he is ready for life as an omelet; he is ready to try on an Eggs Benedict hat! I want to give rehabilitation some of that grass-roots appeal. I want to point out the obvious and show that others have been here and to provide the newly injured with an alternative way of mastering all the softer, the more emotional aspects, which accompany all those, very important: physical, occupational, speech, psychological, and psychosocial therapies.

The technicians: the doctors, the neurosurgeons, all the therapists are quite familiar with what they are supposed to be "practicing," they all are in place just as they should be. What they are missing, however, is that certain level of empathy. This aspect is a very good one too. I wouldn't want to be operated on by a physician who's witnessed my own degree of Traumatic Brain Injury.

I'm not fixated on talking to them; my background is not medicine.

They have already employed so much of the tried, tested, medically researched, and scientifically validated methods of rehabilitation. However, most of them are still without a touchy-feely connection; they have no empirical contact with what they are doing.

MY schooling, while in the helping field, wasn't nearly as intensive as neurosurgery. I've been there. I've been down in the coalmines. I've had to work those veritable smithies of life. My observations in regards to this aspect of the human condition while maybe avant-garde, veritably raw around the edges, while maybe just a little too ripe; they are the real thing, they smack of this life!

All of this is indicative of my studies alone. Still, I hope they are able to help any great number of others each with their own, personal, innovative attempts in mastering this satellite, this planet, this earth.

Broken Brain Bric-a-Brac

If you'd like me to say that this is my calling? Then that is what I am doing, I'm calling for abstracts, essays, pictures, stories, bios. I need to get a feel of what's out there. I want to have a solid understanding of the widely differing circumstances of everyone who belongs to this new society of broken brains, a society into which I found myself thrust without intention October 2nd, 1980!

I want these abstracts, these essays, these pictures, stories, and bios to present a picture to me.

I'm trying to do more than establish a source of affirmation for the families, the friends, and all of the associates keeping vigil at the bedside. I need to get a feel for how everyone who is now speaking the language of broken brain is doing, a feel for how they're managing their lives. I need to understand how they are managing life in this hugely unforgiving society. I'm not writing this story as a catharsis for myself, but as a sort of tour guide. A map, if you like. I want to entreat everyone who reads *The Iliad of the Odd D.C.*, or has it read to them, with one man's understanding of what it is like to journey through a traumatically specialized life. To marry, establish and manage the lives of an entire family... So far only 4, but soon maybe more.

I'm not going to try and design a better toothbrush nor reinvent the wheel. Then again, maybe I should...nah! My wheel wouldn't travel up and down the avenues, the lanes already in place: of pavement, of concrete, or cobblestones, dirt, or bricks. I would encourage people not to follow the signage for direction. There won't be any! On this entirely new landscape, there are few road signs, fewer maps, and probably no experienced porters either.

As a recreation specialist, I've always wanted to be a cruise director, a travel agent, to be able to introduce people to new experiences. I've always wanted to show people places they've never seen before. I now want to take them where no one has ever been (except by reading the Bible or the Book of Mormon), somewhere not included in their annual vacation itinerary. There won't even be a chance to call ahead and make reservations.

I'm sure all of this is beginning to sound pretty sad, but what I want to do is give everyone a traumatic brain injury. I want to manage the experience for them without them having to take a sabbatical from their jobs, without their missing their child's next birthday, without forgetting the last one, or even forgetting their own birthday.

Viewing the Hospital as Church

I would go to church to have my ontological appreciations reinforced, and the hospital to have the base of all appreciations strengthened. Not entirely unlike being excommunicated from the Orthodox Church, it feels like abandonment when the hospital kicks you out the front door. In the hospital, all my meals were prepared and brought to my room. Outside the confines of the hospital, there was always the chance that lunch would be late, or dinner wouldn't arrive on the table until it was cold, even if I was able to prepare it.

A church is there to give a person their own personal guidance, spiritual guidance; the hospital was established as a sanctuary of good health.

The church was established as a bastion of thought, a veritable fortress of emotions. The university is also created in the same fashion as both the hospital and the church. At a hospital, a person is given all that they need in terms of their physical health: stomachaches are investigated to rule out possible hernias, ulcers, and disease of all sorts. In church a person must attend to their own spiritual-sic religious health; they have their own ministers, and clergy who pass out pacifying ointments and drugs, i.e.: the sacramental bread and the blessed wine or water.

The similarities are astoundingly in sync with one another. Robert Pirsig[*] had his church of reason and at the university, I've got my church of disability and the hospital.

Therapeutic activities can begin to seem a lot like they are out to get you. If it's not one thing, it's another. An explanation of this has its foundation among a banker's MO (*modus operandi*). That is to say, if you begin to get to comfortable, that's when entropy sets in. That is when life begins to seem just a little too cozy. You begin to settle back and accept what you're doing as correct. JUST

---

[*] Robert Pirsig wrote "Zen and the Art of Motorcycle Maintenance," William Morrow and Company, 1974.

REMEMBER... HERE'S ALWAYS SOMETHING. IF IT'S NOT ONE THING, IT'S ANOTHER. If it isn't a catch in your step, it's the weakness in your left hip. And if it's not your left hip, it's in your right hip!

Another fairy tale written as a way of explaining to young children an injury to older siblings is Gulliver: a person who stands remarkably taller as he progresses through his therapies

These days, there are so many attempts made to reach that mystical/mythical point of ultimate satisfaction, so many "wounded" people coming forth with all their humility saying that they can solve the pain and loneliness shared by humanity as a whole. They effortlessly proclaim that for the startling low price of $9.95 they will include your name on the list of those already assigned a number in heaven!

No, I don't really mean that! Surely, you already knew that. We search for the minister, the preacher, the reverend who in all of their humility can find that pathway for you, that gate through which lies the mythical land of pain free timelessness.

They are not our parents; they atone to no one. Heck, if that's what you're looking for, you can send all your money-not tax deductible, I'm sure, to me! Or you can minister to the needs of your neighbors. We are, after all, all ministers, every one of us.

This is not a book to offer to everyone, least of all to you, a thought, or recipe that will move you beyond where ever it is that you find yourself. Get a clue! If you listen to, atone to, practice and support anyone except yourself, and of course, your children, I really think you need more help than this book has to offer you.

Get out of your thoughts! Let go of your mind! We, as the insignificant human being, should all be satisfied with that which we are presented. We don't have the capability to master any more than what we've been given. I am convinced that this is a perfect world; there is little we are able to do that

70

affects the perpetual motion of the solar system. It seems quite presumptuous of man to boast that the carrier pigeon has become extinct through the wanton carelessness of his actions, or to get all up in arms over the depletion of the tropical rain forests.

Surely, I too consider it healthy to identify ourselves as the "agents" of destruction, as having "man"ifested the demise, even the extinction, of countless numbers of microscopic zooplankton saturating the ice flows, which lay "just off the coast of the South Pole."

Everyone with the traditional 6th grade level of education should know that the North Pole has no coastline.

As taken from the Talmud, "Jesus has given this story a new fullness by making his own broken body the way to health, to liberation and a new life." Thus, like Jesus, proclaiming to care for not only his own wounds, and the wounds of others, but to then make his wounded body, "into the vehicle through which others could also heal themselves."

I make no claim that I am the savior Jesus! My name has always been Dave or David; and since my having gone to the university and found my 'id', I no longer honor the name Dave with so much as a raised eyebrow!

This may be the last manifestation of my being broken, I don't know. It has brought on the next level of our wounded condition, e.g., loneliness.

The separation, the isolation, the alienation. Jesus too was so lonely. I know loneliness and I've learned to embrace loneliness. If not simply because of my intellectual wish to associate myself with this life alone, as a protective shield, entombing my body but very effectively allowing me to keep on keeping on.

After having lived through this loneliness now for just over 32 years, I've been able to wholly and entirely "get it" that this life is predominantly a lonesome process. The injury has allowed me to see beyond the limitations of intellectual processing and see what I've got to do with my life. My life

71

has shown me, in ways which I needed, that my life was not meant to be spent in the confines of an agency protected by that omniscient cloak of insurance. As a matter of fact, I do not stand the chance of ever being considered "insurable." It does not seem to matter that I am able to lift three times my body weight. I'm still not healthy enough to qualify for insurance. Sure, before sustaining the injury, I was involved with weight training, however, at the time I never even thought about one day being able to control over 600 pounds.

It seems to hinge upon man's illusionary loss of self and the individual ways in which we seek to answer this hunt for ourselves.

We're not really trying to find ourselves but trying to locate a new attachment. That is to discover a yin to set-off the yang, Lewis Carroll wrote of this hunt with the metaphor of a looking glass. From breath-one, everyone seeks to answer the question of death. We all seek that illusionary messiah, and until we find it, we bitch and complain. I have found it! I have seen over Pink Floyd's proverbial Wall. Intuitively my answer is that I haven't learned enough to evacuate this plan.

Or maybe, I haven't learned enough of the unique opportunity I've been so entrusted with. C'mon folks, I died. I know what's in store for you. Surely, you don't want to behave like Peter Rabbit and go through your life with your head stuck in the auspicious hole of ignorance!

The awareness of our loneliness could just be stimulus to escape, to break that proverbial sheet of ice existing between yourself and the rest of humanity! Don't just simply tolerate this life! For the soul, the spirit, the had flawlessly chosen this plan in order to learn something! If you don't learn it, so sad, you'll have to embark on this journey all over again... from point zero. This is not a pick up where you left off kind of a game. I get this from the image of myself while I was growing up. I grew up a "very old soul," and it wasn't until I died that I chose to embrace childhood for the wealth of lessons that childhood offers.

So, how do you see your injuries as having afforded you the opportunities to grow and heal yourself?

I must have walked poorly, for it took a broken toe to teach me that I had better begin picking up my foot. I must not have seen enough of everything, for I now see everything twice.

My thinking that I might even hope that my experiences, my words, might be of interest, might even be beneficial to another, did not come in a present wrapped for the Christmas ritual; and even as I now speak, my fear of rejection, that uniquely human trait of wishing to have an impact, is always in existence!

I don't want to behave as a hypocrite and say, "follow me!" Instead, I want to impress upon you the need to follow your own counsel, and also let you know that your path, though never before taken, has been mapped out from afar. I cannot offer empathy, for I've never been where your feet have walked. I don't want to show excessive sympathy and sound less than sincere and committed to my words. I want you to walk with pride; to say, "Hey, this life really isn't that traumatic." If I can stand before you today and wish you a happy birthday, or a very good-morning, or say "good-bye and have a safe drive," I know nothing else could ever feel so real!

And every time I cut my finger with a knife, I must acknowledge the pain and attend to the source of that Nile of escaping blood. As I do this, however, I must also recognize that the blood, as it flows, is an indication that I am actually alive.

By my academically indicating for you my path already traveled, I trust that the way is not too steep and the path is not overgrown. Although, how can I hope that you will follow me if I still occupy my steps, and I do!

This paradox takes me back to the Zen teaching: I cannot make a clap with only one hand! Nor can you follow me without you first watching me, or my telling you where to go.

10-27-93

Paradoxically, you cannot go anywhere if someone else is already there. So, even as untrained as I may be, I will minister to your needs. I will get out of the way. I don't want you to always have to reinvent the proverbial wheel, so I'll share just a little fodder, just a little encouragement. I will tell you where I've been, and cover the roads I have walked if only to speed up your process. I will do this to allow you to spend more time healing than exploring the innumerable possible routes to health. TRANSCRIPTIONS: Society has had to work hard to keep us down, down at Hammond. When people tell me that I act just like an animal, I don't know how to think or if I should think about it. Are they implying that they are so unable to fathom why I do what I do, am I so injured that they are unable to understand what it is that I am saying? Do they mean that my bathing habits resemble those of a feline, or like the arctic white Owl, bathing only when there are 9 months of food with which to survive? I almost think that I am too closely linked to the processes to be able to take that step back and take a subjective view of it. To be subjective, I've often been told, is just to foster your ego. I'm also far too healed from the issue to be objective, but if I can't be subjective, and I can't be objective, what kind of jective should I be?

I have moved beyond survival. I'm better fit for some other occupation, so I've taken on a sort of responsibility. I am responsible for people I don't even know by being so closely intertwined with the process that they are involved with. Now as a "survivor," better known as a "thu'rivor," I have to also shoulder the inexorable responsibility of "cluing society in!" I have been christened with the authority, although many of us are unable to articulate the specifics.

Does not the person who stumbles over the Arc of the Covenant become responsible for learning more about it? Does the first person to discover an alternate route up Mount Everest become responsible for making the route known to those in the world who want to know about the new route?

I do not mean to imply, or to advocate, that everyone needs to listen to me for a better way to injure their brain! I don't think you are on that level of understanding.

That's almost analogous to the need for children to stick their fingers into the candle's flame; I'm referring to the activity not the effect of the activity.

In the Rock Opera, **Tommy**, Roger Daltry sings, "IIIIIIIII'mmmm Free! Freedom comes with a responsibility!" It is we who are free. We've been to the heights of life. I know I've seen over that proverbial Wall. I'm satisfied for the time being that there is more to be learned while here on this planet, in this realm of the Universe. It is not I who should be pitied for having been down to Hammond! It is I who should be acknowledged for having been to see the other side of Pink Floyds' Wall; however, the secret is that Hammond is where you go and never return. Everyone is shackled with the great weight of ignorance, of naiveté!

Club-Med is how I grew to refer to Community and Memorial hospitals. My life is so perfect; I've been richly endowed! I grew up in the land of milk and honey. Even the fact that I had no form of major medical insurance is perfect because I am hugely displeased with the conventional methods of healing a person's wounds. I have no argument with the ICU programs, but beyond this, the hospitals are far too invested in maintaining their job security! By doing this, they create the forum for fostering co-dependency! The ill health this perpetuates begins to border on pathological-even libelous degrees of treatment. It gladdens my heart to see Hillary Rodham Clinton initiate the process for healing the hospital!

I think it was Ernest Hemmingway who said it best when he said, "This world breaks everyone and there are those who are able to go on even stronger (sic) the broken places." Man needs to learn to forgive the trespasses of others if they want to get on with their lives. I forgive, Joseph Lynn for his error in judgment, yet I cannot realistically give him any latitude when I review how profoundly he impacted my life in a financial way. He stuck the great claw, arm, in on my movement towards self-actualization!

I always wanted to stick up for the under-dog, to be altruistic, although I cannot hope to affect such a noble state of affairs if I don't already have reserves from which to draw. No man can!

Write an editorial. What you think about expands, so by encouraging everyone to focus the glut of their daily thoughts on violence - on "disempowering the violence," we are actually working to give violence more energy, more power.

This book, although touted as a self-help book, creates an oxymoron with the title self-help-book!

I encourage everyone to write their own story, and I'm more than certain that there is a much more exciting story in the minds of someone else. There are so many different aspects to such a multi-faceted issue; to write only one book covering it all would be to effectively write another Bible! You've got to do it, if not for a living, as a way of staying alive yourself.

It is somehow different, but what really is it? Do you not feel that there is enough room, that there is space for health, for a healthy relationship? OR do you instead only see my being injured as somehow having had an effect on my personality? Is there no room in your life to take a chance and meet someone new? Or are you so lazy that you don't want to invest the time to again learn about a new person? Have I become responsible for all aspects surrounding the redevelopment of a friendship? A relationship that now holds such great promise, our not having to muddle our way through the traumatic episodes involved with growing up. Do you want to not always hedge your conversation so as not to offend me or step on any unprotected toes? Is this not what occurs in every budding relationship? Am I a burden? If not a 200-pound physical burden, a 17 year emotional burden?

I now feel burdened as well. I now have to always educate you about the many and various aspects of my injury!

This is what enables me to empathize with elementary teachers when they hoot and holler for an increase in their salaries.

I am sorry, all my old friends, let us hold a funeral or memorial service to eulogize the death of a dear and much beloved school friend, David Cole! Maybe this way we can get on with our lives! Please, whatever you do don't spend too much time attaching an increased amount of personal involvement with having a chance to meet someone new. There is an equal amount of strife for both sides in this new meeting. In getting to know someone new, I am entirely unwilling to shoulder the greater burden! Just as with the beginning of any friendship, there needs to be a time of reckoning, of adjustment, of getting to know the other person. If you feel that you have already spent enough time getting to know me, I thank you for your honesty. Or if you are already over taxed in your efforts in your own life, I can understand! Don't waste your time! Don't waste my time either! Maybe you feel that somehow the accident was in some way my responsibility. If this is how it is for you, I appreciate the Zen in your thinking; however, I am unable to give you the latitude or longitude. I can just forgive you; it's okay! You should've come! I consider myself to be one of the greater friends in your life, so I am throwing a party, a memorial party. I want to eulogize a great boy. We don't get to go back to high school for this party; rather, we don't have to. Instead, this is to be a party full of lovers, a party to fill the night full of fun! I want a party full of good friends who think their lives are too filled to come. At this party there won't be a need for nametags; everyone should already know each other.

In my days, I had grown hugely. I learned how to put everything in its place, to compartmentalize my days; however, I had already reached a jumping off point. I was between my youth and the rest of my life; however, I was given a new playbook at the last moment and expected to execute every step of every play with faultless direction. I was also placed on the field of play for the full 60 minutes of regulation time. I was not even accorded the standard 3 time-outs per half, and there was no one, but no one waiting on the sidelines to run in and give me a breather. It always happens this way. If you're not given the full score to a play, you are still expected to exceed the demands. It's never, "you don't have 3 so I'll only charge you 2;" instead, it's "you don't have 3 so I'll charge you 3.5 or 4!" I was not only disallowed a chance to succeed, I was expected to make the big game-winning play besides. I'm not asking for much. I only want the chance to warm up first.

This book isn't meant to be difficult to read, nor is it meant to teach unlearnable lessons. It hasn't been intentionally put together so that only the learned professor of Anthropology can gain anything from reading it, neither is it meant to come off as a "good read." It is not to be confused with a coffee table book. If given an age appropriate rating similar to the movies, it might get a PG-13 rating for adult language. Parental Guidance, a PG rating, might be used if you are using it to read your children to sleep. If you are mature enough to ride your bicycle on streets where cars must also obey the double yellow in the middle of the road, you are old enough for this book to be a testimony you should hear.

It is a piece of reality. It may necessarily be my reality and it may be your reality as well. While it is an autobiography written by me, it isn't really an autobiography at all. I wasn't the car!

My assailant may even have had a personality like Herbie, the Love Bug™. That is to say, the car that knocked me for a loop and right out of the loop of my life might have meant something to its owner but it is no more. The insurance adjuster totaled it. They qualified it as rust fodder 23 odd years ago and it is probably metallic dust by now.

This is my story.

It is about me. Yes, but not just a recreation of the horrors, the bloody results of a head on collision between a 3 ton vehicle and a 32 pound bicycle at the cumulative velocity I conservatively guesstimate to have been between 65 and 70 M.P.H.

I was late for dinner at (Libby Hall) and had been

traveling downhill. The Volvo® had been passing a slower moving vehicle on a 45 M.P.H. highway. The road, the boulevard: Canyon Blvd. The canyon was Boulder Canyon.

It is mostly documented by myself, as well as gleaned from the journaling of others. MY memory has been compromised. It actually isn't! There just isn't anything there to retain anything, except for locker combinations, phone numbers, and faces. I put the remnants of my "grey matter" through a colander. This is what I was able to retrieve. It may twist and bend the way you look at and otherwise deal with the world in which we all live, like looking through a broken prism that has been glued back together again...probably by all the King's horses and all the King's men.

The actual purpose behind trying to create such a novel document, some more cat litterature, is that I want to provide the entire world with the entirely unsanctioned series of nontraditional steps I've taken in my rehabilitation and then examine where I've taken my brain-injured body.

Are you saying that you want everyone in the world to become injured?

Not exactly.

What I want to do is show people how life is with a traumatic brain injury, then to get up on the morrow (in the Morning) still able to work, able to speak, tie their shoe laces, to love their children and/ or their husband, their wife. I don't want to cut anybody's vacation short, or to have them schedule a stepped up series of physical therapy exercises around a visit to relatives, their education or whatever other activity they're invested in. I don't want to injure the world; I just want to try and clue the world's population in as to why a person might not be able to cross the street while their signal is still green (says "WALK"), or why it is they are having a difficult time understanding the checker at the grocery store.

It isn't that I want to level the field on which I play, or for everyone to have a traumatic brain injury. What good would that be? We need doctors; we need Taxi drivers. For me to structure my book with such a curious MO (*modus operandi*) might even be considered libelous, or delinquent. It might even readjust or otherwise erase and reconstruct your appreciation for a life after death. I don't want or need to have any more printers' ink flushed into the nation's water supply. However, I do want to immerse my readers in the experience of having all their neurons, their brain cells displaced.

I was a 60's child, or shall I say everyone born before they grow up fits into such a notorious, curious, noble categorization: a child. No, I wasn't birthed to a marijuana-induced mother.

I was delinquent though. I hadn't yet registered for the draft, my military service. My dormitory roommate was ROTC. I could never envision myself getting up so early just to run and do push-ups. Then, even before I was able to explore my American advantages, all the opportunities I had right there at my fingertips, to try my wings, or prior to my making an impression on the social fabric of the world, I was "killed."

Clinically, I had not died. Physically, I don't think my heart ever stopped beating. Legally, I had never had to... to stop paying taxes, nor had I received a reprieve from registering for the draft. My societal status, however, was changed forever! This may be where I was to feel the greatest pain just to exist through the challenges of living an impacted life!

Beginning soon after I was awake enough to actually write legibly, I was presented with a journal: a book of pretty much nothing.... and a pen. I've thus kept journals, notebooks, and many other, less appealing forms of documentation: a blood and urine stained garment I'd worn on my legs while comatose, a few pictures, mostly of old girl friends, and my high school graduation celebratory excursion: a bike trip "down," the West Coast, from Seattle, WA to Santa Barbara, CA.

1980

We find me having just graduated from Boulder's Fairview High School with a 3.65 G.P.A. and enrolled at the University of Colorado, Boulder as a civil engineering candidate. There I am, October 2nd, 1980, out on my bicycle getting some fresh air, clearing my head, and otherwise gearing up for the exam I am now thinking I must have had in the morning.

My social political atmosphere had just begun to form and otherwise have an affect on me. The year was 1980. I was born 18 years earlier. Politically, I was just coming into my own sense of power, and I could vote! Ronald Reagan was the Republican candidate running against the incumbent, Jimmy Carter. Mr. Reagan had previously been an actor, a great performer, who would begin his reign on the greatest nation in the western hemisphere... the world, just a month after David Cole was to have witnessed his own mortality, but this one wasn't my fault.

John Lennon, my idol, much of my life's' inspiration, would be assassinated some 2000 miles away. John Lennon was coming into position to affect great peace in the world. This was not my fault either. Each of these globally significant events took place entirely without my affect or my having any effect. My Mom had an absentee ballot there in the hospital room. I probably wouldn't have voted him (Reagan) into office. My political leanings certainly would not have ingratiated such a puppet to lead our nation. The Metaphysics of even speaking his name are not good!

Once discharged from the chronic care setting, the hospital, I was to go back to high school in order to stimulate the remnants of all those brain cells, to get them going again. I began to have strong thoughts of going back to the university, back to the collegiate structure of education.

Who was there to care that I could not walk? Who cares that my speech patterning sounded like I was drunk? Who cares that I could not drive? I was driven!

No, I wasn't a frequent customer of Yellow Cab®.

I was 18 years old, still a virgin. There were so many things I still hadn't tasted and wanted to experience!

1983

Fall Quarter. Winter semester, and I'm back at it, plugging away! Who cares if I could not walk? Who cares that my speech patterning sounded like I was drunk? On weekends, everyone strengthened and maintained society's structure and continued our quest, which was to further man's existence on the planet.

On my first try, I had room #109. I was strong, adventuresome, and full of youthful exuberance and testosterone, a prime candidate as a date. My second try was taken on the second floor. My room was down a long hall, around the corner and just a couple rooms further. I was weakened, jaded, older and disabled, still full of testosterone, only much less encouraging to future, prospective dates.

Does it make any sense to you?

By the following fall semester/quarter, the fall term, I was enrolled in Greeley; I continued my studies at the University of Northern Colorado, the alma mater of a great writer, James Michener, author of Centennial. Upon graduation, from the college of Therapeutic Recreation, I was only too soon to discover the enormity of an unforgiving society in which we all live.

1989

It's 9 years after my high school graduation, and I am all set to graduate with a Bachelor of Science degree as a Therapeutic Recreation Specialist. Some people just call it a BS. Or refer to it as a TRS.

Yet another significant milestone, with the #9 attached! All the other #9s: I was born on the 9th day of the 9th month weighing in at 9lbs and 9oz. There are 9 letters in the name David Cole... the list goes on!

Now was the time that I woke up. That I woke up and smelled that proverbial cup of coffee! It smelled a lot like what has been my elixir to get every morning off to a very good start!

I would then discover that my major, TRS, was not in as great a demand as I was led to believe. My experiential learning in such a capacity was not as singularly sought after as I was led to believe! I had so much empirical understanding to offer my clients, my patients. I did not realize that my experience was as much a liability as it was a blessing. Would you want someone who had a severe stroke as the physician performing a brain procedure on you or your children?

1995

Then, upon my meeting an extraordinarily beautiful woman while acting as counselor/maintenance technician at The Easter Seals Handicamp, now The Rocky Mountain Village, I chose to get married! Our marriage has opened innumerable doors towards the success I had envisioned clear back in 1980. I have only my wife's wit and spunk to thank for this!

1998

May 15, our first child, a girl, Aberdine Gena-C is born.

2000

By this time, my wife is expecting our second child. I am dawdling. The book has been written; the first copy, the rough draft is somewhere in our home. I am frantic; I can't find it.

I have a full time position working for Marriott. Again, I am shown that the level of forgiveness society has in place and scheduled for the benefit of everyone doesn't exist. After 380 aught days as the dish room engineer/a custodial character, I finally smell the coffee once again. No movement, up or down, in the hierarchy is evident! Entirely unconsciously, I must have "master-minded" my dismissal. I think it was referred to as, "terminated?"

It was as though I was killed, and we have our second child, a son Malachi David (Doc).

About this time, my wife begins to feel it might be appropriate to have some land, a yard on which to raise our children.

So, we head south to visit her family. While on this trip, we find Utopia, only it's here, in southern Colorado. The name of our Utopia... is Calhan! We found a spot of land, half an acre, our own little piece of utopia, on a street named Boulder. It lies only a couple of blocks immediately north of the school.

The character who sold us our Boulder street address had sold us a piece of land outside the city limits. There would be no city hook-ups, city services. We would have to drill our own well, even if we were able to find water on the property! So, we took what should have been our first step all along, we hired a realtor, Ensign Reality.

Now, we are about 5 miles out of town, but we're in such a prime location. The views?

Our kids love being somewhere where they can scream to their hearts' content. No one can hear them. Cats and cows don't really count.

Since 1990, when I moved out on my own, I always tried to have a soothing activity, a recreation, a garden. In Louisville, I had to get the okay from the homeowner's association. They allowed me only 28 square feet. I had to move all the gravel and rocks. In Loveland, it was hard to grow anything on 1/6th an acre. It was possible, just not real calming. Now I have 5.2 acres on which to grow stuff, two children and a book to be published. Calming?....Exhausting!

I don't want to encourage everyone to undertake raising children without first getting married; neither do I want to discourage anyone from having children. MY having chosen to join the Church, my having married a Latter Day Saint, may have given me the resources, the strength, I needed to undertake such a daunting life's' chore.

85

MY wife, Gena (pronounced like a gem, not the jeans you're wearing), is also quite remarkable. She experienced a CVA (a stroke) in 1991. The miracles she has brought into my life, Doc and Abby, are significant testimonies to the real staying power of the human body!

Interview/presentation

The person with whom this interview was conducted has asked me not to use her name; however, that was when the discussion took place. I've since lost contact with who it was. I apologize if this is no longer the way you wish to have your testimony handled!

"How many times have you had doctors who don't understand you?"

How about the people, who are the patient, who they don't even diagnose for having brain injury? And anybody can understand the problem, nobody can see, nobody can tell. Maybe you look okay, but there's the trouble. I'm not the only one; I'm sure there are lots-lots of others, and I just think that what my heart tells me, that everyday there may be thousands of other people that go on not being diagnosed for understanding, for having anything wrong with them.

Maybe they only bumped their head on the kitchen cupboard. And maybe something happened and they're different now; people say, "you must be crazy," or "you must be depressed, must be drunk, must be stoned, or doing drugs." And nobody understands, nobody can see, nobody can feel, nobody can say, "Wow, there must be something wrong, something must have happened here. There must be a difficulty; there must some problem with what's going on. And not one person is the same as another, everyone is an individual; everyone is special. No one's ever the same. But then I say to myself, umm if I have to experience all these tons and tons of things, how many more, many many more people are there having these same problems? And no one but no one can help. How about you, you're more sensitive now, right? When you are brain injured, you are more sensitive. You can see things in people's eyes, in their face, in their voice, even by how they act towards you, in their vibrations, in their total energy. You can tell how they treat you, can you not? I can. God blessed me a lot! I can see how they treat people. Sometimes they're smiling to your face, but they're really saying how can I get out of here? They are scared. They scare themselves a lot. You know what really scares them? That maybe someday, they might end up and be that way.

I used to call myself mud, when I hated myself. I've climbed many mountains. You go up up; up up up up to the lake, then I went to the place where my friend died and I spread her ashes, and I buried a rose and sang a song of peace for her. God gives you sometimes lessons in this life. Sometimes you don't want to, but still you've got to learn them. Nobody understands - truly understands - the inside of your heart, the inside of your being, of who you are, of what you are." "When you are disabled, people do not know. They cannot feel, cannot understand, what it is about you. What it is that is inside of you, inside of your heart, and your life. That is what I think the world has got to know, but most of all, the quite "big time medical people" who profess to be helpers of people who are injured need to know- the reality! And truth. It's taking on a big mountain?

I think I've got to do that, have to, ummm, teach them! Because I don't think they know; they only know parts; they don't know all. It's important to get out there and let those people know what we know. I'll bet there are a lot of people - lots, lots of people, who are walking around and nobody can understand what has happened to them, but nobody understands. They say, " Umm, something's wrong here," but do they bother to find out? They just slough it off, i.e.: You're drunk or stoned or depressed." And that's not fair - not at all. I've had enough mistreatment for all this stuff and I don't want it any more! You know what? You can even have seizures and doctors are just too stupid to even get it. Just one day at a time, to do good.

How Must I Begin?

Wednesday, 10-7, 1993: 10:15 PM.

After these last few great words of such hugely felt inspiration, what am I to do? Where shall I start? Here are my words, my attempt, if only a little inspired. I want to create a forum, to establish an avenue-a new route by which others can obtain an understanding of living a specialized life. I want to give a measure of comfort which I had never had available. I feel the responsibility for helping others get where they need and/or want to be.

It has taken me all of 16 years, and for the last 15, I've just been ambling along at quite an uncomfortable breakneck speed trying to find the strength, to find some encouragement. I've been trying to find a reason to speak up, but first I had to find a voice, the voice by which I could speak out of all the misery, the discouragement, the triumphs and exciting moments of discovery and encouragement. These were the moments I would discover my reasoning, my purpose for living my shattered life, to stay alive and make my life out to be more than a statistical memory, to be more than a corpse. I now want to impart the world with that inspiration, that ministration, that empathy that has been expressed to me in the preceding letter.

My injury was not so similar; however, I am confident that I have not tarried so long that this ageless message no longer applies. I was more fortunate though. I don't have epileptic moments. However, I too was counseled not to hope for too much recovery. My family was drawn a grim picture by the medical practitioners. I don't want to go on record as sympathizing with this style of coaching the bereaved. I am more of the mind to encourage with nothing short of positive, self-loving affirmations. It has been my experience that to speak in pessimistic tones only encourages failure.

We are at that point in our history when the individual needs to be realistic and feel a greater share of the control. The doctor is not a surrogate God. You've got the power people; don't relinquish all of it to these poor medical practitioners.

If you want, you could begin just as I had: by grasping and groping at anything and everything that even smacked of offering a chance at life. I spent all my time looking for that guru, the wizard. Merlin has always and will always exist in the minds of man. To find the Merlin in your life all you've got to do is go look in the mirror.

What I have found are the similarities between my own injury and child-hood fairy tales. Have these fairy tales always been there as the softer, less psychologically intrusive, more age appropriate way of entrusting children with the wisdom to watch out-to just say no?

Sixteen years ago, in 1980, I did not have the mind to really see anything. I had only heard the stories of trolls and witches and fairy godmothers as stories of trolls and witches and fairy godmothers. The stories I was aware of were lived in those old forests which have since decayed and been formed into books and stories. All these books and stories have found storage in the damp, musky smelling shelves of the public library.

Cover Letter

Even though this book could have been gleaned from the experiences of hundreds, even thousands of children, as lived, every day, every afternoon, every morning, or every night, I like to think this story is being put together first hand, from the school of hard knocks, the result from an untutored, experiential education, which lends credibility to the humor and much of its message.

While I was in the hospital, and then while trying to live in the unstructured confines of a very unforgiving society, I was at a complete loss. A couple months, a few years, the actual duration is really of no importance, I was scared. I wanted to know, and I'm more than certain others like me want to know, "Hey, what's happened/is happening to me?"

I was new to life in the hospital, and equally, if not more so importantly, the throes of an impacted life beyond incarceration. I was without a foundation; there was no baseline from which I could build my profoundly altered life. My having, "been down to Hammond" and maybe having seen over Pink Floyds' proverbial wall might very well have been more of the structure I needed. It's a very good thing I was appreciative of the musical arts.

I feel that rehabilitation needs to have some grass-roots appeal. All the restorative therapies need a contact, a referral. Unable to locate an authority on the subject, I have volunteered my life services. This is my life's calling. My credentials don't list medicine or physical therapy as being among my knowledge or background; therefore, I'll leave much of that to those more in authority. However, most of them are without the touchy-feely contact; their bedside manners may be great, and while this is hugely important, what's missing is that first person, experiential learning empathy.

While I have been through the university since my injury, I make no claim to understanding Einstein's Theory of Relativity, or the practice of neurosurgery; however, I have been there, and I am still down there in the salt mines, the veritable smithies of life. My observations with regard to the human condition while they may just be avant-garde and virtually raw around the edges, maybe a little too ripe; they smack of this life. With a little refining, they could be quite useful to this life!

More Bits and Pieces!

We (TBIed persons) have got to get together and get this message out. We have got to tell them; maybe it's simply the process of reminding them.

When I look at the newspaper, I am horrified. Surely, there's got to be much more going on in the world than the sensationalized docudramas played across the front pages of so many newspapers across the United States. Wake up people. Wake up and get the picture that life is happening! Find out you've made an investment and now you've got to participate; you've got to complete your own existence on earth.

This may be a hard one for you to get but I was never more alive in this society than for the 5 months that I was comatose! I've never yet been able to muster-up so much support. I've never had the opportunity to learn so much. I wasn't expected to successfully complete any test.

This message is for all TBIed persons. I was amazing. I never thought perfection was so close, so palatable, so tangible, or even so possible. I was "killed", but I wasn't left to die. The medical community saw the possible fast buck they could earn by saving me, and I'm glad they did; however, I am not so sure they really wanted to unleash such a maelstrom. This one, I feel, was probably the biggest mistake society has ever made. Sure the world wars were pretty bad but by having given me the opportunity to experience death and be able to live to tell about it, might be that when I was in school, it was a real struggle not to be "in the groove" with everyone else. It was more you must be uncool to be "cool" in circles I hung around in. My Mom and I have discussed my future plans.

The ER (emergency room) has been set up as a facade. An icon established in order to create and support the illusion that society actually gives a damn about the health and welfare of the general population. In the ER there are actually people who thought at one time that they would get out of medical school and move on to save people's lives. They may even

93

have felt that their presence was destined to create a better society. They are there to "save our lives," or is it in order that they can have fun killing us a little more methodically, in a manner a little less traumatically, more controlled?

"As I was walking, there were marching bands. I cried and cried without even stopping. That was December, so it was 2 what 3 months into your coma." Open the book with a marching band-the drummers-the "shuffle!"

I have the sense that the playing of the piano was just a primary activity, a way of establishing a sense of stick-to-it-tive-ness. That this was just another means, a way of getting me through life to reach the end! I don't know about you, but I love this life. I have very few things to point to with any kind of complaint. The end for which the means enabled me is where I am now, or where you are at this point. But because I don't stand a chance of knowing where that is, I cannot hope to address what it is that you are looking for!

As a newly injured TBI patient/survivor, or even after as many as ten years, I found myself beset with the basest of fears, the most primal personification of me. With all the baggage I unsuspectingly picked up in the course of my travels. It was only after studying for several years and experiencing life for several years more that I was able to really appreciate the ancient Biblical story of Cain and Abel, and then only after having heard it spoken of by Hermann Hesse in his book entitled *Damien*.

I related to the aspect in which the character, Cain, becomes so feared and therefore so powerful, simply because his forehead is marked a mark so intense, almost a scar. What I related to was that this Biblical scar is in fact corroborated with all the scars that result from injury.

I now am able to develop the new sense that what I had often taken to be anger towards my new appearances or towards the rate of my gate or my speech was in fact a simple case of the willies, or fear! And even more similar, a fear created by the mark on Cain's forehead! My new state, physical state, was somehow strangely emasculated. My current state of affairs had begun to appeal to me and was like the Chinese Yin-Yang philosophy. Through this, I was able to correlate my "down-time" with that ineffaceable period of cleaning house. Of pillaging the neural synapses (brain cells) of a greater number of their connections, enabling me to refill, reprogram, so many neural transistors.

Tradition, however, had experience on its side. The only experience I had was with playing the piano and riding a bike! The spasticity in my arms and in my fingers precluded my effortless return to the piano, and as a result of the complications, the Eustachian tubes, my balance and subsequent return to riding the bike was severely impractical. I also was a weight lifter, but this activity was hugely discouraged by my physical therapist.

I wasn't a quitter. I wasn't easily distracted from my search for the Holy Grail, and I didn't see much validity in the scientific school of prognosticating a man's rehabilitation. Just maybe the reason doctors give the worst-case scenario is to avoid giving patients, parents, spouses, and children grounds to be "let-down." Having reached the levels I have reached and having learned in the course of having taken dire directions, I want to put it out there that there is much to be sifted out of meta-physics and the power of positive thinking.

Because I never was given opportunity to think that there was someone out there to reach out their hand and point me in the correct direction, I never had a chance to think that this journey would be up to someone else. Early on I "got-it" that if I didn't make plans to be going somewhere, I was never going to move beyond where the emergency room left off!

My friends were there to give me the initial urgings. They were just lazy and unwilling to face the possibility of losing a friend, and all humility aside, a good friend. I think that I was able to keep up my half of a great number of friendships!

For me, the continual process of life was moving ahead,

sometimes even too fast for my ability to grasp all the lessons availed, while for many of my "friends" it seems to have ceased to carry on. I cannot point my proverbial finger, I cannot hope to master control over so many divergent souls, so I simply let them! A number of them however, were not let from my life without some apparent perseveration on my part, but just as soon as I was able to "get-it, that proverbial it, I would mourn the loss and quickly get back in the saddle.

Something, never really there in the physical, tangible sense, but intuitively I must have known that there was something greater than myself. Just like the Flatirons I had grown up under the shadow of, or the massive buildings of New York City, Chicago, Boston, Dallas, or the tides, and the storms availed by the ocean, or the fear of God struck into the psyches of the land-locked farmers, living in the states of the North American interior, I knew that there was something greater, more powerful than myself. If you've been raised Christian, then that image has taken the form of God. If you've been raised on the seashore, that image takes form as the water. Mythology has always played with this institution, by creating the gods of Olympus, to create that intangible image upon which everything inexplicable can be attributed.

I grew up with the Western image of Christianity, of God established in my head, but this has become only as useful as is any other tool. As long as it serves a purpose, I am first in line saying that the Western image of God exists. But when the head of the hammer becomes loose, I had better find another tool to get me through this life. If I don't the head might fall off on the up-stroke or on the down-stroke? The images of life are analogous to my life's behaviors.

It's not that my way to health is necessarily a given route, or that the path you've chosen won't also lead to where you want, or need to go; however, as author of this book, I must assume that I have some authority. I need to tell you of the direction I've taken and of where it has taken me.

It is because I've chosen to embrace pain. Pain taken for what it is intended: A signal of violation in the homeostasis, as an indication that there is a point in the system, which has broken down and is in need of repair.

I do not mean that by becoming hardnosed towards everyone who is out there in sympathy for the TBIed of the world, that you will stand a better chance of breaking new ground.... just be who it is that you are meant to be! Help, if you are meant to be a helper, if only to give the medicine(s) you need to yourself.

This message needs to find its way to all the TBIed people in the world if you do not want to become stuck on that proverbial cosmic Mobius strip returning to society over and over and over again to learn the same specific lessons which you had been unable to master on any of your earlier trips. You've got to learn everything out there that your are supposed to learn long before becoming authorized to move on to the next level, that next step, the next stage on which you need to perform, and into that next "grade." It seems too many people are being "held back," are flunking one or more times. There is no use for these people in the great cosmic romance.

Journal Entries

Tired or not my Mother does not realize it and asks me to drive down and get some charcoal and lighter fluid. "Gulf," not (the) "Safeway" brand. Well, just to carry on with my story, I succeeded. The driving was great; having only received six hours of sleep from 9pm to 3am, is not nearly as bad as 6 hours from 3am to 9pm. (Go figure.)

8/3/82

I just drove up to the lake, couldn't find Paul (Klemperer), drove up to his house, "He's down at the lake." Drove down to the lake, found him. We both stretched out in the sun. We got rather hot and went for a swim. We swam out to the first raft, got out and did a bit of sun worshiping, got rather warm and headed back to shore. It was a bit difficult swimming in water that had only been warmed by the sun's convention. It was cold enough to make you snatch a breath of something into your lungs. It turned out to be $O2$ most of the time, but $H2O$ once in a while. Now the human body is not built to accept $H2O$ into the lungs, so I tried to get it out; cough, cough, cough is the procedure I resorted to, to get the $H2O$ (water) out of my lungs. Well, I've just told you so... I must have succeeded in getting to the shore. Well, I've just told you about a couple of things that I've been scarred to do since the accident. Swim and drive. Judy, Judy, Judy, Judy....she plans on being gone for another two weeks.

8/3/82

Monday so rudely interrupted. I was going to take my bike over to Larson Engineering and hadn't put it in the bus yet. We adjusted the wheels so that they were on the ground 96% of the time. That made it hard, if not impossible, to practice riding on only two wheels. We rode down to the end

of Centennial Trail at 55th. Nothing drastic happened. I
RODE THE BIKE, with only one difficulty, two difficulties.
The seat was too low, which didn't allow me even a near full
extension or hyperextension. Because of this, there was no
way to go fast, also cloneus was aggravated. I do believe I'll
be on the bike for the day. Not the day but the month.

8/4/82

I am plain sick and tired of living here at 9=5+4 Gapter.
Mom and I seem to be at the end of the rope between us. The
rope between her and Bran broke. It wasn't a very strong rope.
The one between us is incredibly strong, but my trying to get to
the end just weaves another chord into it. The rope seems to be
beginning to "fray" a bit, which would send me falling. Bran
fell many years ago, but Dad was there to catch him. I was let
off the chord but found the landing too hard and asked for a
pad, so Joe L. hit me very hard, only to hang me back on the
chord, spinning now.

8/5/82

I did it, I did it, nobody wanted me to, but I did it
anyway. I got up really early, didn't hear many cars, and rode
up to Platt. I rode along Gapter to Dimmit, turned left, rode up
to Cherryvale, waited for there to be no cars and crossed from
Dimmit to Baseline. Only had one close call and was able to
recover with amazing grace. Ride up to the Nolands and then
on to Fairview on Monday the 16th. Came back and stopped
by the Turners on the 19th (W). Those actions must wait until
I can ride without the training wheels, probably just an idle
dream, though. All the friends and relatives wanted to know
the day I did what I've wanted to do for so long. One other
lady I need to tell, the woman I went to visit the day I received
the fatal blow to the head, Gail Lurie.

8/6/82

I NEED HELP. I mean I am not the way I am because of something I did and getting back to where I need to be. I need help. It does seem that I will be getting back up on a bike. Yeah. That is just one of a very few things I have wanted to do.

8/7/82

I then squeezed through the bike opening in the Centennial Trail. Problems began when I tried to cross on the western most bridge. I tried to get up the sharp incline onto the bridge and f---- up. I fell over. On the left side, just sit back and get yourself better (oxymoron). They even said it looks like I don't even need training wheels, which is exactly how I see it. The only problem is starts and stops. She was the one who made the urgent suggestion that I go see "a Gentleman and a Sailor." What the h---. You only go around in this life once, for me twice, but never mind. You might as well make it a lot of fun, enjoyable.

8/8/82

I miss her, not so much for what she gives to me, but how she accepts what I can give her... "King of Hearts" is showing at Chautauqua. I rode my bike to church. The topic was marriage and sex. To have my comments last sort of showed me that everyone was tired of the preacher. You can't ride down the West coast unless you can ride a bike, and you can't ride a bike unless you continue trying.

8/9/82

Would be a physical impossibility. Just her saying that makes me want to prove her wrong. I feel like a bad person for leaving her at the apex of the biggest hill in my life and seeing all my fellow class/trip mates, while at the same time I am not greedy, and don't want to keep my accident and recovery from those it would benefit not the most, yet benefit the same. To be an example of strength, which very few people (thank God) are given the chance to try to do. I guess I'm just an egomaniac with a very well to be self-esteem. Coming up very soon is the all the more depressing 21st birthday of Ms. Carefrae. I don't know what to get her except something to go along with the fact that she will probably be getting several bottles of "Hard Stuff," Alka Seltzer®.

8/10/82

I guess I do want to be able to come when making love with Judy. I would also like to get her into a frenzied state of self-being. I do not want to have intercourse with her, at least not now. All it will take is a car and a bike, and the ability to ride it. Once I am at a place with these things, I won't be content. I am glad the settlement was not for a lump sum and a couple hundred dollars each month. As is, if the annuity company doesn't decide to close up, I am set with an O-K wage for all that I have been going through. I know that I really harp on my Mother's problems, but if she wasn't around, I wouldn't be. Friday it is tentatively planned to go up to Platt and attempt to ride with no T-wheels. This evening I drove JB and myself up to R.V.P., no sweat. It was a dream come true. I did miss the turn to get to R.V.P.but that only tested my ability to think fast and get us there. We made it and there was a happy ending complimented with a 1/2 ham, 1/2 green pepper pizza.

8/12/82

The day I am going to initially ride a bike-no T-wheels is Friday, the 13th. A bad luck day for everyone who believes in that stuff. Do I? Naaa, never. Just you watch it turn out to be a true-life occurrence. I think I am going to go look for a car, a Volkswagen® Rabbit. I was to go to the doctors; (Wee) I got a tetanus shot that will last me 10 years, almost wished they needed to withdraw some blood to check for mono. JB and Spring have it presently. What I need to do is get more active physically. Well tomorrow is the big day, or has the potential of being a great day. Tomorrow I am going to attempt an initial try at riding with no, repeat no, T-wheels. I need to get my reso that I will perform to my expectations.

8/13/82

Bad luck, that's what today's date is supposed to represent. I don't think so! I received another card from my love, Judy. Well to the surprise and total pleasing of myself, Holly and Dianne, I did it. I f------ pulled it off. Or should I say, pulled it out of a hat full of tricks. I just rode my bike with no training wheels. Dad's not home from work yet, and neither is Bryan. My Mom is still at work, Bran's in Alaska, and Judy's in Wyoming. Feeling about my being able to get back on a bike. Well, I was really rather doubtful about the possibility of ever mounting a bike again. I would like Judy to get home so that I can tell her the great news. Since I rode today, the question is, was today a fluke Friday the 13th or was it a ekulf yadirf iht hteetriiht?* If the second is the case, I should or shall be able to peddle tomorrow and show Bryan and anyone else who is there to witness the spectacle.

8/14/82

I am taking Kends R. and we are not being driven to or from the theatre. I, Dave Cole, am drinking. Just you watch, because I told you ahead of time, I will f----up. I seem to have worked myself into a corner. With my personality, it's probably the corner in a round room. I miss Judy very much; Kenda could see this and kept bringing her up. A real trooper that Kendall is. If I do go up to Seattle with Cathy, it will be on September 2nd. If this turns out to be the case, I will have to talk to Mr. Bynum about the fact that I will be receiving the

_____

* Ed. note: try reading this backwards. :)

1075 each month starting in September and confirm with Gail Lurie that the first check will be invested in money market certificates. I don't want to think about them anymore. My going to school and repaying Bynum needs to happen soon. I owe Mike $6000. School will hopefully be covered by vocational rehabilitation. The one thing I am having troubles with is my bowels. Now they are extremely full, which is rather uncomfortable. I have drunk nearly 5000 ml of water. Once again I am finding that I miss Judy very much. I also need to practice getting the bike going without sitting on it. If I don't go to the bathroom tomorrow, I will resort to chemical means.

8/16/82

What major am I going to study? I now, at this instant, want to be a writer. The only problem is I don't have a heart set desire to go to CU again. You realize that I haven't ejaculated for many weeks; it must be because I haven't contacted Judy for going on a month. While at the Carfrae's for Kathy's Geburtstag, I spoke with her about the trip, of the vacation. It won't be an all expenses paid trip to the torture chamber; it will take extra funds, but all in all a nice gift for what I am going through.

8/17/82

Judy gets home and ends my vigil. To have conversed and set up times to see the two people is a sure sign that I am getting back into the swing of life. Laurie wasn't there today so I didn't get to kiss her. That's right. Judy is supposed to be back tonight. I don't know what time, but my countdown has gotten down to 400 minutes. By God, I do miss her. By "her", I mean her person, not just the physical attractiveness. She doesn't get carried away when I'm heavy petting with her, but the few times it has happened, I was in total self denial, even enough to tell Steph that we must not do anything we would regret. She is now wearing the facade of being a Mormon.

She is presently in a relationship with Shawn W--. Her brothers do not expect it to last beyond her association with Mr. W--. I hope not, and not for my sake, but for hers. I did the unexpected. I swam out to the raft in a very fading light to the point of being dark. Besides my having not been very visible, the water was colder than a witch's t--.

8/18/82

I went to therapy and got a rash of compliments. Compliments flowed from everyone who knew. Janice didn't know and was extremely displeased. We had a very heated conversation. Not to take that, I said that I had worked too long and too hard not to ride. Meanwhile she came back with, "It's up to you, either you walk well, or ride, but not both."

8/19/82

Now that I have the chance of getting beyond where Janice had wanted me to go, she doesn't want me to go. I'm having a hard time trying to figure out whether it is time to move on, or whether I should listen to her pleas. Maybe if I just increase the amount of exercises I do, it won't have regressive effects if I ride. I took Judy to "A Gentleman and a Sailor."

8/20/82

D---it, I f------ wet the bed last night. Well, I vinegared my bed and wrapped my wedding present, not for me, but for Stinky, "smelly" to go back. I was walking slowly but to the point. I am now walking rather rapidly, but not to the point.

8/21/82

I really think that I have found someone who I used to pity but now pity myself for having not "met" Judy Turner when I was in high school. Going out with Steph my junior year and playing with Editorial my senior year.

8/24/82

This morning I went over to Rich Sommer's house for *Frustuck. Es war gut, sehr gut!* I also went down to CU to talk to a counselor about getting back into the swing of things. I was very very discouraged by his attitude (Richard Klein). I guess I would like to go to CSU to be in school with Judy.

8/26/82

Judy is really helping me keep my senses. I want to go to bed with Judy, not f--- her. I am still a virgin.

8/27/82

Well I shan't count the minutes until Judy leaves for school, or the minutes till I leave for Seattle. 1120 hours until I leave for Seattle, that's 2880 minutes for Judy and 7200 minutes for me.

8/28/82

What she needs is what I have, the ability to listen, make a few comments, let others release feelings that don't need to be stored and walk away for a picnic up Sunshine Canyon. WE were involved with the lunch from 11:00 until 1:45. Then we went about some extracurricular activity. I need to hit my sack of H_2O.

8/29/82

Had a very heavy talk with Judy. Almost to the point of crying, but no, I have lost that ability. Judy, on the other hand, no, both sleeves did cry. The hymn was one that I did know, "Morning has Broken," was the tune. I did have past memories of singing it. Judy came out and scolded her Mom for allowing such people as myself up on the patio! (I'm pretty sure all was in jest). When I get to Tacoma, I am to give him (Uncle Bailey) a call and if his landlord was gone by the time I get there... Or I can stay with Penny, or...or, (I had innumerable opportunities.) It sounds like I am going to be away for a spell. Not to worry, you're coming too.

8/30/82

A certain Johnathon Hopkins came over just as I was getting ready to retire. John continually harps upon the idea that he doesn't sell the Lord, just that he should be the one who is responsible for telling all around him that it is the only way to gain righteousness. I like him as a total person, but his "holier than thou" sort of friendship is not where I enjoy dwelling. Or even more disgusting, that she was in the hospital or mortuary.... she just called and she's alive "just leaving Fort Collins... late."

9/1/82

Of all the good things to happen today, Janice, (my PT), was very positive about my walking. To be leaving for Seattle at such a peak in my life seems almost too good to be true.

9/2/82

I haven't yet been asked to drive and because of how late it is, I don't want to drive. I feel like I am just along as a very definite burden, granted I did pay for gas this stop, still I haven't done my fair share of piloting "Herbie." He either figured that we were unwise, or that there really were "Jack-a-Lopes." Maybe I am just a bit too senseless and unfeeling, so bad that what turned everyone on really was disgusting to me. Maybe the "Head Injury" is what makes me so closed to the rest of society. I should really lead the life of a hermit, isolated from a good majority of the world. Closed off from society, all of society, except Judy.   And I seem to have the identical feelings towards many of my meetings with society. Well, we continued our trip to Burley Id. Once we got there, we were fed, again.

9/7/82

Today we are going to the "Bumber Shoot," (a festivity endemic to Seattle.) At the Davies, I listened to the radio. It wasn't ROCK-N-ROLL, wasn't DISCO, wasn't really anything, just the Wall Street Journal over-n-over-n-over again.

9/9/82

This morning at 4:00am, I wet the bed. (As things have been turning out it was also for the last time.) Speaking 13 years later, it was the last time.

More Bits and Pieces

The ER (emergency room) has been set up as a facade. An icon established in order to create and support the illusion that society actually gives a damn about the health and welfare of the general population. In the ER there are actually people who thought at one time that they would get out of medical school and move on to save people's lives. They may even have felt that their presence was destined to create a better society. They are there in order to "save our lives," or is it in order that they can have fun killing us a little more methodically, in a little less traumatic manner, more controlled.

"As I was walking, there were marching bands. I cried and cried without even stopping. That was December, so it was 2 what 3 months into your coma." Open the book with a marching band-the drummers-the "shuffle!'

I have the sense that the playing of the piano was just a primary activity, a way of establishing a sense of stick-to-itiveness. That this was just another means, a way of getting me through life to reach the end! I don't know about you, but I love this life. I've very few things to point to with any kind of complaint. The end for which the means enabled me is for where I am now, or for where you are at this point. But because I don't stand a chance of knowing where that is, I cannot hope to address what it is that you are looking for!

As a newly injured TBI patient/survivor, or even after as many as ten years, I had found myself beset with the basest of fears, the most primal personification of me. Me with all the baggage, which I unsuspectingly picked up in the course of my travels. It was only after having studied for several years and experienced life for several years more that I was able to really appreciate the ancient Biblical story of Cain and Abel, and then only after having heard it spoken of by Hermann Hesse in his book entitled *Damian*.

I related to the part where the character, Cain, becomes so feared and therefore so powerful simply because his forehead is marked with a mark so intense, almost a scar. What I related to was that this Biblical scar is in fact corroborated with all the scars that result from the injury.

I now am able to develop the new sense that what I had often taken to be anger towards my new appearance or towards the rate of my gate or my speech was in fact a simple case of the willies, of fear! And even more similar, a fear created by the mark on Cain's forehead! That my new state, physical state, somehow strangely became emasculated, and that now my current state of affairs began to appeal to me in ways likened to the Chinese Yin-Yang philosophy. Through this, I was able to correlate my "down-time" with that inefficable period of cleaning house. Of pillaging, the neural synapses, brain cells, of a greater number of their connections, enabling me to refill, reprogram so many neural transistors.

Whereas I had grown up in the traditional Western way, with many of the traditional Western ideals programmed into my head, I now found myself entirely "deprogrammed." I could get really frustrated and seek a return back to all that malarkian brain mush or I could begin anew, afresh, a virgin of traditional steps and processes.

Tradition, however, had experience on its side. The only experience I had was with playing the piano and riding a bike! The spasticity in my arms and in my fingers preclude my effortless return to the piano and in light of the complications the Eustachian tubes, my balance and subsequent return to riding the bike was severely impractical. I was also a weight lifter, but this activity was hugely discouraged by my physical therapist.

I wasn't a quitter, I wasn't easily distracted from my search for the Holy Grail, and I didn't sense there to be much validity in the scientific school of prognosticating a man's rehabilitation. Just maybe, the reasoning behind doctors giving the worst-case scenario is in order not to give patients, parents, spouses, or children grounds upon which to be "let-down." Having reached the levels, which I have reached, and having learned in the course of having taken my direction, I want to put it out there that there is much to be sivied out of meta-physics and the power of positive thinking.

Because I never was given opportunity to think that there was someone out there to reach out their hand and point me in the correct direction, I never had a chance to think that this journey would be up to someone else. Early on I "got-it" that if I didn't make plans to be going somewhere, I was never going to move beyond where the emergency room left off!

My friends were there to give me the initial urgings, but they were just lazy and unwilling to face the possibility of their losing a friend, all humility aside, a good friend. I think that I was able to keep up my half of a great number of friendships!

For me, the continual process of life was moving ahead, sometimes even too fast for my ability to grasp all the lessons availed, while for many of my "friends" it seems to have ceased to carry on. I cannot point my proverbial finger; I cannot hope to master control over so many divergent souls, so I simply let them! A number of them, however, did not leave my life without some apparent perseverance on my part but as soon as I was able to "get-it," that proverbial it, I would mourn the loss and quickly get back in the saddle.

Something. Never really there in the physical, tangible sense, but intuitively I must have known that there was something greater than myself. Just like the Flatirons, I had grown up under the shadow of, or the massive buildings of New York City, Chicago, Boston, Dallas, or the tides, and the storms availed by the oceans, or the fear of God struck into the psyches of the land-locked farmers, living in the states of the North American interior. I knew that there was something greater, more powerful than myself. If you've been raised Christian, then that image has taken the form of God. If you've been raised on the seashore, that image takes form as water. Mythology has always played with this institution by creating the gods of Olympus, to create that intangible image upon which everything inexplicable can be attributed.

I grew up with the Western image of Christianity, of

God established in my head; but this has become only as useful as is any other tool. As long as it serves a purpose, I am first in line saying that the Western image of God exists. But when the head of the hammer becomes loose, I had better find another tool to get me through this life. If I don't, the head might fall off on the up-stroke or on the down-stroke. The images of life are analogous to many of life's behaviors.

It's not that my way to health is necessarily a given route or that the path you've chosen won't also lead to where you want, or need to go; however, as the author of this book, I must assume that I have some authority. I need to tell you about the direction I've taken and where it has taken me.

It is because I've chosen to embrace pain, pain taken for what it is intended: A signal of a violation in the homeostasis, as an indication that there is a point in the system, which has broken down and is in need of repair.

I do not mean that by your becoming hardnosed towards everyone who is out there in sympathy for the TBIed of the world, that you will stand a better chance of breaking new ground.... just be whoever it is that you are meant to be! Help, if you are meant to be a helper, if only to give the medicine(s) you need to yourself.

This message needs to find its way to all the TBIed people in the world. If you do not want to become stuck on that proverbial cosmic Mobius strip returning to society over and over and over again to learn the same specific lesson which you had been unable to master on any of your earlier trips, you've got to learn everything out there that you are supposed to learn long before becoming authorized to move on to the next level, that next step, the next stage on which you need to perform, and into the next "grade." It seems too many people are being "held back," are flunking one or more times. There is no use for these people in the great cosmic romance.

Prom Chocolate Moose

The book should be geared to help inform those who otherwise fallaciously assume that they already "know "what's going on! Target Audiences.

While today's youth are putting into practice the age-old ritual of rebellion, they now have the "artificial" "skill" to actually make it all seem to work! Today, the aspiring generation does not even have the tools necessary to make their own life work; far be it that they would be ready to toe the line if anything really important were to occur. Any assumption that says, "I know more than my parents..." has already missed the mark!

But don't read into this that I am assuming that I know what I'm talking about. All I am trying to say is that my having the fortune to return and try and make something of myself is demanding that I say something.

A muscle, once it is generated demands activity! The child, after he has discovered his own voice, begins to exercise his newfound talent. He'll wail all through the night and day, until his tantrum yields results. If he so chooses, this will become an overt tool of manipulation. (And not until there is the structure, the dictums, as are managed by our adult populace.)

Similarly, a mind once given the opportunity to think, demands the space needed to create! And what allows this opportunity to exist? Well, I think it is the result of experience, and these experiences are managed most effectively through the mundane tedium presented by our current elementary and secondary institutions, grade school, and high school.

Neither my first life nor my second life would've amounted to a whole hill of beans without there having been the chance to learn what I had, my having kowtowed that invisible line and graduating with honorary distinction from high school. If I hadn't already had the founding mental capacity to experience and take from those experiences, lessons, I wouldn't have seen the importance of doing anything, of rehabilitating my physical self, my emotional self, my mental self! You see my intellectual self had the biggest voice. It told me that I didn't want to have any ties to high school...romantic, or other.

Control

In order to affect this system, this world with a left-brained, analytic, American, conventional style, something I could control, I "broke-up-with" that most beautiful, vivacious, hugely intelligent girl I'd known (but not Biblically) since my junior, her sophomore year. The ending started somewhere around November it would seem, and this process took all year long. Like a bad cold, I just couldn't shake it!

It must have been a terrible year for Stephanie Marie Noland: '79-'80, but I didn't want the next fall to arrive and her to feel left behind. I was going away to college, all the way across town to CU; I didn't want to have the images of Steph catching/hanging up on my integrity. I didn't want to have a girlfriend back at my old high school. So, in the brilliance of my teenage intuition, I felt that it would be more honorable to give her the opportunity to meet and fall in love with someone else while I was still in the picture, "To offer support?"

That's what I had been telling myself, all year (all school year). But so? None of this turned out the way I expected. I struggled with her all year, fought with her, "broke-up-with" her; consoled, petted with her for 8 months, I held her at bay. Then the long awaited, much heralded Senior Prom Night arrived! Do I have anyone who I've had my eye on all year? Do I know a girl who will make my high school career seem at all even "worth it?"

Of course not! For all the last 8 months, as well as all of last year, I'd only been seen with Stephanie. Besides, she was rather beautiful and otherwise invigorating, why not? And she was smart, you Idiot!

"C' mon David, you know you want to go to the Prom with Steph!" These were the words of my locker partner and best friend of my academic years. I'd been going to school with Ken Mann since we'd "shot" spit wads across the back of the room at Baseline Elementary School, (The Best although at the time Ken didn't much like to come to class with: Mrs. Johnson, Mrs.Varnwald, or Mrs. Haflich)! In the end, I wanted to take Steph to the Senior Prom. Why else would I have bothered to suffer such a beautiful girl?

So Ken Mann and I dressed to the kneecap (we couldn't afford to rent a tuxedo, to go dressed to the hilt), but we did do, what I thought out-wined everyone else. We both cooked an absolutely exquisite dinner for two of the most beautiful girls at that school! We started the evening off in the hot tub, sipping a Domestic Chablis. Then, after we'd become thoroughly prunized, we began the meal with a green salad, croutons, Roquefort dressing and garnished with alfalfa sprouts. This was all followed by bread, baguettes, and an herbed cream cheese spread. Then we left the girls to tell secrets, or whatever it is girls say to each other when alone, and go to the kitchen to prepare the most succulent cuts of Filet Mignon we could find... With all of this, we had tread quite deeply into a bottle of Chardonnay. Then, the finale, my own concoction of a Chocolate Mousse! And a very fine concoction, I might, in all modesty, just add.

If only I'd been as much a coffee fanatic then as I am now, I might have read the ingredient 2T coffee as the liquid as it had been intended. Instead, I added 2 T of coffee in the only form I knew it to come in. And if they hadn't been our dates, and if we'd been any closer to the city limits, I am secure in saying the grit in the otherwise smooth, wonderful tasting desert would have encouraged them both to call a cab or walk home!

The evening concluded. I don't have even the foggiest idea how the rest of the evening went. Maybe that's the blessing I intended to get from being knocked unconscious for so long. Maybe I screwed up even more in the course of the next 4 or 5 hours. Actually, I don't even think we'd made more than a cameo guest appearance. The arrival and departure to the dance was made in a Mercedes Benz® top of the line for the year, 1980; our arrival was stunning!

Get a clue, you idiot.

I don't see school as being necessarily applicable to life on the immediate, the first level; however, I have been made aware of levels of understanding that go beyond the primary. As Star Trek has most artistically portrayed, "To seek out worlds in dimensions unknown to man..." When I was in high school, I too rebelled. I chose, however, a tamer process.

I rebelled by not being like anyone else. I managed to keep that wool in place over everyone's eyes, by having the external facade of marching to the same beat that everyone else followed in marching band for both my sophomore and junior years of high school. By the time my senior year rolled around, I felt that I had sufficiently kowtowed to the metered system to break away.

$2,000.00 Book

If you've purchased this book, you're probably doing yourself one of the biggest favors of your life! By buying this book, you are dismantling the need of actually having to go out and live this process in the course of human evolution, your own evolution. Just think of all those poor people who are reluctant to buy this book. Now they need to have an accident too, a trauma, to put at risk, to jeopardize their being able to walk, being "able to think," being "able to love," being lovable right back.

The price tag for your not buying this book may shock the daylights out of the finest psychiatrist in the world. I am a teacher, a teacher of a fact of life, one for which there are no courses available in the university system. A course where the only required work before taking, let's just say, there are precious few who survive the first or the final exam. A course which, while there are people who are having traumatic brain injuries every day, no one can walk away from the blood splat on the road, or in the car, and then be able to talk about it to their grandchildren.

I died! For all intents and purposes I ceased to live! My only proof of this happening is that I never stopped having to pay taxes, and I never ceased needing love! There were a number of other indications of my being alive, none of which were in my collective bag of experiences until after I had died! I was never more alive in this age of liability and negligence until after I had the opportunity to get a behind-the-scenes look at what it is like to be dead! At no point in my prior days of youth had I felt so much love. There is no better way of knowing how warm the sun is than by moving to where the sun never shines. When you are young, there is no way of knowing what it's like to be young. Only through having lived through youth, into the different measures of adulthood, are you able to see back. It is the "Yin-Yang of life," it is the pike along which you travel in order to know much about this wonderful thing that is termed by Western, English speaking man as life.

The only way of ever really knowing, of having all the irrefutable proof that you are living, is by dying.

If you want to get that proof, to have a tangible demonstration of life, you've either got to study it in a book of academia, or read my book!

There may be another route. I'm sorry. I don't know where my head was, but there is another way... I think. The other way is by giving birth; however, my not being a woman and never having the chance of birthing another human being, I gathered together all the evidence of this lesson by having to die. I know there are so many other people who experience death as well, but do they know what they are talking about when it comes to being expected to struggle through the initial stages of life, infancy, and receive a crash course in adolescence before having to go through the pains of young adulthood?

I had my initial go of learning how to be a man. I failed the course! So, I was sent back to see if I had it in me to actually be a man.

There was a point in my days where I had had to practice being a man thrice in the course of any 20 hours. I don't know what you want to call it, but I refer to it as my being a stud! I knew three different women, all of very different ages. There was a grandmother whose second child had graduated from high school with me, that's her second child. Her first child already had two daughters of her own. The next woman had two daughters in high school, and the third was 4 years younger than me.

Such an experience didn't actually last very long. It was over after only a couple of weeks.

Talk about the extreme burden, of intellectually knowing how to do something; your muscles have already been trained/guided in the motion but are still physically unable to perform what was already stored in muscular memory. As a child, everything's new and unexperienced. You are devoid of having to be bothered with trying to appease the Ego;

therefore, your pride is still immune to being hurt or damaged. After having been able to tie your own g------- shoelaces for so many years, it's sure to be a drag having to learn how to, all over again, but the struggle with this may be a process you were meant to have. There is no reason not to do it and even to enjoy doing it!

In my travels I would find this message expressed in any number of different ways, still I think it was best summed up by my conversation with Judy Hicks (thank you Judy) "I can see myself even when I get frustrated, or I make a fool of myself!"

To amass even more pain on the already festering injury, while your eyes may not have been affected by the initial trauma and your perceptive abilities unimpinged, what it sees you doing does not fit in with any of the pictures already imprinted in your mind. The levels of frustration this has the tendency to create can only begin to hint at the myriad of other frustrations.

The owning and the training of our Golden Retriever dog seems to fall into place here as analogous to this situation. I was truly without any guiding leash around my neck. I had no instructions, no training to know how to respond to the whistle either. I was free to get on with my life as ever I felt would be best. And I did. I was able to show a little self discipline. I know when not to cross the street, like the Golden Retriever, I was ignorant. When I went to junior high, I was given a note at the beginning of my 9th grade year which said, "David is a responsible individual and I will not write any of his excuse notes."

This was basically giving me the opportunity, the chance to be recognized as an adult! It was something every kid at Nevin Platt Jr. High envied me for.

So, I had all the tools, all the chances to "ditch" any and every class and to then just run away! I had the advantage every red-blooded American kid dreamt about! But I was above all that, I was doing just as I was supposed to do. I was

121

going to school for an education just as I had been doing for the previous nine years. I could handle this; I would do just fine. This policy held precedent for four of my final six years of secondary education, and it worked! I towed the line; I made the grade. No ink was wasted (in the form of absentee notes) by the school writing notes of concern home to my Mother.

During the 18 years preceding my own injury, I was a terror, I was so wild, no one could even hope of controlling me, Judy.

That Entirely Necessary Shift

When I've taken myself out into society, I don't have the ability to see myself as I am perceived by another human being; therefore, I am able to use my left side, as represented by my left arm, as a measure of my destruction. Even while I have my bad side, I have my good side too, my strong side, my right side. My left gastrocnemius is a more graphic representation of my down side. When compared with my right gastrocnemius, it is seen in conjunction with my right gastrocnemius, and the level of change, of adaptation becomes very apparent!

Now I hope not to imply that I am any less than human, but the amount and extent of my rehabilitation, I feel, is somehow hugely influenced by my level of attainment prior to the injury. My intelligence before the injury was quite high, and so my ability to achieve the level of education that I have following the trauma actually reflects this.

Not wishing to sound cold-hearted and maliciously cruel, I've got to point out that while my accident was just that, an accident! There are those so traumatized that they might be able to benefit from the different institutions put in place be the government: of the people, for the people, and by the people.

Influenced by my parents, and availed of the opportunity by the institution of spiritual gratification of church, which I was a member, I was able to participate in a great number of human sexuality classes. Therefore, I chose to abstain from intercourse, theoretically, until after marriage, while I was in high school. I was in no way asexual though! Don't think I am inhuman! I had opportunity. I chose not to let those opportunities slip away. But I also didn't feel obligated to act on my impulses. This was surely my downfall.

However, living with the ability to have known what it's like to die. My having died, and able to talk about the experience, is what I feel has given me the opportunity, nay the obligation to make it clear to society. There is a song written

123

by Peter Townsend of the WHO, and sung by Roger Daltry whose words have impacted me and my obligations in this life are as follows: I'mmm free!"

Humpty Dumpty's Fall

While I had never actually qualified for that one-way journey to the ICU, or the coroner's office, for the next several months I had been entirely unable to make a positive, affective contribution towards the advancement of the human population. It seems that for the next four to six months beginning October 2nd, 1980, I was on hiatus from the cold of a miserable Colorado winter. Instead, I had been sequestered in Boulder Community Hospital's Intensive Care Unit for the last few months of 1980, and then to the Boulder Memorial Hospital's Intensive Rehabilitation Unit for the first five/six months of 1981.

According to the official hospital records, I had been out for only 99 days; however, my primary physical therapist had been unable to passively involve me in therapies other than range-of-motion activities for darn near six months.

So, "All the King's Men and all the King's Horses couldn't put Humpty back together again." Wait a minute though. What is it that fools us into thinking we can affect a return to normalcy? In fact, did Humpty even want to be put back together again? If it were me, I really don't think I would have wanted to return to the dull life of a simpleton egg. No, I would want to become an omelet, or maybe even better yet, a soufflé or quite possibly an eggnog.

I just cannot help but wonder where I would be if I was limited to getting back to the way I'd been before, that is before being the end result of a driver's instant of miscalculation.

I shudder to think. Would I have passed the examination I had been scheduled for that very Friday? Would I be able to find a girl friend? Sure, I had had a number of friends who were girls, but a girl friend is different. To me, a girl friend was someone who was always there to take out to dinner. And who would've always been there to help me write my term paper in another one of my more boring classes.

I must have been "a prude." Maybe that was why no one wanted to be my girl friend. As it would turn out, I was rejected by one girl after another for what seemed the better part of 25 years, but that's another story.

As I began to be able to structure some form of reality out of those moments of terrific pain, it was my masculinity, which seems to have pushed me along the antiseptic hallways of the hospital. It was my brazen attitude, and what there was remaining of my bravado, that seemed to keep my spirits up and to keep me alive.

That is just to say that it was my own personal spirit and the spirits of so many friends. Everyone, or most everyone in my hometown, Boulder, Colorado, who had received word of me and my injury, turned out in droves. They were able to donate more blood to the Belle Bonfils Blood Center in my name than there was in the Belle Bonfils Blood Center altogether.

The nurses at the rehabilitation hospital had enough foresight to place a sign-in-sheet on my hospital door for each person who came for a visit to record their name and relation to me.

These pages, 16 in all, have long since been thrown in the trash. I wish I had considered their disposal with a more lucid mind. Instead, I threw them all away in a moment of fury.

What is there that gets in my way of making any/good use of the ingenuity, which my God has given me?

What is there that stops me from trying to hold a place in that fabulously underpaid world of work? It surely has nothing to do with the loss of any intelligence, and I haven't developed narcolepsy, e.g., I am quite able to be out of bed with plenty time to "go to work.

NO!

What has been compromised in my head, however, has nothing to do with the mechanical regions of the brain or my human physique. There is nothing wrong with me that man now, or in the conceivable future, will have the ability to "fix!"

I've been able to return to my old- stomping grounds, i.e. the "weight room", and I've been able to squat-lift 605 lbs. I never lost a child's ability to bounce back from injury, e.g., the resiliency to recuperate, heal myself *ad nauseum.* I've fallen off my bike, and in the shower, I've separated great regions of muscle and bone. Just the other day I fell down a flight of my stairs and did not, I repeat-knock on wood, did not break my neck or any other bone what so ever. Blood, however? You'd think I'd been giving blood, but I was still able to get to the emergency room!

A lot of superficial lacerations are all I received and some stitches.

What I feel has been compromised in terms of my psyche is in no way connected with the mechanical, affective regions of my brain. My physique in no way lost touch with the directing centers of my brain. There is not now, nor in any perceptible length of time, injuries that a man can fix....or a woman.

Humpty Dumpty sat on the wall, and he had a great fall, or he got knocked in the head! "All the King's men and all the King's horses couldn't put humpty back together again."

So, if Humpty Dumpty and the King's men are personified by the paramedics and doctors, that is all the doctors who had ridden up on their great, charging steeds, professing that they had all the required education, and that they had obtained all those necessary documents to have understood what was the matter with me, made me to be just like every other H. Dumpty but none of them knew ME! I've not found that there was anyone who could have ever predicted that I would "bounce-back," not to the levels of recovery I've since managed anyways.

None of the doctors who has prognosticated all those dire predictions of my limited to nil chance of ever walking again, or of my ever having the ability to talk, to think, or to ever become a contributing member of this society again, none of them had even a clue! I think they were calling the glass half empty and had been trying not to set themselves up, or set anyone else up for disappointment. They didn't have that proverbial clue of all the magnificent mystical capacities my/our God had been sure to include with the original blueprints.

I hope none of this violates the integrity, or offends all those proverbial, well-read academician Dr. Presleys, and all the Dr. Scaers out there, they had been and are still inextricably necessary, but not for me. These doctors have done a necessarily poignant, a magnificent job in keeping me alive right up until they looked in their crystal ball so muddied with documentation to have predicted how far I would go, to what level my parents and friends could realistically expect my rehabilitation to reach!

Why they did, I'll never know, but by their saving my life, they have quite unwittingly... or maybe even un/intentionally unleashed an energy maybe equal but entirely dissimilar to Einstein's $E=mc^2$. What is even more freighting is that as I age/grow wiser and older, I am in fact getting fatter... e.g., more mass!

I just don't want anyone to have the idea that either having an insurance policy with all the money in the world would or will necessarily guarantee a full and complete recovery, or that being injured having lived all your life in the ghettos will predispose a person to not be able to become healed entirely. What I hope this story will bring to light is the responsibility of the individual. Life in this world is meant to be taken with that proverbial "grain of salt."

All the Dr. Presleys and all the Dr. Scaers need to be installed in the works and to have been put in place with absolute perfection. Their abilities have been established in order that the initial procedures, all the ER (emergency room) and the Tx (Therapy) activities are to be implemented "flawlessly;" thereby, creating the best possible environment and opportunity for an injured person! And as a human being, I cannot and do not claim to be without flaws, without fault(s).

Intuitively, I probably understood all of this, or I must have at least had the wisdom to toe that proverbial line and practice, practice, practice the entire regimen anyways, because practice makes perfect, and if I couldn't be perfect, I'd at least want to be human! If this had not been the case, I probably would not have exercised in excess. I probably would not have dedicated much of my professional education to the institution of health.

I don't know how this is coming across to people. Something tells me that a supreme attribute in the course of my recovery had been my general attitude.

It's hard to remember this one, but it seems that I was quite perturbed about not being allowed to soak in the hot tub-the whirlpool- naked. I'd never worn a suit in the hot tub before the injury. It just seemed so out of place to be wearing a swimming suit while sitting in a tub of hot water.

Another indication of my general demeanor may have been my creative rehabilitation. It seems that everyone wanted me to return to the state I existed in before October 2nd, 1980; so to help complete this picture, I began to experiment with my sexuality. I knew the nurses were quite attractive, but they were all so far away. My penis quite often would grow erect; subsequently, I would feel the wonder of sensation to be had by stroking it. Shss.... don't tell anyone, but I felt that the most important indication that I was on the road to recovery was my masturbating! The census data on this one will probably arrive soon, but once I discovered this, in my new state of affairs, I must have participated in such unseemly behavior at least four or five times before my being "abandoned" by the hospital. That's the way it felt anyway.

It had seemed to me that the hospital had seen fit to get my life back on track. Only then to abandon me, they thrust me back out there into the world. The winter of '81 was a hard winter, euphemistically as well as atmospherically; the world was cold as s---- after a couple days. Back in the hospital though, everything was warm and so well protected.

Before the injury, I only had the image of life as it had been programmed into my head through my initial, institutional education: K-12. That's 13 years of structural assimilation muted if not obliterated. With only the collision of a bicycle and a car, so much time, so much energy, so many relationships and such a powerful personality had come to a conclusion. But it doesn't really seem to have been at an all conclusive juncture. It now seems to have been only a more structured form of Mrs. Varnwald's erasing the blackboard.

The Tao masters will work an entire lifetime on trying to reach a level of nothingness, h---, I managed to do this in a matter of seconds.

The idiot and the Odd DC...is it just an inflammatory statement, a pejorative. It's obviously not something every red-blooded American man would really like to write home to Mom about!

While poor Humpty may really have wanted to make a return this complacent or not former existence as an egg, I wasn't anything like your average Dumpty. While initially I may have desired a chance to return to the very same life I had known prior to 10-02-80, that stemmed from my life having seemed the best available; the best life I had known up to that point. I had only just turned 18, my birthday had occurred less than a month before.

That is... the only life I had ever known, the one I was living just prior to the collision; I have since lived with the fall-out from the impact with my own destiny for going on 18 years. I do not want to come across as a naysayer to life or to discourage others. Don't allow your son, your daughter, your parent, or your spouse to lose their perspective.

So what perspective is that? From my place in society, I see them having become <u>disenfranchised from the life they knew and quite possibly also from what they</u> have, for all intents and affective purposes, died. Their return to the planet earth is no longer among the capacity of man to control. This is just a story about me and how I chose not to simply become just another statistic. Actually, I wanted to become more than a stat, more than another simpleton Dumpty. It just didn't feel good to be numberedamong Colorado's 1980s highway fatalities. I didn't want to be listed, to be counted once more, then filed away, or have my name written in a letter, which would probably have gone straight to the dead mail pile at the Denver or Boulder Post Office; however, I cannot help but wonder. Where would I have been today if I hadn't been there to point out some of the errant driving habits of someone who I had never and still have not had the pleasure or more lucid opportunity to formally meet?

Sure, man has invented the automobile, and sure, we've managed the distillation and purification of crude oil. But is this what has created the seriously mistaken impression that we have even an iota of control, if only the underdeveloped, fraudulent authority over our mortal existence?

Are we justified in assuming that we, as human beings, have managed the extinction of the carrier pigeons? Or was the bird already on the planet's extinction wannabe list?

While it does concern me that poor Mr. Dumpty fell from his perch on the wall, quite possibly it was because of some marauding band of street thugs, and they pushed him off the wall.

Don't you sometimes wonder, have we actually lost something, or was Humpty's existence only as important as the inspiration for another nursery rhyme?

We assume that Mr. Dumpty is grieved at his new, sorry state of affairs and that all he wanted was to return to his complacent existence as an egg. I don't think so.

I may be too optimistic, just a little bit pushy, but I'd like to think that Humpty aspired to greater things. I think that H. Dumpty aspired to be an omelet, or better yet a soufflé or nog... or maybe Eggs Benedict with a perfect Hollandaise sauce.

I have never been at the level of a triage discussion, and

I don't wish for you to assume I know what I'm talking about or feel any authority over suggesting anything relating to this aspect of an injury!

However, I haven't just been surviving for almost 2 decades; I have been alive, "thriving" for 17 years. I have been to the university to complete a hugely adapted career choice through my undergraduate exercises. I've lived with the fall-out, all the badges of my injury (s), and I have since married back into traumatic Brain Injury. I met my wife working as a counselor at a summer camp for adults, their having sustained a TBI.

I have lived with several of the innumerable aspects of the injury; the only one I haven't experienced, I would really rather not become an authority of. I do not feel inclined to live through Traumatic Brain Injury as the parent of a patient.... my child! My parents, however, have undertaken the task maybe without even volunteering, but hey neither did I. Besides, they seem pretty darn good at it. Maybe I should encourage them to write their own book.

I don't want to encourage anyone else to go out, put my stories to the test, "to just try it, see what it's like." I do want to discourage everyone! It is a very long haul, and there is no coffee break at 9:00, no one-week vacation, ever, not even after you've put in 43,800 hours. This is just my gross estimation. I'm not accounting for days off due to the most recent snowstorm, Christmas, Thanksgiving or even President's day. Just read my book and it'll probably be far less of a financial outlay than trying to verify all of my data. It would be nice if none of my math was correct.

I do not want to discourage anyone from being a risk taker either. We need all the Christopher Columbuses and all the Sir Edmond Hillarys in this world. We also need all the personalities which otherwise would have been sacrificed if not for all the medical technologies of this 20th-21st centuries. None of these stories are meant to be discouraging. In fact, all of them have powerful endings. Don't allow your son, your daughter, your parents, or your spouse to become discouraged or lose their perspective.

For all affective intent and purposes, I ceased to live for quite a few years. I ruefully conclude that neither will your family member. However, that'll be when the fun begins!

Aside from my carnal form requiring maintenance, I did not contribute to the existence of the human race. My return to the planet earth was beyond any man's control.

MY primordial existence was in the query. I must have chosen not to just become a statistic. I didn't feel good filling the ledgers with another statistic. I very easily could have contributed to Colorado's 1980 measure of highway fatalities, but I wanted my death to count for something bigger, I must have wanted more.

I am a genius. An absolute, died in the wool genius! And I did, I died in the wool; I was 100% virgin anyways.

What is there that gets in my way of making any/good use of the ingenuity, which our God has given us?

What is there that stops me trying to hold a place in that fabulously underpaid world of work? It surely has nothing to do with the loss of any intelligence, and I have not developed narcolepsy, e.g., I am quite able to be out of bed with plenty time to "go to work." The Bourgeoisie?

No!

What has been compromised in my head, however, has had nothing to do with the mechanical regions of the brain or my human physique. There is nothing wrong with me that man now, or in the conceivable future, will have the ability to "fix!"

These doctors have done a necessarily poignant, a magnificent job in keeping me alive right up until they looked in their crystal ball so muddled with documentation to have predicted how far I would go, to what level my parents and friends could realistically expect my rehabilitation to reach!

I just don't want anyone to have the idea either that having an insurance policy with all the money in the world will necessarily guarantee a full and complete recovery or being injured and living all your life in the ghettos will predispose a person to not being able to become healed entirely. What I hope this story will bring to light is the responsibility of the individual. Life in this world is meant to be taken with that proverbial "grain of salt."

The hospital: If you're not there, don't enroll. They discourage fraternization with coeds while on campus. Then they go and program every hour 5 days a week.

If you're already in the system, treat yourself. Heck of a deal. Go on hiatus. Take a vacation, a working vacation albeit, but a holiday none the less. Listen, you'll have to afford it one way or another. Use the facilities as they were designed. You put in for a little RnR and you certainly deserve it.

However, I didn't do this. Sure, I may have gotten it early on that I was on vacation. I was a workaholic though. Even though I ate like I was at a Roman orgy, I worked and exercised very hard. Don't think that the calories you consume in a hospital are any different than the calories you consume when not in the hospital. You'll still get fat. Because they don't let you use the stairway, there'll be a lot fewer opportunities to exercise the calories out of your system.

Why'd This Happen....To Me?

"So, how did you come up with such a self deprecating title? Surely, you don't consider yourself an idiot just because you were hit by a car. Or are you trying to maintain a little humility in spite or maybe in light of the circumstances you've witnessed? Is this book maybe just a moment of your own catharsis?"

Yes, it could be construed as my moment of catharsis; however, why would I expect you to want to afford $2,000 unless I felt there was a need for you to get that experience?

"So what experience is that?"

I think one of the biggest lessons afforded me along with my having the opportunity to do some real life, first person, in depth research, was the opportunity to make a contribution toward the research and development of methods of reducing, even eradicating such a multi-faceted, life altering injury.

There have been moments of my wanting to shoulder some responsibility for the accident. My only contribution that evening was maybe choosing to get a little exercise, conserve a little gas, maybe clear my head of school...get a little recreation.

Actually, I don't think I made any contribution to the injury what so ever! As a matter of fact, I may have unwittingly contributed to the lessening of any vehicular violations that Mr. Lynn was subsequently assessed. Beginning, maybe 4 years prior, I began the activity of weight lifting. This is in conjunction with the big level of cardiovascular conditioning may have allowed me to reduce Mr. Lynn's infringement from vehicular homicide, or involuntary manslaughter, to careless driving, or whatever it was he may have been responsible for (assessed.)

In this society with all of our rules and laws governing what we do. So before the "accident," I was trying my best just to enjoy this life. I could read about all the death, destruction and general melee associated with calamities of all sorts, but I didn't appreciate the chance possibility that any of this could enter in and otherwise become my life!

Nobody from my class had ever really died. Not in the fashion as portrayed by the media anyway. I had been an Idiot. Not in the fashion as mortality, an idiot towards the mortality of anyone in my surroundings. I'd basically been without an empirical clue about my life, and that necessarily included my death.

Instead, I had been intent upon measuring up to the fabled expectations as would've been meted out by society. However, I only had relation to that proverbial child, the same child that exists, or should exist, in everybody. And here in lies my predisposition towards being the martyr I've become. This was the construction of the bullfight arena in my psyche. This would eventually become the Corpus Coliseum, where my left-brain system found itself frustrated, disillusioned, and having to compromise.

There while the commercial is selling the truth. When it says, "Your doctor knows best." Or, "....it's the brand doctors prescribe most." If a doctor prescribes it, why is it then available for you to purchase across the counter? I mean get the proverbial clue people! A doctor is educated to know the entire etiology of a disease and its treatment, it is then up for you to decide whether or not a particular therapy is necessary. Only you can decide if the needle sticking from your arm is painful or not.

Dr. Spock has revived society's desire to know how to raise a child. I don't have any children. Why, you may very well be inclined to ask. I like to think that it has very little to do with my having injured my brain. I also feel confident in concluding that it probably doesn't have much to do with my reluctance to have sexual intercourse for my first 25 or 26 years.

Personally, I think it has a lot to do with my general disillusionment with society's current family structure, family being the only reason for being so emotionally and legally involved with a woman . Sure thing, I am proud of being quite fond of beautiful women. However, I've also had the fortune of a rather curious series of events, with my bachelorhood not being a topic of much conversation or apparent concern in the frequent carnal discussions at the dinner table. I can only assume that my sexuality...

I was hit by a car

but it wasn't very far

to the hos-pi-tal.

I couldn't pick my nose.

I couldn't say a word.

I could not stand up.

So how was it that you've been able to hire a lawyer, go to the university, and buy a house?

These are the types of questions I've been entirely unable to answer with what could be considered complete satisfaction; however, for you, I am going to try.

What Happened

A very brief overview of more medical ramifications!

What this injury seems to have managed in my life is to have set me up as an example; it's all just been one big set-up!

An example not to be emulated or followed but one to steer as completely clear of as possible. A *reduxio ad hominem*? Based on the assumption that this life hadn't been put in place as a torturous existence.... I've chosen instead to try and uncover the bigger picture, to be able to identify more precisely what the lesson for me actually is. Or maybe I've already done all this-been there, done that, and that the hiatus I'd put in for eons ago has finally come available. Now, I've become caught-up in a void, stuck out there, somewhere between where everybody is, and where everybody else wants to be!

You see, it must be very difficult to be my friend. I have the curious scepter of disposition, of my trying to never be the very same person from one sentence to the next. No one can ever hope to "get me pegged." The purpose behind such an eccentric behavior stems from my boredom with society. I just get so sick-n-tired of hearing the same newscast over and over, day after day, ad-nauseum all about the Presidents' indiscretionary behaviors.

Maybe that's what "they" want? Could it be that the NEWS is in cohorts with the other media industries, the movie industry especially? I've found myself having to go to a flick every week or two. What really becomes a drag is when the only theatre selections available are oxymorons, real-life dramatizations.

It's curious how my universe is working out the details for me. For so long, I'm not sure exactly how long, but I've been entirely unable to tilt my head backwards without there being intense amounts of pain, so, what do I do? I decide to strike out on my own and reinvent the travel down a flight of stairs, so did I make it.... to the bottom? Yes, of course I did. Gravity still exists in my universe.

I decided that it probably wouldn't take quite as long if I were to dive down the stairs; was I correct? Of course I was. Upon reaching the bottom of the stairs however, that was where the lights really began to blaze.

Explain what you know clearly, if not just concisely. Make the arrangement come off as an art. Write bearing information; explain what you know, well. I've frequently heard it said that what is important about learning how to do a good job at writing is to satisfy the reader, give the reassurance that all is well at the helm; well, if I were to give any energy to this as credible, I'd be a very clever writer of fiction. After you have presented all the facts and reached all the conclusions you have wished to attain, quit!

It does not seem ethical just to speak of my life as a rosy picture. To embellish the realities until they begin to resemble Hollywood.

All is not well at the helm; this chaotic route through life has not been particularly satisfying.

There Once Lived a Prince!

I simply ignored all the warnings that I should maybe wear a helmet. I was under the mistaken immortality syndrome; my infection had been "fatally" complicated by my having survived, an earlier car/bicycle collision, sustaining only road-rashes.

I have tried to structure this book around the storybook model. The following stories were initially inspired in1980 and the following 15-16 years of my rehabilitation and have been documented in written form, starting from the time I was able to get my first typewriter. I hope that these words do not solve any problems; I am just looking to create the chance, a forum, opportunity for self-actualization. I learned self-actualization in my Psych 110 lecture hall, sometime around September, 1985.

Because discoveries have always moved microcosms of society to new levels of understanding, I have been granted the opportunity to have, for all practical affective purposes, died. I have died and been allowed the chance to share with people my experiences.

I don't have any cognition from my unconscious state of affairs. This story is focused primarily on how I was able to achieve some semblance of life beyond the ICU. And then, how I was able to succeed with that, this life. That is life existing in an enormously unforgiving world. My world didn't much resemble the apocalyptic images presented by any number of the more popular late 20th century movies; however, now there is resemblance with the fairy-tale images which society, if only unintentionally, instill the children with.

There Once Lived a Prince

Once upon a time, in a land far, far away, there lived a prince, and what a handsome and strong prince he was; he led such a beautiful and unencumbered life. He sported the hay fields, his many games so oft taking him o'er the lands to fields, to ponds, and "up to the lake." He studied the sciences;

he learned to love mathematics; he studied the arts, and he roped and lunged and learned how to be astonished by languages not born to his tongue. All the while, he was learning of the great many new things to be astonished by; he also learned how to love, and he found such lessons of life exceedingly pleasant though often not fair.

He learned to love an enormously beautiful woman with hair so straight, so long, so silken, though not so fair. It crescended over her shoulders; it hung so clean and so straight before encircling her not so voluptuous waist. Her shoulders were strong and so straight; the breasts swell forth from a pure and freckled chest. Her face quite pleasant, and what a royal prize it would be to speak of love, and to mingle, and to dance with this chaste maiden.

So, David (that was the prince's name) invited her to the most royal ball.

Dear David

Dear David,

You don't know me, but I am a friend of Betsy's and this whole past year, I have been a neighbor of yours at my parent's house there on Gapter Road. They are Jan and Bob Johnson. They know you. My Mom always gave your little sister and brother their Halloween pumpkins, if that places it for you?

David, I knew about you before I left Colorado, but your condition was so that I could not see you. However, I have followed your progress closely through friends in the neighborhood. The whole neighborhood was and is very concerned about you. You have a whole lot of people really pulling for you and praying for you because they really care.

You and I have something in common, David. We both had severe head injuries that required surgery, which caused such dysfunction and paralysis, though our injuries were not caused by the same situation.

I was a healthy, active person like you.... coordinated, athletic and minding my own business when bam!! Like a sniper's bullet, as unsuspected and equally as fast, and through no fault of my own, I awoke to the grim reality of over-night becoming handicapped with paralysis, some blindness, and later, epileptic moments due to lesions on the brain from surgery.

Living with it is at once frightening and curious, curious, and frustrating.

I know the frustration you're experiencing. I know what it's like to try and be brave both for yourself and also for them, to watch the anguish in the faces of the people you love and who love you, hurt because they love you yet are so powerless to help, at times even unable to conceal their hurt; its often being expressed in angry manners when you've affected another of life's trivialities, done something so innocent, so blameless!

Still you need so much love and tender ministrations; hating it because of the circumstances of needing it. I know the frustration you feel at not having control over any of it, no matter how hard you will yourself or want to change it, first of all not having any control over your own body and speech; wanting to scream, though not daring or able if I did. I know of the whole schmear because I have just recently been through it too. I thought it might be some small consolation to you to know that there is someone else who can really understand it all. The people we love and who love us can only surmise with what they see, but they can't really know or understand what it feels like, no matter how they might try.

But David, this is my reason for writing. I licked it, I am still licking it, and so can you! And so you will!

With enough determination and hoping to have finally enough courage, I intend to get it all back, and you will too!

Mine was not caused the same way yours was. I was teaching class in a college and an artery burst in my brain, swamping the brain with blood, which put the brain in shock; this is called a stroke. Like you, I was in intensive care for a month, hardly aware of anything. Like you, I was in a hospital for 3 months after that. In the interim, I had three brain surgeries, of course I lost my job which I loved, missed a marvelous trip overseas I was planning to go on that week, and began the arduous ordeal of learning to do, all over again, every little thing that I'd already been doing so automatically for so long that I'd never given it much thought. I lived for this past year with my parents; not an easy thing to do when you've been out of your parent's home for years, raised your own children, and had your own way of doing things to then become completely dependent on your parents again isn't an easy chore for any of us. But one thing positive that has come out of it, and I'm sure you've discovered this too, is that there is so much love in this world.

If it hadn't been for my family and my friends' incessant reassurances that I wasn't doing this alone, and that maybe, just maybe, love had had its hand with working such a

144

fast rehabilitation; that and a little determination.

David I am driving again. That in itself makes me feel so much more independent. However, I did trade my stick shift in for automatic transmission because I still have some residual paralysis on my left side; therefore, I'm not able to feel the clutch.

And David, I am able to live by myself again, in <u>My Own Home,</u> with all my own things surrounding me, once more being in control of my own life. I've come to Indiana, because prior to the stroke I'd been accepted to study here for my PHD, with the top man in the world in my field. The letter of acceptance reached me while I was in the intensive care ward where I wasn't expected to live. Can you imagine? My life-long dream was coming true only to be lost due to some technicality. What a disappointment! But I'm here now, and I am going to, no holds barred, get that PhD!

But I am not as young as you, but still pretty young never-the-less! I am the same age as Betsy. Your being so much younger gives you even better chances than I have. Don't ever give in to it David, or give up. You are going to make it and still be able to pursue all your dreams. You have time, you have love, and you have youth; you have the determination!

David, the doctors told my mother, "It isn't realistic to even presume that she will ever be able to walk again. She may never get out of that wheelchair." If I'd heard this, I thought I'd rather die, for I had too many things to do, to die now. I didn't have any time to waste. Three months later, I walked out of that hospital with the aid of a cane and a leg brace. Another month and I was walking the Centennial trail with only the cane. I was scared that if my ankle flopped over, it would flop over and break before I even felt it. Three months later, I walked the trail without the cane. I was determined to run by snowfall. That's where I'd met Betsy; limping, but trying to run! By January, I was able to run. Winter came and I was faithful about my exercises, but I longed to be outside running, for before the stroke, I'd lived in

California, and would run along the beach with the wind in my hair. I had run 2 1/2 miles again every morning. And you will too! I and you will ride your bike, and dance with your girl, if you really want it and can discipline yourself enough you can have it all, do not give in to despair or give up trying! David, when you can write, let me know your progress, and I'll keep you posted of mine. We're tough! We'll do it! I love you more than you can ever know, P.S. We'll race each other to recovery, the only loser being the one to stop trying.

I do not wish to plagiarize anyone that is everyone who was there in the beginning, even though I may have forgotten any enormous number of individuals, the injury having left me with so much amnesia.

Even though sadly incomplete, it could have been worse; I could have not had a journal in my hands as soon as I had, without it so much, even more of this story and most of these people would have been lost on God's golden rolodex.

I'm sorry; I just don't know where my head's going. There is another route to take towards the understanding of TBI, although I don't stand the chance of ever gaining any first-hand, empirical evidence. I'm sorry women, I'm sure that giving birth, while not usually as traumatic or presenting so severe a list of repercussions, and I've been told it is one of the most wonderful aspects of being a woman.

Infancy: We've all been there, and we've all done that. Well, I've been there; done that twice. I've had to go through the whole process, less the growing pains; I've done it twice. I think it was Sigmund Freud who is the author of triad emotions. During the "id" stage, I was without any sense of dignity. When I saw a shiny chocolate éclair, I'd want that shiny chocolate éclair. And because of my body's instinctively sending signals to my bruised and otherwise compromised brain that I was hungry.... all the time, I ate! All the time.

While I was in this stage of neurological development, there was also the oral stage and the anal stage. SEX: In the first, the initial stages of becoming a man, it seems I failed all the course work. I was sent back, or left here as the case may be, to see if I actually did have it in me to be a man.

There was the period, a short period, in which I "made love" with three different women in less than 24 hours. I don't know how you'd care to refer to such a sexual hiatus; I think that I must have been trying to exert myself, to make up for all the lost sexual episodes.

Of the three, two were already mothers, one was a grandmother, and the third was four years younger than me. Disgusting? Well maybe, but I wouldn't want to associate such abrasive terminology in reference to something our Heavenly Father had provided us with, for our own use and enjoyment! I also might add, I'm glad that it happened; I'm satisfied that I was safe as I should've been. Sometimes I wonder, maybe I should've followed the footsteps, or the bedding of my peerage and started earlier. I was 25 by the time I lost my virginity. Please let your own conscience dictate the timing of your agenda. Right now, I'm married have been since 06/12/95, my wife is entirely appraised of my less than seemly behaviors, and she is now the best sex I've ever enjoyed.

Talk about burden, I'll talk to you about some of my burden. To have full knowledge, to be intellectually aware of having been able to do something, only to find yourself having to struggle with a motion you have done for so long. It's hard to have already trained your muscles to do an activity, and when you find the coordination is no longer stored in your muscular memory, one of the difficulties in this life becomes apparent.

When you're on the first go-round, there is no need to appease the ego; your pride is still immune. After I had been able to tie my own d--- shoes for 18 years, my ego was having a hard time going back to the beginning. That's the situation I am referring to when I say, "You've got to get out of your ego!" I've had to take a moment review the scene, and get out of my ego on several different occasions. My being married is instructing me to leave the latches on my ego off their hooks

147

more that I'd ever done before. There is no reason.

In my travels, I've found this message present, though expressed differently in many varied traumatized personalities. It was best summed up during a conversation I had with Judy Hicks, "I can see myself even when I get frustrated, or when I make a fool out of myself. It creates more pain on top of the pain already festering on the existing injury. Your eyes may not have been affected in the initial trauma-your perceptive abilities unaffected; but what they see you doing does not fit into any of the images already imprinted on your mind, into old learning."

"This almost seems analogous to the training of a dog, the training of my Golden Retriever in particular. I was without that leash around my neck. I had no instructions on how to act. There were no instructions on how to respond to the whistle. I was free to get on with my life as ever I felt would be best. And I did, but I was able to show a little self-respect, a little discipline. I knew when not to cross the street.

My last four years of school, ages 14-17, my mother sent a note to the school. It had said, "David is a responsible individual; I will no longer be writing his excuse notes."

This was great; I had effectively been given licensure to do as I pleased. I was being recognized as an adult. Of the kids at school who knew, everyone envied me. I had the tools I needed. I could "ditch" every class that I wanted to. It made me feel real good; I was the envy of what seemed every American kid! That was because I didn't want to miss any of my classes.

The psychological burden this placed on my shoulders, only now am I able to pick out the huge amount of responsibility my mother had given me and expected me to carry. I was just a kid; I should not have been expected to conform to the adult world.

Meet Peete

This is a story about my redeeming opportunity of meeting Peete, Peete Punque (the last 'e' is silent!) For the person who is given this as an opportunity, let them not relinquish the chance! It may sound brutal, and it may not be something everyone wants to run out and undertake, but as analogous to the art of lifting weights, No pain-No Gain! It is at the same time both a royal pain-in-the-a--, as well as presenting possibilities of untold riches. To "Meet-Peete," to be given the chance of a lifetime. To be given the chance of peeking over that infamous wall artistically encapsulated by Pink Floyyd. We are about to embark on a journey, a journey which I hope you will "enjoy."

This will be a journey to visit Pete Punque that mythical-often realistic character everyone celebrates yet is trying to avoid! To give body to the concept, Peete, is to give form to a fear everyone at one time or another experiences. By giving form to this fear, there is the chance of controlling it. There is no way of avoiding it, so let's give it a name so that we can at least control it. That's what this entire Western life is all about, isn't it? Transylvania is that land with the opportune chance to be associated with the more playful aspects surrounding this topic: death,

Peete is death, or the visceral wall between your living and your being dead. Peete is: a concept.

a new way thinking,
a posture, an opinion,
a sentiment,
a way of thinking,
a theory,
a moment of irrational prejudgment,
It is to have- to possess a prejudice, and we are all prone to this. It may not be a matter of ignorant, or to remain an ignoramus!

You don't Peete something, but if you don't live your

149

life like there's no tomorrow, there may very well-for you....
not be one! Now I don't want to come across like I wreak
doom, or that I am a naysayer to life, yours or mine! I do want
to make the point that there's not a whole lot to get strung-out
by. That if you've chosen to live beyond your means, well
then there's not a whole lot that I can say that will assist you in
your regaining your sanity.

What really is there to be too hugely concerned with?

We all live, no joke about this! And we all die! This is
where I am prone to chuckle....and quite often do!

In the movie *Pretty Woman*, there was the line in
reference to the street on which a woman walked in her
profession, "That's just geography." Let us create the illusion
that TBI is just a matter of the route one chooses in getting
through life!

Don't have another "Bad Hair Day," Meet-Peete! In
other words get the stick out, develop some courage! This life
is not out there to encourage any single individual to live.

No, it's not!

What it's there for, I haven't a clue. If we want to get
ourselves back into the swing of things, we've got to take
control, We've got to become more brazen, we've got to be
brash, we've got to assert ourselves..... We've got to prepare to
Meet-Peete!

Every man, even in childhood, is born a myriad of
possibilities of likelihoods and of accidents. Even in youth, he
is already a composite being, an aggregate of potentials. I was
a sunny child; I was quite often taken up in playing with
Baffin, our Labrador dog, or playing the piano. My familial
household was pleasant, unencumbered with strife; however,
we were not entirely without upset, and this was maybe good,
maybe necessary that I'd not been without the founding
background to withstand trauma. It was fortunate that I had not
been inoculated from life before my having the chance of
building up my own, dormant immunities. This may have been
good, it may have presented to me a theatre with the stage on

which my life was meant to unfold. The paths I was meant to take. No one in my family had ever suspected what we had no way of articulating. I was only 18 years old, just initiated onto the adult plane, although not entirely entrusted with all the secrets, all of its keys...!

In line with the precepts of that wise old author and sage, Pearl Buck, I had intuitively undertaken my life with absolute regard for the doctrine of moderation. Never laugh too loud, nor whisper so soft!

And just as often as my peers would bolster my pride with comments and much talk of how handsome I was, I would seek for humility, often to a fault! My sense of self, my ego; my esteem in cohorts with all my other faculties had been gauged to have taken me into such humble levels of our already mundane existence, with predestined position in life (my name and my family life posed mutual exclusivity: David: beloved, and Cole: worker) I had only the scarcest opportunity to comprehend: I was a Cole, a worker, scheduled to have assumed a workers' role, to have taken my position in the mines, and in the smithies for much of my gainful life! This I had always known. I had scheduled myself to always be trying to make the break from the cycle, to have forged for myself and any subsequent children, a comfortable life. A life want of the drudgery of such enslaving toil!

In high school, I had often witnessed the exact opposite. I have seen children, my peers, born into opportunity. I could see them so incredible burdened with the misfortunes of privilege.

> *From wrath and envy keep they soul*
> *In mildness never fail*
> *For though the godless get more gold*
> *Their wrath's of no avail*[*]

I don't mean to make this injury appear as an odyssey everyone should be looking for, some new experience

---

[*] Ed. note: David thinks this is from Tolkien, though I cannot corroborate.

151

everyone should plan into their next vacation. I do want to point out to the people who have un./fortunately been blessed with the experience, that there is still life out there (here), and in order to not have to become stuck in the never ending cyclical track of carnation-reincarnation, we've got to learn how to get everything that we were sent here to learn while here on a single and necessarily the maiden visit; however, that is then to say that any particular visit is either the first of subsequent voyage, and we really have no way of knowing. But that is just to say that I have no way of articulating such an experience. Not to say that I have ever had it. I don't know; now there's a catch-22: I can't tell you where I've been because where I've been is keeping all the images.

These days, there are so many attempts made to reach that mystical\mythical point of ultimate satiation, so many "wounded" people coming forth with all their humility saying that they could solve the pain and such loneliness shared by humanity as a whole. They effortlessly proclaim that for the startlingly low prices of $9.95 they will include your name on the list of those already assigned a call number to take their place in heaven!

No, I don't really mean that! Surely, you already knew that. We search for the minister, the preacher, the Reverend who in all of their humility can find for you that pathway, that gate through which lies the mythical land of pain free timelessness.

They are not our parents; to no one do they atone. Heck, if that's what you're looking for, you can send all your money-not tax deductible I'm sure, to me! Or you can minister to the needs of your neighbors. We are after all, all ministers, everyone of use.

This is not a book to offer to everyone, least of all you a thought, or recipe that will move you beyond wherever it is that you find yourself. Get a clue! If you listen to, atone to, practice and support anyone except yourself, and of course, your children, I really think you need more help than this book has to offer.

Get out of your thoughts! Let go of your mind! We, as the insignificant human beings, should all be satisfied with that which we are presented, and we don't have the capability to master any more than what we've been given. I am convinced that this is a perfect world, that there is little we are able to do that affects the perpetual motion of the solar system. It seems to me quite presumptuous of man to boast that the carrier pigeon has become extinct through the wanton carelessness of his actions, or to get all up in arms over the depletion of the tropical rain forest.

Surely, I too consider it healthy to identify ourselves as the "agents" of destruction, as having "man"-ifested the demise, even the extinction, of countless numbers of that microscopic zooplankton saturating the ice flows which lay, just off the coast of the North pole.

As history demonstrates, Jesus has given this story a new fullness by making his own broken body the way to health, and a new life. Thus, like Jesus, proclaiming to care not only for his own wounds, and the wounds of others, but to then make his wounded body into the vehicle through which others could also heal themselves.

I make no claim that I am Jesus! My name has always been Dave or David; and since my having gone to the university and found my 'id', I no longer honor the name Dave with so much as an eyebrow raise!

This may be the last manifestation of my being broken, I don't know. It has brought on the next level of our wounded condition, e.g., loneliness.

The separation, the isolation, the alienation, and <u>Jesus too was so lonely.</u> I know loneliness and I've learned to embrace loneliness. If not simply because of my intellectual wish to associate myself with this life alone, as a protective shield, entombing my body and very effectively allowing me to keep on-keeping on.

After having lived through this loneliness now for just over 31 years, I've been able to wholly and entirely get it, that this life is predominantly a lonesome process. The injury has allowed me to see beyond the limitation of intellectual processing what I've got to do with my life; my life has shown me, in ways which I needed, that my life was not meant to be spent in the confines of an agency, protected by that omniscient cloak of insurance. As a matter of fact, I do not stand the chance of ever being considered "insurable." It does not seem to matter that I am able to lift three times my body weight; I'm still not healthy enough to qualify for insurance. Sure, before sustaining the injury, I was involved with weight training, however, at the time I never even thought about my one day being able to control over 600 pounds.

It seems to hinge upon man's illusionary loss of self and the individual ways in which we seek to answer this hunt for ourselves.

We're not trying to find ourselves, but trying to locate attachment. That is to discover a yin to set-off the yang. Lewis Carroll wrote of this hunt with the metaphor of a looking glass. From breath-one, everyone seeks to answer the question-death. We all seek that illusionary messiah, and until we find it, we bitch and complain! I have found it! I have seen Pink Floyd's proverbial wall. Intuitively my answer is that I haven't learned enough to evacuate this plane.

Or maybe, I haven't shared enough of the unique opportunity I've been so entrusted with? C'mon folks, I've died, I know what's in store for, surely you don't want to behave like Peter Rabbit and go through your life with your head stuck in that archetypal hole of ignorance!

The awareness of our loneliness could just be the impetus to escape, to break that proverbial sheet of ice existing between yourself and the rest of humanity! Don't just simply tolerate this life! For the Soul, the Spirit, the had flawlessly chosen this plain in order that it learns something! If you don't learn it, so sad - you'll have to embark on this journey all over again...from point zero, or not. This is not a pick up where you left off kind of a game. I get this from the image of myself. While I was growing up, I grew up a "very old soul," and it wasn't until I'd died that I chose to embrace childhood for the wealth of lessons that childhood offers.

So, how do you see your injuries as having afforded you the opportunities to grow and heal yourself?

I must have walked all together poorly, for it took a broken toe to educate me that I had better begin picking up my foot. I must not have seen enough of everything, for I now see two of everything.

My thinking that ever I might even hope that my experiences, my words might be of interest, might even be beneficial to another did not come in a present wrapped for the Christmas ritual; and even as I now speak, my fear of rejection, that uniquely human trait of wishing to have an impact, is always in existence!

I don't wish to behave as a hypocrite and say, "follow me!" Instead, I want to impress upon you the need to follow your own counsel, and to also let you know that your path, though never before taken, has been mapped out from afar. I cannot offer empathy, for I've never been to where your feet have walked; I hope not to show excessive sympathy and sound less than sincere and committed to my words. I want you to walk with pride; to say, "hey, this life really isn't that traumatic. If I can stand before you today and wish you a happy birthday, or a very good-morning, or say good-bye and have a safe drive," I know nothing else could ever feel so real.

And that every time I cut my finger with a knife, I must acknowledge the pain and attend to the source of that Nile of escaping blood. As I do this, however, I must also recognize that the blood, as it flows, it is there as an indication that I am actually alive.

By academically indicating for you, my path, already traveled I trust that the way is not too steep and the path is not overgrown. Though, how can I hope for you to follow me, if I still occupy my steps; and I do!

This paradox takes me back to the Zen teaching: that I cannot make a clap with only one hand! Nor can you follow me without your first watching or telling you where to go.

10-27-93

Paradoxically, you cannot go anywhere if someone else is already there. So, even as untrained as may be, I will minister to your needs. I will get out of the way. I don't want you to always be having to reinvent that proverbial wheel, so I'll share just a little fodder, just a little encouragement; I will tell you where I've gone, cover the roads which I have walked if only to speed your process up, to allow you to spend more time healing, than exploring the innumerable possible routes.

(Transcriptions: Society has to work hard to keep us down, down @ Hammond.) When people tell me that I act just like an animal, I don't know how to think or if I should think about it. Are they are implying that are so unable to fathom why I do what I do, am I so injured that they are unable to understand what it is that I am saying. Do they mean that my bathing habits resemble those of a feline, or like the Arctic White Owl, bathing only when there are 9 months food with which to survive. I almost think that I am too closely linked to the processes to be able to take that step back and behold a subjective view of it. To be subjective, and I can't be objective what kind of jective can I be?

I have moved beyond survival. I'm better fit for some other occupation. So I've taken on a sort of responsibility. And I am responsible for people I don't even know. By being so closely intertwined with the process they are involved with, I. Now, as a "survivor," better known as a "thu'rivor," we've got to also shoulder the inexorable responsibility of "cluing society in!" We've been christened with the authority, although we are unable to articulate the specifics.

Does not the person who stumbles over the Arc of the Covenant become responsible for learning more about it? And the first person to discover an alternate route up Mount Everest becomes responsible for elucidating the world of who wants to know the new route.

I'm surely not meaning to imply, or to advocate that

everyone needs to listen to me for a better way to better injure their brain! I didn't think you were on that level of understanding.

That's almost analogous to the need for children to stick their fingers into the candle's flame; I'm referring to the activity not the object of the activity.

The Rock Opera, Tommy: "IIIII'mmmm Free! And freedom has a responsibility!" It is we who are free. We've been t the heights of life, I know I've seen over that proverbial Wall. I'm satisfied for the time being, that there is more to be learned here on this plane, in this realm of the Universe. It is not I who should be pitied, for having been down to Hammond! It is I who should be acknowledged for having been to see the other side; however, the secret is that Hammond is where you go and never return. Everyone is shackled with the great weight of ignorance, of naiveté!

Club-Med is how I grew to refer to Community and Memorial hospitals. My life is so perfect I've been richly endowed! I grew up in the land of milk and honey; even the fact that I had no form of major medical insurance is perfect because I am hugely displeased with the conventional methods of healing a person's wounds. I have no argument with the ICU programs, but beyond this, the hospitals are far too invested in maintaining their jobs-security! By their doing this they create the forum for fostering co-dependency! The ill health this perpetuates begins to border on pathological-even libelous degrees of treatment. It gladdens my heart to see Hillary Rodham Clinton initiate the process for healing the hospital!

I think it was Ernest Hemmingway who coined it best when he said, "This world breaks everyone and there are those who are able to go on even stronger the broken places." Man needs to learn to forgive the trespasses of others if they want to get on with their lives. I forgive, Joseph Lynn for his error in judgment yet I cannot realistically give him any latitude when I review how profoundly he impacted my life in a financial way. He had stuck the great claw-arm in on my movement towards self-actualization!

I always wanted to stick up for the under-dog, to be altruistic, although I cannot hope to affect such a noble state of affairs if I don't have any reserves from which to draw. No man can!

Write editorial: What you think about expands, so by encouraging everyone to focus the glut of their daily thoughts on violence-on "disempowering the violence," we are actually working to give violence more energy more power.

This book, although touted as a self-help book, creates an oxymoron with the title self-help-book!

I want to encourage everyone to write their own story, and I'm more than certain that there is a much more exciting story in the minds of someone else. There are so many different aspects to such a multi-faceted issue, to write only one book covering it all would be to effectively write another Bible! But you've got to do it, if not for a living, as a way of healing yourself.

It is someone different, but what really is it? Do you not feel that there is enough room, that there is space for health, for a healthy relationship? Or do you instead only see my being injured as somehow having had an effect on my personality? Is there no room in your life to take a chance and meet someone new? Or are you so lazy that you don't want to invest the time to again learn about a new person? Have I become responsible for all aspects surrounding the re/development of a friendship? A relationship that now hold such great promise, our not having to muddle our way through the traumatic episodes involved with growing up? Do you want to not always be hedging your conversation so as not to offend me or step on any unprotected toe? Is this not what occurs in every budding relationship? Am I a burden? If not a 200-pound physical burden, a 17 year emotional burden?

I now feel burdened as well. I've now got to always be educating you of the many various aspects of my injury! This is maybe what enables me to empathize with elementary teachers when they hoot and holler for an increases in their salaries?

I am sorry- all my old friends, let us hold a funeral or memorial service to eulogize the death of a dear and much loved school friend, David Cole! Maybe this way, we can get on with our lives! Please, whatever you do don't spend too much time attaching an increased amount of personal involvement with having a chance to meet someone new. There is an equal amount of strife had by both sides of this new meeting in getting to know someone new. I am entirely unwilling to shoulder the greater burden! Just as with the beginning of any friendship, there needs to be a time of reckoning, of adjustment getting to know the other person. If you feel that you've already spent enough time getting to know me, I thank you for your honesty, or if you are already over taxed in your efforts in your own life, this I can understand! Don't waste your time! Don't waste mine either! Maybe you feel that somehow the accident was in some way my responsibility, if this is how it is for you, I appreciate the Zen in your thinking; however, I am unable to give you the latitude, or longitude, I can just forgive you, it's okay! You should come! I consider myself to be one of the greater friends in your life. So I am throwing a party! A memorial party. I want to eulogize a great boy. We don't get to go back to high school for this party; rather we don't have to, instead this is to be a party full of lovers, to fill the night full of fun! I want a party filled by good friends, who think their lives are too filled to come. But at this party there won't be a need for nametags, everyone should already know each other.

In my days, I'd grown hugely. I learned how to put everything in its place, to compartmentalize my days; however, I had already reached a jumping off point. I was there between my youth and the rest of my life; however, I was given a new playbook at the last moment and expected to execute every step of every play with faultless direction. I have also been placed on the fields of play for the full 60 minutes of regulation time. I've not even been accorded the standard 3 time-outs per half, and there is no one waiting on the sidelines to run in and give me a breather. It always happens this way; if you're not given the full score to a play, you are then expected to exceed the demands. It's never you don't have 3 so I'll only change you 2; instead, it's you don't have 3 so I'll charge you 3.5 or 4! I'm not only disallowed a chance to succeed, I'm expected to make the big game winning play besides. I'm not asking for much, I only want to have a chance to warm up first.

David Cole

Dear Humanity,

I grew up in Boulder, Colorado! I completed my elementary and secondary levels of education, and I even began my collegiate career there in Boulder, then after only a little more, or less than a month at the university I died (was mortified) right there in Boulder.!

Maybe died is too strong a word. I was subjected to a Traumatic Brain Injury there on Arapahoe.

Without guidance, I'm directionless. Without a mentor, I am at a standstill. I don't know what style, what language/s what format I need to prepare and/or address my manuscript to follow.

I am ready though. It is my 2004 Resolution! Not that it hasn't always been my resolve, I just want 2004 to see *The Iliad of the Odd D. C.* on bookstore shelves, on coffee tables, in the library, stuck in the Web, headlining The Boulder Sunday Camera.... and many other similar periodicals all across the state, across the nation, all over the world!

Because traumatic Brain Injury isn't exclusive to the United States, but endemic to humanity, I would seriously like to work with translators from Germany, France, Czech Republic , the former USSR, Mexico, Spain, Switzerland, Austria, Italy.... anywhere where there are people.... with a head... In order to be counted you've got to have a head!

I want to go all over as a veritable ambassador. Almost as an ambassador in search of a country, in search of survivors in each and every different governing state. I want to encourage these people to represent themselves, their country, to document, collect, and compile similar such manuscripts, to spiritually, intellectually, maybe even financially embolden this new society, this army of Traumatically Specialized persons!

To become Philanthropic Up-themalogists! However, I'm not so certain that Up-Themallogy translates correctly.

163

Dear University,

Without guidance, I'm directionless. Without a mentor, I am at a standstill. I don't know what style, what language, what format I need to prepare and/or address the manuscript to fit.

I've found at least a couple hundred pages of documents collected over the past 23-4 odd years since the collision, that's right, it wasn't collusion; however, the fallout of the collision dulled my speech, it may have sounded like I said collusion.

Not to Expect Miracles

In terms of my recovery, I have been counseled not to expect the miraculous. Much of the implication has been not to expect any sort of return to a life so similar to the one I had left there on the Boulevard. I don't want it to go on record that I even sympathize, much less support such a pessimistic, though entirely safe, form of bedside manner, of post mortem council! My thoughts apply to either the traumatized patient or their family.

Even though I can't support the idea of establishing a false sense of security, or to set a person up for a major let down, it seems to me that if you do not aim for all the strengths you once enjoyed.... as well as those you've never been acquainted with, what chance is there of our attaining a level of ability any higher than the one to which you've awakened?

It may be accurate to remind me that I had only wanted to manage a return to everything I had neatly tucked away in the normalcy, which I had at my control on October 1st. My sense of grandeur, at that time, had been extremely limited. I could only see what the four walls, the ceiling and the floor held within them. I was lucky; I had a window opening onto the Flatirons, four of which I had climbed, but they seemed so far away, so unattainable. It is true that, initially, I might have only wished a return to the familiar confines of my own comfort zone, but it was the love, the conversations, often only monologues, and the human contact, which gave me the courage to keep on keeping on, to shatter that glass ceiling of therapeutic prognosis.

Once I had the chance to get out of my comport zone, after I was allowed-able to explore beyond everything which I had already known, that was when I was able to finagle a return into the university system. It was here that I would find my "id,"and it was here that I was able to establish an MO (*modus operendi*) that would provide the tools I needed to get through this life...namely, a wife!

No, all joking aside, it was not until after I had successfully negotiated the ivory hills and walked on the alabaster floors of a university (actually they were mostly all just concrete and dry wall)! It was pretty much not until after I had my Bachelors' Degree and had the chance to formally become Self Actualized, that I felt worthy of supporting myself and eventually a wife. This new relation necessarily spawning children, Aberdine Gena-C, and then Malachi David!

On Calling the Question

So, you'd like to have a Traumatic Brain Injury? For the life of me, I don't know why, but for the sake of Chocolate Mouse, please allow me to pack along for the ride.

So, are you saying you'd like to have a Traumatic Brain Injury? If that is why you chose to omit a helmet while out foraging for fun, on your bicycle, allow me to complement you. You see, that is precisely the way I had chosen, for lack of a better verb had chosen? I have never felt more alive than during the three, maybe five months, in which my having chosen to remain engaged with this celestial plane was on the floor of debate. I am satisfied with my God's having decided to "call the question" when he did.

How I Died and Lived to Tell About It!

Begin with me in high school- indicate that I was on the road to great things; however, only great things as I could see about the life I was living. I had no thought of there being anything different. I don't know that I wanted something to be different.

I was relatively popular, I had the expected girlfriend, and I had gone to several of the dances. Even here, there had always been the anticipation, the fear of rejection, but no. I was just a HO. A hunk of (Coal) Cole.

Our high school had had "Spring Frolics," a time to get out of the building, to run, jump, to let your proverbial hair down. I had signed up to ride in a bicycle race: The Fairview Classic. The course had been a circuit around the school. My having ridden the eight miles to school every day for the last two years had piqued my anticipation. I was going to win the race; it was just about that time that I had an instant of altruism. I saw that if I was to win, it would mean I would have to ride faster than Bryan Thompson. He had been the boy I had ridden the eight miles to school every morning with.

One of the girls I had gotten to know in high school; gotten to know-not in the Biblical sense , but whom I had dated, had been Stephanie Noland. For the duration of my junior year there at Fairview, she had been my "one and only." Time "rapidly" moved on. I became a senior, she had only become a junior, and she was what I thought was my second moment of altruism

I could see that come the next year, I was going to be at the university. I would be among all those "college babes," but there would be the unspoken while being very well understood "hands off policy." I didn't want this to come between us. Maybe I was only acting selfishly in wanting Stephanie not to know the stresses of being without a boyfriend....maybe? Maybe I was chicken. Was it my own fear of being without

Stephanie that encouraged me to be the martyr? Anyway I foraged my way through the last nine months of my secondary education knowing only Stephanie Marie Noland, so what was I to do for the infamous, sic notorious Senior Prom? Surely, I didn't feel safe or sane in asking any one of the other "complete strangers" to the dance. Surely, it would seem odd to anyone else except Stephanie Marie, after having only been seen hanging around with "Steph," everyone just called her Steph all year, and so did I.

Then there would be the summer vacation, holiday." The following semester I would be studying my brains into a tizzy at the University of Colorado- CU. I didn't want to undertake such an arduous process without my having at least followed in the footsteps of my "best friend." He had gone to Germany and ridden his bicycle through the land, after all, I had studied German *ins der Hoschschule unt Den Gymnasium* (in the high school and the junior high). I followed the example of my elders. I was convinced that everything would follow in due course, and that I would graduate eventually and would be sought after by engineering firms all over the country. At the time that's what I thought I really wanted; however, the universe, my universe, had different plans for me. It saw the opportunity to use my young resilient body as a sacrificial object.

That is, I don't believe that I led such a woe-begotten life, not that I'd been destined for anything other than the riches of Western life as I had developed in my mind.

I wasn't exactly sure whether that mind was such a brilliantly powerful mind, or just a never-say-die persevering one. I had not entirely met up to such predetermined schedules of secondary life. I hadn't received straight A's, as had my best friend Bryan Thompson, and my best girlfriend Steph had, but I had been able to graduate from high school with Honors. I had "gotten my cords," and that's all I really wanted to accomplish at the time.

So, there I was, just out of high school, gold honor cord wrapped around my neck, and was accepted into the only

168

engineering school I had ever really known, CU. I was on my way.

But first I had to do this expected graduation thing. I had to make the summer holidays after high school really mean something. The bicycle had been a very big part of my life throughout my high school tenure; I guess I figured it should maybe somehow be a big part of my celebration. I didn't have the financial reserves necessary to go to Europe; I was still "wet-behind-the-ears." Still, I wanted to take a bicycle trip and because I had no close friends in high school, I turned to the only person I related to, Ken Mann, my locker partner. The boy with whom I had completed my elementary and secondary course of study, but he was not to graduate that year; as a matter of fact I don't think he would get out after four years in high school, but he graduated. So many others had not had any sort of tribulations in their childhood education, but Ken had. He had led a life so fraught with peril. He hadn't been among the great number of us who just came up and moseyed through education having always "toed the line," no, Ken had realized early on that life was to be lived, not to be guarded, not to be sheltered; it was meant to be lived and enjoyed. In our sophomore year of high school he had been out there; he had the opportunity to see over that proverbial wall, the chance to "go down to Hammond". To have been living life to the fullest, and because he followed the motorcycle circuit, his vision of what real life was all about came to him in the form of a motorcycle accident, but that book is for him to write.

I decided that my senior year escapade was to be taken in America. Certainly cheaper if only like a domestic vintage of wine or beer. That was the beginning of things happening. I was going to have join me on the excursion, my best girl's brother, Jimmy. While we had been organizing the expedition, my Mother's boyfriend, Terry (who would later become her second husband) had spoken of his joining us in our ride. My Mother thought this was a very good idea, after all, we had only been high school graduates, what did we know about life? I ventured this proposition with Jimmy. We discussed how we didn't really relish the thought of our having been under the

169

guidance of a parent figure, and decided no. It was supposed to have been our trip, our chance to taste of life before we were to become embroiled in the tedious struggles of academia; however, we were still under the guise of our parents, This meant they had veto power in our lives, and they vetoed the entire journey unless we were to go with a chaperone, in this case Terry Shantz.

He buckled down; we compromised and decide that he would only go along for half the journey. So it was settled, we were to be allowed to go, only after having agreed to entreat Terry on the voyage half the way. As it turned out, we had ridden much faster than we ever thought. We were young, energetic, and out for what we'd envisioned would be our last final hurrah before real life would begin. Towards the end of that very trip, a couple days after Terry had separated from our company, I was hit by a Volvo®. An old derelict Volvo®, but a Volvo®.

In that collision, I had been able to hold my head up off the asphalt, maybe only an illusion, maybe only a metaphor for life: life presents any number of obstacles and it is man's task to accommodate and grow from these obstacles. Maybe I should have taken warning from the incident but I didn't. Instead I only took the message that I could hold my head up from the trials that life had in wait for me. Sure. My skin was not as hard and impervious as a tortoise shell, but it also grows back together again.

At this time in life, I had never heard the term Head Injury, nor did I conceptualize the repercussions of receiving one.

They say that ignorance is bliss. I agree. If you don't know about something, there's no need to waste time worrying about it. The metaphysical ramifications alone are there, posing a challenge, which education is in place for the purpose of circumnavigating. They also say that ignorance does not imply innocence. This world is so full of contradiction, for what purpose do we artificially institute even more?

I had been at a birthday dinner party up at the home of Gail Lurie which had been up Boulder Canyon, up Sugar Loaf Mountain. While I'd been at the dinner, I'd forgotten a pair of dark glasses. On the evening of October 1st I got a call from Gail. She told me that she had my dark glasses, and would I like her to bring them down to me in the morning?

I realized that I'd had an examination in the morning and it would be so cool to be able to walk in wearing a pair of dark glasses. I'd never had a pair of dark glasses, and everyone was wearing them. I said I could probably use the break, and that "I will come up tomorrow to get them before my test on Friday."

The next day, two coeds from the floor just above ours, Kelsey Harvey and Eileen Powell, came down and snuck into bed with me very early in the morning, being sure not to wake Paul Harris, my ROTC roommate, whom I despised. We were sure that such wanton sexual behavior, even though there had not been any contact of our sexual organs, would infuriate my roommate. *Ménage a Trois* had then become a part of my sexual fantasy.

I had recently been to the homes of Kelsey and Eileen in Evergreen, an idyllic mountain paradise. It gave me an image of the free times I should have been enjoying, maybe even ravishing. Classes had, after all, become such a tedious undertaking; I was ready to move on to something else. Maybe this was an early warning, an indication that there was more to life than maybe I even really wanted to know about.

It came to me in the form of a lesson. Not too much unlike the course in Miracles, having since been offered. I had not been allowed the opportunity to say yeah or nay to being enrolled in the class. I didn't even get to choose which section would have fit into my schedule the best.

There is a radio announcer in the back-ground. "This is a required course. You cannot choose the scenario in which to take it. There will only be homework, the class will meet for lectures only when you are least able to attend, and you are expected to complete the course before you will be allowed to move on!"

All this should fill up ten minutes of the film. Then we go onto the accident. I am seen riding, very powerfully, up the mountain. There is also a short interchange with Gail.

"I've got to get back down to the dormitory before they close the line for Dinner."

Gail asks, "Do you have a light?"

"Why yes, yes I do, a leg light."

"That's not very good you know."

"Yes, but it's the best thing on the market," I say as I swing my left leg over the top bar of the Univega®I ride." Take the camera in front of me, showing just how useless the leg-light really was, even though the light in the sky wasn't yet gone.

Show the hurried trip back down the canyon.

Flash to Joe Lynn, show him looking hurriedly at his watch, show him step on the accelerator, and show the car speed away from the camera.

Flash back to David as he pulls off of Canyon onto Arapahoe. Show him looking at his watch, show his black chamois shorts, and show his legs: their being so unusually large. Go to his face, beautiful, calm, serene. Slow the film down at this point; show David looking down at his watch, flip back to Joe pulling up behind a slower moving vehicle, show Joe again looking down at his watch, and show him stepping on the accelerator as he pulls to the left to go around the car in front of him. Then jump to David's eyes. We see him assess the car against the test he has, then flash to his memory of the California accident, then to images of the exam, then to his thoughts of there needing to be some way out of the exam, then to images of the payment check from the California accident, then to Joe's view of the scene. Show his stepping forward, hard on the brakes synonymous with the collision, there really was no time to react!

The screen is dark, in the background there are voices, indicating how this accident traumatized more than just the two players at the scene. Kelsey says, "Just last weekend we had gone up to my parent's house."

Eileen, "Remember how we were trying to piss his roommate off?"

Give some measure of how much blood was being donated in David's name. Kelly Allan's being pissed that she was disallowed from donating any blood because she had just had her ears pierced. Show the sign in sheet on my door, show it's filling up with ghost writing.

Flip to Joe Lynn's pleading for forgiveness from everyone at the hospital; we hear Dad say that "there just isn't enough room in our hearts to give you any sympathy; please don't come to the hospital anymore."

Craig Balsley, "Hey Cole, you've got hair growing on your legs after all."

New scene. David begins his rehab. I did not need a sugar coating of the process. I hadn't benefitted from any secrets, if there were any which had been kept away from me. I hurt more to build up an incorrect prognosis in my own head, just as most of us do as we go through life, only then it's not called a prognosis, it is called looking ahead, anticipating, dreaming. I had no one who knew exactly what the matter with me was, and therefore I hadn't been afforded the large amounts of attention that is usually given any child. That is, after all the closest approximation available to the level of my physical abilities. My psychological necessities were of a much higher level of development than my physical abilities; therefore, I was frustrated by knowing what I had been and to see it so hugely compromised. Maybe I was a freak? Maybe there are more head injuries that have need, or are in sync with the level of rehabilitation available than there had ever been cases like my own. I don't know.

Hey, don't cozy over telling me what you know is going to be. Give me the worst case scenario, and allow me to

173

judge how I feel about it.

In most situations, this is how I was treated; I'm just saying there should be no information that should be kept from a patient for whom it applies.

Of course that may enable more people to commit suicide. I'm wondering, with the population of the world nearing an absolute saturation of the globe, why are we so fixated on the need to save, to birth, to resurrect every living person? Call it heresy if you must, but I think the time has arrived for people to become less concerned with frustrating a system for which God has already created, a built in system of reproduction that is, for all intent and purposes already self perpetuating ad nauseum! Show the blood, the pain, the seemingly interminable length of time rehab takes. For me, time had begun to move like cold molasses, and just as if I were again a child, I exhibited infantile stages of development. I went through Freud's Oral stage; I ate everything I could get my hands on; then I went through the anal stage, which I equate with my being hugely constipated. Where as while I had been in the hospital, and under their "expert tutilage," they had been able to have given me colace...*ad nauseum* as a stool softeners. However, after I was out of the hospital and away from so many drugs, I found that I had become chemically addicted, though maybe only psychologically dependant (lazy).

New scene: David begins his second life. He goes back to the university, CU, and is intimidated by the size of the campus. I realize that I must have jumped the starting gun. I decided to give my brain a little more time to heal, thus I went to Seattle with some high school friends. I spent about two weeks there.

DC *alle finé*[*]

 This injury seems to have been one big set-up. For 18 years, I had been quite able to have managed my own life, a bachelor almost as if I were in preparation for the odyssey which I was to begin in my 18th year aboard this planet: I had been in fabulous cardiovascular condition, my physique had been at least minimally accomplished in the weight room, and my mind had been constructing any number of neural synapses.

 Unlike the examples outlined by Homer, this odyssey is one not to be emulated or even to pretend to follow. This one, I encourage you to steer, as completely clear of as you possibly can. These lessons are almost geared as a *redusio ad hominem,* i.e.: I am hoping to show you how wonderful life can really be, by showing you how rigorously trying a near death experience actually is! I've based my arguments conclusively on the assumption that my life, like your life, wasn't established as a tortuous existence.... I've chosen instead to try and show you the image of what life can look like after I've had the redeeming opportunity to die while trying to live. And that one's based on the assumption that it's fair for me to say that for all intent and purposes I, or that, David Cole died.

 Actually, the David that died remained out of circulation and had been out of circulation for just about 25 years. That was the age at which I had taken "Introduction to Psychology" with Jerri Chance.

 Jerri now was an older woman by only 1 or 2 years, and a very beautiful woman, and just about a year older than I. My first day in class had found me in the very front; the first row of the soup-bowl like lecture coliseum. There was the traditional period of getting to know one another, several hours with the lights down exceptionally low, and then came the explosion. Sigmund Freud had only been in the chapter about 4 or 5 pages, and I..... well, that's when I found my id.

---

[*] DC *alle finé* , a musical term, according to David, meaning "go back to the beginning, play until you encounter the symbol again, and then skip to the end."

175

I must be very difficult to have as a friend? I have the curious disposition of trying never to be the very same person from one sentence to the next. No one ever stands a chance of 'getting me pegged.' The purpose behind having such an eccentric behavior stems from my boredom with society. I'm just so sick-n-tired of hearing the same news cast over and over, day after day, *ad-nauseum* all about the Presidents' less tactful behaviors.

Maybe that's what 'they''want? Maybe the NEWS, working in cohorts with other media industries, is in place only as a stimulus for the movie industry, don't `cha think? I have found myself having to go out to a movie house just about every week or two, but only as often as I can realistically afford the admission price. What's really a discouraging reality is that often the only theatre selections available are oxymorons, e.g.: real-life dramatizations.

It's curious how my universe is working out the details for me. For so long, I'm not sure exactly how long, but I'd been entirely unable to tilt my head backwards without there being intense amounts of pain, so, what do I do? I decide to strike out on my own and reinvent the travel down a flight of stairs. So, Did I make it...to the bottom? Yes, of course I did. Gravity does still exist in my universe.

I decided that it probably wouldn't take quite as long if I were to dive down the stairs; was I correct? Of course I was. Upon reaching the bottom of the stairs, however, that was where the lights really began to blaze.

Explain what you know clearly, if not just concisely. Make the arrangement come off as an art. Write bearing information, and explain what you know, well. I've frequently heard it said that what is important about learning how to do a good job at writing is to satisfy the reader, give the reassurance that all is well at the helm; well if I were to give any energy to this as credible I'd be a very clever writer of fiction. After you have presented all the facts and reached all the conclusions you wished to attain, quit!

It does not seem ethical just to speak of my life as a rosy picture. To embellish the realities until they begin to resemble Hollywood.

All is not well at the helm. This chaotic route through life has not been particularly satisfying. The only reassurance I am able to share, to speak of adroitly, is of the satisfaction that you are walking. If you are able to speak, and if you do not move through your days as only an enigmatic intelligence, I want to re/assure you that you are on the right path!

Write as the provider of information, almost as a tour guide. Leave the reader with a single bit of new knowledge that will keep him reading.

Begin with a few hard details that tell the reader why this has been written, and why he ought to read it.

Attend to the details and worry not about entertaining the reader, that is their responsibility, they love it.

Be able to "hook" the reader with allusions to my rebellious attitude in rehabilitation; thereby leaving the reader with the information how I've been able to emerge from the injury, a much happier man than the boy with all the hopes and dreams so deeply embedded. The call of all the glorious American work ethics embroidered so firmly into his pants and up his sleeves. Allude also to the fact that Fred had been a hugely prolific stitcher.

I find that the best temperature for me to write in is when the temperature is where I can be sitting at my typewriting desk wearing a pair of shorts, a hat, and booties. When the steam off my coffee cup doesn't just rise slowly, but curls seductively from the porcelain white pedestal cup I'd been able to pick up at the closing sale of Lillian's Espresso, a wonderful coffee and a meal kind of shop.

"When you lift your leg, make sure that the arc is behind you. Don't use your quadriceps. We are trying to strengthen the tensor facialatte." Already I had been trying to come up with a logical, if it were only the mythical, explanation for my being alive.

I had been told that I was hit by a car while riding my bicycle back to the dormitory, after going to retrieve a pair of sunglasses I'd left behind at a birthday party at the home of Gail Lurie, which had been up on Sugarloaf Mountain.

Graduation means different things to different people. Me? I was going on a bicycle trip!

The Bicycle Trip after Graduation

Down the Coast of California

It's Finished!

Waking up in the hospital wasn't all bad.

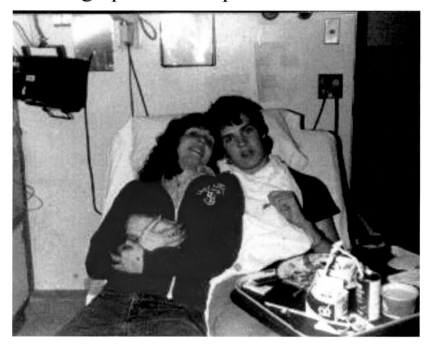

February or March 1981

DC *alle finé* 2

Why did this have to happen when it did?

I've got an exam in the morning, and I'm scheduled in the kitchen at Nancy's Restaurant on Saturday.

All this injury has managed to do for me in my life is to set me up as an example; it's all just been one big set-up

An example not to be emulated or followed mind you, but one to steer as completely clear of as possible. A *reduxio ad hominem*? Based on the assumption that this life hadn't been put in place as a torturous existence.... I've chosen instead to try and uncover the bigger picture, to be able to identify more precisely what the lesson for me actually is. Or maybe I've already done all this, been there, done that sort of thing, and that the hiatus I'd applied for eons ago had finally become available; that now, I've become caught-up in a void, stuck out here, somewhere between where everybody is, and where everyone wants to be!

You see, it surely must be quite a task just trying to be my friend. I have quite a curious scepter of disposition. I've chosen to live my life trying to never be the very same person from one sentence to the next. I want there to be no one who can ever hope to "get me pegged."

The purpose behind such eclectic behavior, I think, stems from the basic boredom I've found with society. I just get so sick-n-tired of hearing the same newscast over and over, day after day, *ad-nauseum*: All about the Presidents' in discretionary behaviors, the recent development of a major tropical depression in the Gulf; or the Oklahoma bombing and the O.J. Simpson investigation.

Maybe it's just what they want though. Maybe the NEWS is in cohorts with all the other media industries, the movie industry especially.

All reality shows and real life newscasts are oxymorons; all those real-life dramatizations, or the short paragraph at the end of a mini-series on the home television, ie: "Mr/s. X was found guilty, and is currently serving the final months of his/her 25 year prison sentence. Very soon though, they will be back on the streets, as members of our society.

MY universe seems to be working out all the details in my life, for my life. There was a long period of time, I'm not sure exactly how long, but what seemed such a very long time. I was unable to tilt my head backwards. If I tried to, it often was not without there being great amounts of intense pain, so what do I do? I decide to strike out on my own and choreograph a new means of travel down the last flight of stairs.

During the course of my trying to manage my new life, I've found enormous fortune in the persons who entered in my life's continuum, and several discoveries which I have since incorporated into my life.

When I started to write this manuscript, I was down weight bearing information. To try to satisfy all my readers. To assure the reader that all is well at the helm. So I tried. And tried, and tried. My injury had made my common sense oblivious. What I had failed to realize, entirely failed to understand, was that if I continued to try and write for everybody, I would continue to remain STUCK, stuck in trying to solve all the ills of the world. I'll leave this one up to the rest of society. I am more than certain that there are a myriad of stories, a library of good books out there; and I am sure that my own story of injury and subsequent rehabilitation, would grow weak and pale when set aside your own story!

One of my personal discoveries, one I am sure every red-blooded Sicilians has known about for many centuries, is garlic! Garlic is that magical substance so often used to keep vampires away, and to spice up that pizza or spaghetti sauce. Well besides keeping Count Dracula at bay and most of the senior high cheerleading squad, garlic is also a wonderful elixir when trying to keep mosquitoes away, and useful in helping rid oneself of that persistent cold. The first cloves of the fruit will immediately set about trying to purge your system of any

186

toxins and other uninvited guests. I have found this to result in a rather unpleasant odor to exude from one's mouth and pours. As soon as your body, your blood, is empty of the sludge that causes "BO," you"ll be able to enjoy the fruit of the garlic as often as you wish.

It does not seem ethical to speak of my life with a rosy background. It doesn't feel correct to my nature to embellish the realities, the truth until it would begin to resemble a story that Hollywood might latch onto.

I'm sorry; all is not yet very well at the helm. This new, this chaotic course through life, necessarily my own; it has not been a detour on which I would hope you could join me. That then is just to say that I am the master of my destiny.

I am not!

All that I am able to share, to speak of with sincere authority, is of my satisfaction that if you still have the capacity to understand even a smidgeon of what I have written, then you've got the foundation from which to make your life persevere!

Write as the provider of information, as a tour guide.

Always leave the reader with a single bit of new knowledge that will keep him reading.

Begin with a few hard details that tell the reader why this has been written and why he ought to read it.

Attend to the details and worry thee not about entertaining the reader; that is their responsibility, their love.

I find that the best temperature for me to write in is when the temperature is where I can be sitting at my typewriting desk wearing a pair of shorts, a hat, and booties. When the steam off my coffee cup doesn't just rise slowly, but curls seductively from the porcelain white pedestal cup I'd been able to pick up at the closing sale of Lillian's Espresso, a wonderful little coffee and a meal kind of shop.

'When you raise your leg, make sure that the arc is

behind you. Don't use your quadriceps. We are trying to strengthen the tensor facialatte." Already I had been trying to come up with a logical, if it were only the mythical explanation for my being alive."

What I had been told while reclined there in my hospital bed was that I had been struck by a car head-on. It seems that I had ridden up Sugarloaf Mountain in order to retrieve a pair of sunglasses, which I had left behind me at the home of a friend and sponsor of my eighteenth birthday dinner, Gail Lurie.

The Moat Between Them

Two castles, your horse can gallop up to either one of them, individually but still, she cannot jump the moat that lies between them!

Write the first chapter or more about the perfection of the universe, leading up to the first and second accidents!

There Once Lived a Prince

Once upon a time, in a land far far away, there lived a prince. A very handsome and fair prince was he.

There once lived a prince. And such a fair and beautiful prince he was, and what a beautiful, unencumbered life he did lead. In high school he had even loved a woman, and she was a beautiful princess as fair of face was she as of order. It wasn't that the father of this gallant Prince was displeased with his choice of brides, nor was the relationship discouraged by the woman's family, for they never had royalty sleeping among them. But still the relationship was plagued by a mysterious force driving it forever further into the abyss from which few who enter even return!

The year of which I speak really is of no consequence, for the story is told and retold by innumerable Princes from everywhere and has been told and retold in so many different languages, in so many different countries, for so many different years, but this one is a tale which few, if any predecessors, could boast. None, so articulately anyway. There are of course fairy tales told and Halloween stories sold, but none have actually been lived, in the first person, by any of the expressed or apparent authors. This, it should be made note, is not a short story. As a matter of fact, it's pretty long, so long in fact that I doubt very seriously that any publisher would willingly print my entire story, so I've eliminated much of the less note worthy jargon.

I begin my tale, my biography. An autobiography, whichtakes placein the fine years immediately following the decades housing wars and such abundance. His time had followed the years just after the world was at war. The digital enumeration beginning, 197.... I grew up, my never actually having to fight, claw or kill, nor did I need to spend my time reading the newspaper, hearing the television news, or watching others commit any of the atrocities of which I have just spoken. Instead, I was more interested in just being a kid!

There were many tales told in the days of the round tables and about the world without any problems. I'd rather tell this story from the point of view of persons unable to articulate their processes, their struggles; all the myriad of issues which they face, but feel that these topics are of little if any interest to people who are struggling themselves trying to exist, just exist! I cannot feel empathy for these people; I don't want to take away the power of their pain. Instead I wish for this book to focus on illuminating facets and angles which everybody who has ever struggled with an injury to the locus point of affect, the head. I seek to open up the world and show them the inside intricacies of an event which we all stand the opportunity to experience. No one wants to face the reality; no one has the gumption to examine the myriad of possibilities that exist.

The smallest being is the infant child; not yet entirely human, but neither a part of anything else either.

Kennedy was to be assassinated only shortly after the day of my first birthday. H---, I didn't care; as a matter of fact, I couldn't have given a s---, but I probably did. I probably soiled more than one cloth diaper; we didn't have the disposable kind yet, or was it that my Mother was bent on living her life almost ascetically? A life of struggle.

The education of my early days was preoccupied generally witha big brick building- a school building. Twelve years later without any due or undue hoopla, or fanfare, I successfully maneuvered my way well beyond my first days in preschool. I had begun high school in an institution some seven miles away, at Fairview High School.

I so readily tired of riding the school-bus for it had

come by my house about an hour and a half before class would even begin; and because I'd lived farther along towards the end of the route, I would often get there with a little more than an hour to wait in the building for my first class. I couldn't imagine what it was like for kids at the beginning of the route.

Besides, I had a friend who lived directly across the unpaved, oily, greasy, dirt road, and he had an older brother, who could drive. We spent so many a long hour of the imperceptivity shortening days. And because the days never seemed to get any shorter, the length of the school year always seemed to increase. It grew and grew that is, until Saturday, June 7, 1980. When I was given a little red book, and no, it wasn't written by Mao Tse Tung. This little red book was a diploma. On the diploma is written:

"Having fulfilled the requirements as prescribed by the Board of Education of the Boulder Valley Public Schools, District Number Re 2, Boulder County, Colorado, David Fredrick Cole is entitled to this Diploma given this seventh day of June, Nineteen hundred eighty."

This memo failed entirely to mention anything about the "with honors" part. But I had; I had been hugely successful and graduated with honors. This was the last anything I would complete with honors for the rest of this, my first life! And now, I had life to look forward to. I could now enjoy all the freedoms accorded an adult. My birthday was only about three months away, and I would no longer need to be so devious in order to get my beer.

It was the summer of '80, the summer after my high school graduation, and quite possibly my last summer to be taken off; I wasn't legally or morally obligated to work, yet. Instead, I had chosen to work. I didn't want to always be a slave to tuition; I wanted to always be one step ahead of the tuition. But this was to be my final summer to spend lollygagging about the fields. H--- I just graduated from high school with honors, and since I was scheduled to begin college in 3 months, I didn't want to work. But I did work, for I didn't want to graduate like all my friends... many thousands of

191

dollars in debt, so I worked a couple of fabulously low-paying jobs; dissonance, cognitive dissonance, is the word which comes to mind. On the one hand I wanted to enjoy my last summer off, while on the other I did not want to follow in Uncle Sam's footsteps. I did not want to be enslaved with debt for the remainder of my natural born life.

The jobs I took were in the sun; therefore, hot. The first job was inside a garage at a car dealership, as a go-for. (Go-for this, go-for that). The other was outside directly in the sun tying re-bar at a concrete form, assembly manufacturer. All this was okay though; I was only 17 years old, an honor graduate just out of high school, I was flying. I didn't mind being made out as a slave, and as a matter of fact, I even considered it to be a privilege, assigned to go out into the cool morning air to get the doughnuts for the 9:10a.m. coffee break, every morning at 8:30a.m. It was as though my high school graduation entitled me with promises for good, and now that that had been done, I could settle into a dull state of lethargy.

That's just how my mind was working at the time. I was finally finished with the tedium of scholastic exercise which every child is plagued with for 12-13 or so years. I now had everything planned out; my life was going to find me with a wonderful job, working for a wonderful company, and maybe I would even own this wonderful enterprise. I simply could not conceptualize, thank goodness, that there was much more beyond high school that I needed to experience, but I was ready. I was ready to take on the world. And after so many years of dull tedious work, I almost considered it a given that I should get a break, a little time off. I didn't expected this gift to be presented to me as I walked across the stage at the high school commencement, but I'd done my part and just as well, maybe even better than possible, I figured. As a reward for all my hard work, I was ready for a little R&R. I felt that it was now my obligation to make plans for a wonderful vacation. I was going to go on a bicycle excursion that summer. I was going to invite Jimmy and we were going to peddle our bicycles down the West coast form Seattle WA to Santa Barbara CA. We thought we had the world in the palm of our hands, and we had. So as a graduation present to myself, I was going to take a bicycle tour; I was going to ride the Western edge of the United States.

There was only one woman who I dated in high school for more than a week. She had one older and one younger brother. Now Jimmy was no slouch when it came to academics; however, in the field of social rapport, Jimmy was lacking in large volumes.

There I was, on the top of the world! I was a winner. I had great riches laying in wait for me. Surely I couldn't be so callous, so selfish, so rude as not to include Jimmy Noland, an alum, in my holiday plans, for I'd just finished well over a year of almost living at his house. I never slept there, but I sure spent several very early mornings and steamy late nights there courting his younger sister, surely I couldn't plan a high school graduation vacation without him; you see, he was also in the class of 1980. Now looking back, I'm sure I very easily could have married her at that time, but it just wouldn't have set right with my Mother, or either two of my girlfriend's parents, or with Jimmy, and therefore not well with me either. I had been a pleaser, a brownnoser, a cad. Call it what you will. I was altruistic to a fault.

So, with Jimmy I planned. We mapped out all our destinations. We called ahead and secured several maps for our holiday of a lifetime. We were off to tour the Western edge of the United States, bicycle in tow. What could be more fitting for a student who had just completed 3 years of peddling the 15 miles to and home from class every morning almost every trying day for the previous 3 years, than to get back aboard his bike and to travel the 1800 some miles down the west coast, what indeed? For the lesser half of the trip though an older companion would accompany us. He too had graduated from Fairview but had done so maybe 2 decades before; however, I might allow him to join us, even though it just didn't seem right but I was willing, I was accommodating. I would!

In the nape of my neck, I was sure that we were being

193

set up, and set up I was sure for something big. At the time, however, I just wasn't really prepared for the initial political, much less any subsequent familial ramifications; I wasn't ready for the epitome of perfection as, eventually, it was to become. At its onset though, it didn't look like much, it had even felt like a vacuum, but I wasn't about to take that laying down, coma or no coma. I was out to make the world, and I wasn't about to let anyone let alone anything get in the way. I forget whom it was who said, "If it doesn't kill me, it can only to make me stronger!" And I can feel the frustrations had by the car, a Volvo, which was later to be stripped for used parts and then sold for scrap metal, probably melted down as scrap metal.

Almost as soon as I "woke up" from my traumatically induced coma, I began to learn all over. I could hear people say, "It makes me so angry that you were hit by that car; I just don't know what to do with my anger."

My life was obliterated, not over, just made out to look like death and I was the lucky one. By not muddling around in all that damaged hardware, I was able to reassemble myself with only a little guidance, some assistance given by so many ill paid therapists, that I was able to get myself off to a new beginning, if just a little rough around the edges. I had the raw material with which I could create a monster of anger, or something a little more constructive. What evolved was a dialectic rapier often more scathing than a serpents' tongue.

But there was nothing else; I had little way of knowing that I had the freedom to choose the entertainment that I wanted to attend. But right then I had no other choices, no further choices from which to choose. So, what did I do?

I began exhibiting characteristics clinically termed as agitation. I was agitated; I was pissed as h---, but that's not clinical. I was set up for the fall. At this time, I was organically disallowed from speaking, of communicating what I really wanted to say, and I didn't even know that I hadn't known what the heck was happening to me.

194

By not having any further input, I had no further examples. I readily adopted these messages as the way things really were. And I too would become angry. I too felt the need to place blame, but because I was rendered incapable of articulating my anger, I had to act out my anger, and it evolved very much as though I was just a child. But this time I had the foundations from which to build. I didn't need to go back and begin at point zero. I was very fortunate! Like the child growing up hearing only English, or only German, or only French being spoken, I had only anger in my system. Bravo that this was soon replaced with more constructive pictures of possibility, of growth, of altruism.

The child, who learns only one word for every object he witnesses in his surroundings, knows everything by only this one word. Because I didn't have the opportunity to view my "lot in life" except with only what I was given, and because I wanted so to please several of my therapists, I too became angry.

You may be asking yourselves, "I don't get it; David's writing a book in the same genre where there have been so many hundreds of other books written before."

If this is how you see it, this is where I must correct you. I have paused for 12 going on 13 years so I might find something different, a new way of lending what I have witnessed to others so they might be better for the experience. Therefore, they can die when it is time without needing to go on having to afford rent and food and heat and light in the night.

1980

1980, what a grand year. Actually, what a very big year too so packed with life and death. A very big year in the life of the United States as well, in the life of music lovers everywhere, and in the life of a recent high school honor graduate. That's me.

If there is a toll collector at the pearly gates, I'll need to plead insignificance that he'll need to allow my passage regardless of my being financially able to balance the fare. I led a fairly blessed life. I did not swat too many mosquitoes; I helped a number of "old-ladies" across the Pike. Surely, I deserve to get beyond these gates. I am innocent. I played no part in the fall of this, the golden empire of the United States. I wasn't available for comment or vote by proxy when Ronald Reagan got hold of the White House, and I had no part in the slaying of John Lennon, who wasn't even offered a chance to be assassinated for a second term. For both of these calamities, I was "dead;" I didn't vote absentee either! I was dead! Just when you think you have some control of world order, and it doesn't even matter that you're working so hard to assume greatness, it could all get snuffed out like the stadium lights.

And I'm sorry! I am entirely without any responsibility for all the calamities which 1980 wreaked. I was dead. My heart may have been beating, but for all intent and purposes, I was deadened towards affecting world affairs. And just maybe, I set this one up. So much has occurred since I began to entrust the universe with my needs and problems, that maybe I set the stage for all this to happen. I had been a weight lifter in high school, and graduated with honors, a 3.65 grade point average, and a diploma signifying only that I had, "successfully fulfilled the requirements of graduation as prescribed by the Board of Education of the Boulder Valley Public Schools. District Number Re 2. Boulder County, Colorado!"

I don't need any more chances handed to me. I hope not to appeal to your sense of pity for the poor; I only ask that I not be assessed as incompetent because my appearances indicate such as so many scream for; instead, I need less willfulness to pre judge me just because I don't walk the straight and narrow. Fewer stigmatizations, defamatory remarks, some made publicly and others less evident to the unaided eye or ear, but made never the less, metaphysically.

The precursor or secret phase: This is an examination of a person's life before the actual onset of trauma. This is where I hope to be able to make the greatest difference. I figure why the h--- spend so much of my waking existence writing anything if it doesn't affect something? Even the checks I write; if they didn't affect something, I'd be less inclined to draft them at all, but without writing them posthumously, I would have been most entirely unable to write many of these words.

The measure of everybody's life; their actual successes and their less so realized successes and even just their attempts at living a life as a temporarily able bodied (TABED) human being, is quite often reflexively aligned with what I've lived and witnessed in others. Don't be concerned that the measure is skewed because I am only one individual and there are so many other people being afflicted-affected by TBI. Persons whose lives were never cut out to take on an active-constructive role in society, and all those who have never had the gumption to relate their experiences to the larger society; and therefore, they've simply gone on to take their place on some accountant's data register and are heard from no more! I am entirely unwilling though to concern my writing with these persons, or fully examine their rationale, reasoning, or guiding *modus operundi*. However, I am able to grant them this latitude, for I have no respective perception of their lot in life. This may make me out to be the fall guy, that bad cookie, the aberrant author who is so callus, so rude, and socially estranged. If this should be the categorization, which you have assigned to my personality, then, so be it. I cannot hope to refute your sense of integrity, but I can hope to get you off the dole, to get you on your way and lessen your susceptibility to becoming just another statistic.

While I say that I want to address health and potential, I need to acknowledge that we also need statistics, but if you are reading this, what does this indicate? We need them, but only as a way of showing statistics to others, to impress, digress, and otherwise ingest society with even a single iota more control over their lives. This serves to make them happy, to pacify their need for affecting other, more impacting calamities such as rioting in Los Angeles, or garbage workers striking in New York.

In the discovery/ chaos phase, I had a clear identity about who I was, what my strengths were. I was on my way to impacting society in a measurably sizable way, but what I was entirely unaware of, was that something could go wrong. I was without an internalization of the processes involved with that metaphor, death. Now, after the fact, my illusions of death, of immortality, are actually reinforced.

To me, death has always been reserved for the grandfathers of the world, the men who went to battle, and then only for me. This was only to be after I had married, procreated two or more individuals as a way of, at once, having affirmed my existence, of announcing that I, David Cole, had actually once been here, and sought an experience everyone needs to undertake at least once in their lives. I was entirely committed to living. Almost pathologically invested in this life; I was serious about making this time a good time, a prosperous time; however, I hadn't actually had anything to go on, nothing to judge how things were really going, but then reality is such a nebulous term. There is no baseline, not even one from which to gauge my hunger.

Was I really hungry? Or has all this been somehow incorporated, programmed into my sense of reality, like a computer program in which you've got to set the stage, you've got to make the input understandable, and you are responsible for any mistaken results had by the machine. So, because I was shown the possibilities of what life could be like, had I chosen to be birthed into the wrong culture?

My homeostasis might never have known eating into a

sickened state of gluttony. My equilibrium may have been adjusted to always walking upside down. Upside down being as is related to the conventional, this 20th century Western sense of right side up.

We might never have even known what it was to breathe oxygen. Now I seem to be delving off into metaphysical arenas or ontological realms.

As a young adult, not even an adult yet, still a teenager, 18 years old, and I was just beginning to expand my parameters of experience. So far, I had less than 30 days to enjoy life in this new legal new category, though for all other purposes, I was still "wet behind my ears," as well as in front of the ears and in the ears too. I was wet all over, except if I had wanted to commit a crime, then I wouldn't have fallen into such a nebulous position where my level of judgment would become an issue. I have been tried and hung as an adult. This is the way it has all seemed to work out; I wreaked some terrible calamity on some poor unsuspecting soul, and so for the rest of my life, I now have to pay for such an infringement.

So you think you know how I think? You're sure that you have all my answers for me. That isn't really how this world is geared to run! I am the only one who knows how I think! Are you frightened of me when I enter a room? Do you have questions, questions that I may be able to answer? Before a homicidal maniac kills anyone s/he is treated with all the rights and responsibilities afforded other people in society, so why am I treated with manners fraught with fear? Do you really enjoy treating me as though I am mentally retarded? I don't really think so, yet you do! This area remains clouded over and impenetrable, yet I am more apt to greet you, befriend you, anger you, love you, and be loved by you, than that homicidal maniac I mentioned earlier!

I am able to love, be loved, make love, and be hurt, but it's okay if I make you feel uncomfortable, you'll get over the uneasy feelings. What really pisses me off is when I am neither accepted nor rejected, but glanced over. It's one of the most useful combative ploys. It's like the Denver Broncos on

200

the defensive line, but instead of hitting the offensive player, they just step back allowing the offensive man come at him. It is a martial arts form of causing great destruction... Just take the energy being directed against you and convert it into an energy to protect you, aikido?

As it were, though, I have been hung without first having been tried; without ever having been found guilty by a jury of my peers. No, they all have been at home, in the dormitory, or in class. I have fallen between the proverbial cracks and the fall was to take me through not only the cracks in the roadway, but also through the cracks in the law, and the cracks in the medical profession. The abyss into which I had been cast was to hold alterations so profound that I wasn't about to take them on alone. It was a relief to know that emergency medicine had advanced to the levels it had.

After patching (stapling) me up enough so that no more bodily fluids could leak out and stain my shirt, pants and socks, they were able to arrange the pieces in a bed for the next 3-5 months, after which time I was to begin the stepped up regimen of bodily reeducation.

Before I could be scheduled to undertake this long lonesome process, I first had to master a couple of rudimentary abilities.

Because I wasn't expected to access that infamous next level of recovery ad nauseum, I became a freak, an aberration, a disorder of the mind. However, none of this with my mind!

Indeed, I also was able to navigate the Western most border of the United States, that's Highway 101 and 1, by bicycle from Seattle WA. to Santa Barbara CA.

After reaching Santa Barbara, ill fate lay in wait and dashed into traffic before I finished crossing an intersecting road of travel. Maybe this was meant to be a warning; maybe it should have alerted me not to ride my bicycle in traffic anymore, but it didn't. Instead, it only reinforced my sense of immortality. I was now even surer that I was invincible. No car could injure me! Nothing could knock me out of

201

circulation; all my years of weightlifting were paying off in sums immeasurably huge.

The awareness polarization phase. The recovery-rebuilding phase. I just want to bare this spot and have it known by everyone who helped me in the critical, crisis. emergency moments may have already been paid by my insurance adjusters as well as myself. I am forever in your debt, whatever that may mean to you, and that too is good.

Idiot and the Odd D.C

Definitions according to M. Webster

The Iliad:

An epic in the Homeric tradition. A series of miseries and disastrous events. A long narrative. Iliadic/adj

The Odyssey:

An epic poem attributable to Homer recounting the long wandering of Odysseus usually marked by many changes of fortune. An intellectual wandering or quest.

****

Definitions according to D.Cole

The idiot

An epileptic in Davidian nomenclature. An encapsulated series of miseries, of fortunes, the verges of misfortune and other illustrious events.

The narratives of a Philanthropic Upthemallogist[*]. Idiotic/adj

The Odd D.C.:

That's David Cole beyond simple survival! An epic: recounting the heroics, fortunes, misfortunes, changes of fortune: since, beyond and because of a Volvo's impacting upon his head; an intellectualized, often fortuitous quest, on hiatus, a spiritual wondering

The Iliad and the Odd DC

The good fortune which you may or may not have quite unwittingly, without any malice or fore thought just bestowed upon yourself is probably not entirely evident at this point. These benefits are manifest either directly: their being activities, which I probably should not have been involved in,

---

[*] David defines his function as an Upthemallologist as himself, walking the mall doing random acts of kindness as part of his self imposed rehabilitation

or conversely: their having been programs I had not been involved in, which I probably should have investigated a little further.

Such as wearing a helmet whenever I rode my bicycle, whether on campus or off; however, it had been the late 70s early 80s, 1980 to be precise. The nautilistic design of the bicycle helmet had resembled that of a motorcycle helmet, "too hot, too bulky, impedes my vision." For many of these very same reasons, I had never even owned one, now I can only wish that maybe I had worn one of those hot, clumsy, miserably distracting appliances.

Thursday, October 2nd, 1980, that's less than a month since I had been obligated to register for the draft.... I hadn't obliged. That's when something else entered the picture. It was bigger than me, bigger than the draft! It might have even resembled tomorrow's Wall Street Journal, no one could see it or could have heard the impact of a young cyclist head-on with an errant automobile, or read that he could now be reached in the Boulder Community Hospital's ICU.

Now that one's funny! This being less than 30 days since my becoming eligible to vote and legally obligated to register for the draft, and already I was a casualty. Without even being inducted... no draft, no Boot camp, and already I was a "corpse." I could have used an honorable discharge but no! None of this was on Uncle Sam's ticket; I had to foot the bill alone. Actually, my insurance had to, but I had to have it and quite fortunately, my Dad did!

Friday morning: Expository writing, 101, and there I am missing the morning's exam. Darn, I may need to see what I should do about that one.

Let's go back a day, okay? It's a Thursday. I'm in my dormitory, the clock on the wall reads just about noon, and I am more than a little anxious about Fridays' examination, in the morning. The Hallett Hall communal telephone ring breaks through the institutional "silence." The call is for me; my hopes soar. Would it be my instructor calling to announce the cancellation of tomorrow's examination? Ha, I think not!

It's Gail Lurie. She's calling to ask if I want her to bring my "shades" with her when she comes down to Boulder in the morning on her way to work. It seems I left them at her house at the recent celebration of my 18th birthday. I hesitated, that would be easier, but I was sure my tired butt would enjoy the bicycle ride, "no Gail, I'll try and pick them up later this afternoon."

Having never lived outside the United States, or Colorado, Boulder since the age of 3 when my Dad became employed with IBM, I was entirely unfamiliar with the old English ritual of jousting. It had not been among my more noble afternoon sports. Besides jousting not being offered that semester; it wasn't in the engineering curriculum, and I don't think I would have voluntarily chosen to duel with an opponent weighing easily 2700% as much.

I may have just been a freshman, still wet behind the ears, that is just plain ignorant; however, I doubt very much I would have voluntarily chosen to wager my masculinity, my ability to play the piano, to ride a bicycle, or to love a girl. My not being a gaming man, I don't think I would have risked my life either; the Colorado lottery had not yet been installed.

The suggested retail price you've been asked to afford, i.e.: $1,980.00. Besides being the year of my redeeming odyssey, there in Boulder Canyon, it is my attempt to immerse you in the experience without your actually having to go out and put your ability to dance, to love, and to be lovable right back.... to put it all on the line, to risk it all on the spin of life's bicycle like roulette wheel, or the role of the dice. I hope that by having created this trail map, I have done you a small favor.

In this era of professionalism, all the issues of liability, and the need to find a specialist to pull all the thorns-of-life from the paws I've taken in my day, I have a sense that I have, quite unintentionally been traumatically specialized. How about you?

Why are we here? Now this is a question so thoroughly

205

squabbled over for so many years that by now society has abandoned any further processes of examination, or verification, of trying to discover another reason for it. Instead, we have all just come to accept our existence and have all gone the way of our fathers and their fathers before them. We have grown, sought an education, propagated our species, and died, and we've done this and have been doing this for probably too many years to bother keeping track, but as a smitten of entertainment, or a past time, we've chosen to bother keeping track of all this.

When a man is born into this world, he comes in a package, which is neither complete, nor adjusted to take on his environment; there is a whole lot of assembly required. That is why we have developed the institution of childhood, and why this is then ruled over by those strange and mystifying entities, the doting parents. Even though these creatures are huge and terrifying, scream and holler and cry as much as we might, we just don't appear able to free ourselves of their control. However, there is something else out here which, no matter how frightening these creatures might be, that is even more horrifying, even less controllable than what we've come to refer to as a parent. Those maladjusted, usually underpaid scabies, those sitters.

When I would throw a piece of paper wadded up, and wrinkled, it was so very similar to my being an infant. There was very little accuracy, and I would become so frustrated! I didn't even have the opportunity to "GET IT" that my perception(s) of the movement, the world, were utterly inaccurate. I had no way of realizing that there were other ways to see the world, but I was unable even to realize that I didn't know that I didn't even know!

I am assuming, as inaccurate as the process of assumption can be, that by the time you've chosen to read this manuscript you've had the basics, the beginning fundamentals, a few rudimentary cognitive abilities to develop a picture, to "see" what it is that I am saying instilled in your head. I am assuming that you've all, by now, probably had a 6th grade level of education. Don't get me wrong, I'm not implying that only persons with a 6th grade education are eligible for head injury, only that before the age of 12 or 13 a person is typically so guarded and otherwise over-protected from traumatic events, that there is literally no reason to elucidate them.

Why do I hope, even dream, of enabling you to understand what I mean when I say that I can see two of you? That I can reach out and touch each one of you, individually, but I am entirely unable to put my hand between the two images of you that I have, and that isn't because I am unable to coordinate my manual dexterity to move my hand in such a direction.

If this book, this story, has been written, and consequently read without raising a few eyebrows, without raising a person's interest, or calling the question, I would be living without integrity.

The price you paid, e.g.: $2000, is meant to pour the foundation in order to give you an inkling- one iota of what having a Traumatic Brain Injury entails and what it is like.

The title comes from a book written by or compiled by Homer, and if you thought you knew what this book would be about, if you had wanted to be in control and to know what I intend to tell you, I beg your pardon!

This story, this book is just the chronological measure of my life. It is almost a biography... of sorts. It is almost an autobiography... of sorts. It could be considered historical fiction but I wanted to leave the control, the perfection, the association with that to my mentor, James A. Michener.

Before October 2nd, 1980, I was an idiot; however, after October 2nd, 1980, and after "living" a little more, my life experiences left me looking rather odd, and my initials are D(avid) C(ole).

It was about 1978, I was in high school. My primary girlfriend was SM Noland, and she was exceptionally studious- 4.0 GPA, I wasn't necessarily that studious, but she had been taking a class in which the textbook had been written by

Homer. The Iliad and the Odyssey. I'm just not that creative; I had to borrow the title of someone else's book as the leaping off point for the title of my own book. Therefore, I'm almost a plagiarist.

You ask why you consider yourself an idiot. Allow me to use my affective synonym for idiot: ignorant? I was an idiot; I was ignorant; I was without a clue; I was clueless in Boulder. I was ignorant. I was, is, are, and am an idiot. I am not now though! I think as Ernest Hemmingway wrote, "While this world breaks everyone there are those who continue on even stronger at the broken places."

No Rest for the Patient

These are the words of Barb Richards, who I had only connected with as an acquaintance, except for the 9th grade trip. Even then, she was an R.A (responsible adult). I was one of the 9th graders, and she was someone to be wary of.

But all that.... that was a long time ago, in my other life, when I was just an idiot.

"In this game, so often called, life, 'it's really hard to tell the cast without a list of the players!" So, in this case:

David Cole

Fred Cole, "Dad"

Wendy Wharton, "Mom"

Brandon Cole, "bother"

J.B, also James Cole, "brother"

Spring Cole, "sister"

Barb Richards, "B-mom"

Morgan, also "Morgs" Richards, "stepsister"

Kendall, also "Kends" Richards, "stepsister"

Terry Shantz

David "Doms" Wharton

Toby Wharton

Fred "Grand Dad" Cole

Blanche "Grandmother" Cole

Annabelle

Williamson's

Mrs. Minister Pingle

Mitch (Pingle)

Most Reverend Forest Whitman

More Journal Entries

Friday October 10, 1980

"My dear David.... The following pages are telling your story, all those who love and care for you (particularly your Dad and Brandon) and events as I saw and heard them starting the night before your accident. (10/10/80)

PS: Last night your Dad told me that Annabelle said it was important to have the space of time filled in during your unconscious period. I thought about this and decided I would like to do that as my gift to you. Also a way to fill the/my time.....Which sometimes seems not to move at all!

Wednesday October 1st, 1980

David tonight you had dinner at Manhattan Drive. Your Dad was excited about your coming over since he had not seen you since school/college started. I talked to you on the phone for a while. You sounded so up, so excited: classes were good. I enjoyed our chat... The last time we'd touched base was at the '77 trip reunion at your house. My thought later was that you were possibly being stretched for the first time. Had I been told that I would be seeing you the next night, I would not have believed....................."

Thursday October 2nd, 1980

"I was looking forward to a trip to Boulder. Your Dad and I were invited to a dinner at the Williamson's for dinner. The reason: Mrs. Minister Pingle was in town to do a wedding. Mitch was there and ate with us before running off to his, back-to-school night. Val fixed and served a superb Italian dinner. John had just built a beautiful roaring fire, and the five of us had just settled in for some relaxing talk time. Your Dad had dropped off some books at the "dormitory and last saw you "whole" at 5:15 P.M. At 9:15 P.M. J.B. called your Dad with word that you you'd had an accident, was in emergency and could he get to Boulder Community Hospital Right Away! I asked if he would like me to go with him, replied, "OK, David would probably enjoy seeing you." When we arrived we were placed in a small waiting room with your Mom, Terry (who I really met then for the first time) and a really neat man named Dale, the hospital Chaplain who would spend many hours with all of us. Dale started to tell your story, my friend and I had to take deep breathes------ just to listen. A man had crossed a double yellow line to pass a truck and hit you, head on. Guess what a bike and Volvo do not make good sparing partners... "Anyway, "you "lost," but you gave it your best.

"The word was that there were no vital signs at the scene of the accident. They put you in a pressure suit (maybe you know what they are, but I had to ask your Dad.) It's a suit that works on your whole body like the item they place on your arm to take your blood pressure.) And in the hospital you came. You went into surgery and we were told that you would probably lose a kidney and your spleen, and that it could take 2-3 hours. In my mind it feels like they moved us from waiting room to waiting room. Actually, not knowing the floor plan I (now) know that we only moved once. Realize, without humor life would really be grim.... So, there were a few chuckles. Now starts the parade of doctors 3, nurses, and orderlies who kept us informed each step of the way. Every time someone would come out of surgery they would say, "Mr. and Mrs. Cole?"

"Looking at your Dad and me. I guess my black hair confused things.

The 4 of us would say, "No," this is his father; this is his mother. It was really hard to tell the cast without the players. From time to time Dale would go check and come back with an update. They closed you up after only 1 1/2 hours with a much better report.

(At this point let me say as we walked through the night each update sounded better and better)

"There was a tear in you bowel which they stitched up. Your one Kidney was in bad shape, but the bleeding was walled off and they felt time would take care of this. Next came Dr. Presley requesting permission to X-Ray your head checking for blood clots and any other abnormalities. At this point he took your Dad to sign some more papers. This was the first time he has physically seen you. So we Wait while they X-Ray your head. Oh, David, let me tell you about the one young man who kept going in and out of surgery with his operating greens on---- He was wearing clogs which had paper booties on them.... See what I mean about humorous part?

"Actually by now, it's really Friday a.m. October 3. While we were waiting your friend, Ken Mann, his girlfriend and his father had heard about the accident and appeared in the waiting room.

"Robin Turcott, Sheriff's officer stopped at your accident on the way to another call. She waited until an officer appeared for you** (there is more to this-- look for the …)

"They spent a lot of time talking to Wendy and Terry. I was standing in the doorway of the waiting room when they wheeled you out of surgery and this was the first time I saw you!!

"I understand your Mom and Terry saw you before your abdominal surgery. The word at this point was that we could see you and say good night once they had got you hooked up in ICU in your own room. Wrong. Dr. Presely came out and said he needed to place a screw in your head so they could monitor your cranial pressure. So, we waited. Considering the hours we waited, enough was going on at that time; time seemed to move swiftly.

October 13, 1980

"David, I must tell you I'm behind-- but even through the first night, as you have certainly noticed! Meanwhile, moving right along. I guess because of the nature of that first night, I keep remembering things I've passed over. One very important special person is Brandon. When your Mom called looking for your Dad, Brandon had hoped to and went over to stay with J.B. and Spring."

213

Friday, October 3, 1980

"After we arrived and after I had enough information, I tried to call Valerie Williamson. But of course the line was busy!

"So I looked up the Gapter Phone # to give Brandon an update; I told him what we knew and ended saying, "I love you," and he said, "I love you too." More good things about Brandon as the days unfold.

"I do not remember the time, but the good Reverend Forest Whitman strolled in during your surgery, dressed as always.... Drawstring pants, Sandals. He and Dale (hospital chaplain) knew each other so this added a light touch. The two of them stayed almost until the end, or at least until you were settled in your ICU room. After Dr. Presley inserted the screw we were again ready to go see you... But no, they decided on an X-Ray checking for spinal injuries. This done and no additional information---- assumption: you'd pulled off another plus! We finally went in to see you and say good night. I would have to say you resembled "Lerch" on the Adams Family. Your whole body was/appeared swollen--tubes were going in and tubes were coming out! Your height/weight over-poured the bed and the small room. Your Dad and I left before your Mom and Terry, knowing you were critical, even though it all looks very grim... I just feel that David is going to be O.K.!"

"We got to Manhattan Dr. about 2:30 a.m. Brandon was spending the night at Gapter. Your Dad fixed us each a Very strong drink, and through much conversation, we tried to unwind. At one point your Dad put his head back and said, David, get up and walk away from this." Finally, about 4:30 a.m. we called it a day and got some restless sleep.

Robin went to a meeting at Gale's house and heard that you had taken a ride on your bike in order to re-coup your sunglasses!

Friday October 3rd, 1980

"7:30 a.m. the phone rang-- your Dad's boss, Ken, had

214

just heard the message your Dad had left on Ken's machine before going to bed. We got organized and headed to the hospital. Your Mom, Terry, Brandon, J.B. and Spring were on duty. Today's positive therapy is no rest for the patient. We all talked to you! felt awkward at first, but it got easier each time. We are curious to hear from you what you experienced. They brought a tape recorder and several of your favorite tapes from home. In bed with you was your White Seal hand puppet. What a beautiful warm fuzzy. I said Good bye--- I'm off to work and Vail for a school board conference for the weekend. It was hard for me leaving your Dad, but he promised to call me both nights with an update. Another word about Brandon--- He became one of your very best bedside nurses. Those blue eyes never missed a thing!! He monitored your tubes, the monitor --- actually, he and your Dad had the system down to a science when I returned from Vail.

.. A word about the community that occurs among family and friends who come together in a surgical waiting room. A woman named Kim and her father were on duty that first night--- Kim's Aunt had had a malignant brain tumor removed. They were in the same waiting room with us that first night. She said, "He is in excellent hands with Dr. Presley is tops and really cares. 3 hours after the team of 3 doctors had worked on you, thinking their night was over, Thursday, they were back at it working on Mark Rahlstead, who had fallen asleep at the wheel and rolled his BMW: head injuries and possible spinal injury, collapsed lung-critical. It turns out his girlfriend, Cindy Sprouse's father, works at IBM. That all had gotten together in... where else... the surgical waiting room. Others who were patients or had family there kept/are still keeping up with your progress. Mary Ellen- a perky young woman who was supporting her mother who is a nurse at a clinic nearby. The father/husband(?), Max had a malignant brain tumor (was only ill less than a week) and not expected to live even if he regains consciousness. Pam Fritz, wife of Skipper who came in after running into a telephone pole. He was not in ICU very long before they moved him upstairs. David Sarageni, graduate from Fairview (2 years ahead of you). He has a twin brother named Dale. David had an accident in his panel truck. Severe head injury and was really disoriented and talking loudly, hollering for help. One night his step-Dad said, "I hope he doesn't wake up your David with all his loud talk." Your Dad said, "Oh, let him wake him up--- that would be great!"

Saturday October 4th, 1980

"Last night I finally got several hours of sleep. Your Dad called with an update and mainly a chance for him to debrief--- We talked for about an hour. You had squeezed the hand of one of the nurses. The smallest signs give hope!

"Your Grandparents arrived today... Doms and Toby. Also Bailey, Your Dad had tickets for the CU game which he and Brandon attended... Score: 82-42, alas CU lost, but the change of scenery, away from the hospital for a while, was helpful. Sometime during the afternoon the Reverend Mrs. Pingle and Valerie came to see you. I attended the excellent communication workshops which helped my time to pass. Daily swims and the hot tub at the hotel in Vail felt really great. The Englewood School Board and the Air Academy Board had a "work dinner" at the left Bank. Again I was anxious for the phone call from your Dad; after his good-night to you at the hospital. Today, you had yawned and tears were seen. All good!! This doesn't sound like much, but for those who are waiting for any signs... it doesn't take much!

"By now your Mom has talked with the ambulance driver and we are all relieved to hear that you did have a neck pulse when he arrived, which was less than 2 minutes. God, we are all glad to be able to talk about what we didn't want to discuss!

Sunday October 5th, 1980

"As we drove down from Vail, we listened to the Bronco's winning! My Saab was having some body-work done, so upon my return to Englewood, I borrowed Bev's (the woman whose home I've lived in since June 5th) car and made one of my many "swift" Boulder runs! When I pulled up and

216

parked across the street from the hospital, your Dad, Bandon and Bailey were sitting on the lawn. I met Bailey and said, "yes, I certainly can tell you are Wend's brother!" Fred said, "Brandon and I are getting ready to go eat-- want to join up? We went to JJ McCabes. Before we left, your Dad went in to say we would be back. When finally he had returned, he said, "Sorry it took so long, but I didn't want to talk to Joe." Joe had been the driver of the car that hit you. After he got out of jail on Saturday, he and his wife came to the hospital. Both your Mom and Dad have talked to him, and have been kind and understanding, but he feels terrible. Your Dad said, "I've said all I have to say!" Then to me, "I just want to run when I saw him tonight." We ate, talked, relaxed a bit and returned to the hospital. When we returned, Doms and Bailey were just leaving to take Spring and J.B. home. At this time, I met Doms! Once inside, I finally met with Toby (actually, I saw her at her '77 trip reunion at Gapter.) We run into your Mom and Terry coming out of ICU. Your Mom is teary eyed and visibly very upset because of all the liquid that is going into you. You are starting to retain fluids and the concern is that your heart could fail. David, realize please that I last saw you on Friday a.m. So I'm really impressed with how much better you are looking. You are on a respirator; therefore, your chest moves up and down very fast. I'm amazed at how good the stitches look even though they are moving so swiftly! Your color looks good, you appear lighter, your kidney output is excellent. I feel better seeing you for myself. The medicine they give you begins to work and the area around your heart begins to your. Wendy, Terry and Toby leave just as soon as you stabilize. Brandon, your Dad and I stay late. About 10 your Dad calls your Mom and gives her an update. We leave only after you are settled! Oh yes! The chest X-Ray? You have your picture taken very often to check on your lungs. Janet, (one of the ICU nurses I get to know, she has one long braid, and takes really good care of you). You can tell him good night after they take another x-ray. Fred and Brandon have parked across the street from me. When I start Bev's Suburu, it roars-- refusing to idle. In the dark your Dad is unable to figure out the problem, so it's off to Manhattan (the

217

Arms) we go in the Pinto. A drink. Time to debrief and off to bed.

Monday, October 6th 1980

"Rise and shine- Brandon is off to school and we head to the hospital hoping the car will start. It continues to roar soooo your Dad (in his spare time) drives me to Englewood and Sinclair Middle School where I retrieve my car, and tell Bev her car is sick in Boulder. Your Dad drove straight back to the hospital this afternoon. I have my first experience on the RTD from Englewood to Boulder. We decided that extra cars we did not need. I arrived in time to eat dinner with your Dad and Brandon. Then it's off to the hospital. I walk into your ICU room and start to laugh--- no one told me that P.T. had started today. There you are, only a towel across your lower body... nothing else... but barnd-new white and blue high top tennis shoes. I said, "Hey David, I love your tennies!" I laughed. Tonight I met your friend Craig Balsley. He'd come to see you! What a neat guy. He said, "Hey Cole, you do have hair on your legs!!" He told me the last time you worked out together you didn't have hair on your legs! I can hardly wait to hear from you, what silly stuff you heard.

October 7th, 1980

"So it's off to the hospital again, with all the information of how to get the car started! Success!! Meanwhile, back to Sinclair to trade cars with Bev. This is the 3rd time I've disrupted her classes since your accident. Good thing I'm a school board member or we'd all be in trouble! I worked and then back to Boulder. I told your Dad to ask for what he wanted and needed during this time. He said, "I feel guilty about the gas you are using. " I said that is not the issue-- now, what do you want?

"Today is the day I walk to the mall and find this journal. I went to several shops before I found one that seemed acceptable to me. Then I went to the stationary store and found this blue pen to write with. As I was walking back, your Mom passed me in the VW van. We waved. When I got back to the hospital, your Dad said that she had taken the cat to the vet. When we were leaving, she had pulled in the parking lost. We went over to talk and look at the cat. She asked if I had taken the bus to Boulder? The cat needed to take pills for a month. I gave your asked a hug and said, "Just what you need in your spare time!" she looked weary.

Friday, October 10th, 1980

"Today is the day that your friends (from campus) are able to donate blood in your name. There are signs up all over. Your Mom went by before the donors came with a dozen carnations to give out.... to say thank you.

"47 donors came! (The largest number ever to give blood in someone's name.) Kelly Allen could not give blood because of newly pierced ears.

"Toby was very involved in helping this to happen. It gave her something to be involved with at a time when your friends wanted to help but felt so helpless.

Saturday, October 11, 1980

"Your Dad and I came to see you. Each day looks better and better. They asked us to leave while they worked on you and cleaned you up. We came back to say goodnight and all the lights were on in your ICU room.... (They weren't ready for us yet). We leaned over and peeked in where the levelers were pulled up, and you were sitting up in a lounge chair with Drawstring P.J. bottoms on. When we did come in to say goodnight we talked to you and Janet. She had washed your hair, which we decided must have felt good. Somehow, seeing you sitting up made you look so much better!

Monday, October 13th, 1980

"Today you moved out of ICU to your own room. During the move some missing items were found under your bed in a plastic bag, e.g. your dorm keys, sunglasses*, a tennis shoe, biking shorts.

* The sunglasses you went to retrieve on October 2nd. You were returning to the dorm, with the glasses, when your

accident occured. Tonight is one of the few down nights your Dad has. All I do is care, hold and listen. The eve before the CAT scan is scary--- as this may tell about any brain damage. He gets up to make tea and later I find him on the couch deep in thought. After talking through concerns, we go back to bed to sleep.

Tuesday, October 14th, 1980

"Your Dad arrived before they loaded you up for the trip in the ambulance to go to the CAT scan machine which is housed a block away. He rode over and later came back with you, wanting very much to be part of this important event. You were scheduled for 8:30 a.m. He found Dr. Presley and got the report. As all others have been, it was good news- a badly bruised brain stem--- no abnormalities are there. The only foreign item in the scan is the place where the screw was put in to monitor cranial pressure and Presley said, "I did that so the world we live with is TIME, and it continues to be what we all deal with daily. Dr. Presley says you could wake up in 6 hours, or it could be 6 weeks, it is now up to you, (as it has been from the beginning) your body and the bruise to heal. Tuesday evening you were deep under. It had been a big day, but another hopeful day.

Friday, October 17th, 1980

"Alan drove to Idaho springs to bring your Grandparents down so they could see you for themselves. It is hard for them, too. I met your Uncle last spring before the ninth grade trip when he dropped the lens off at my church for your Dad to use. Today I met your Grandparents for the first time. I like them... I understand your Dad more- the keen sense of humor and intelligence. After they spend time with you, Doms and Toby, Wendy, Terry, J.B. and Spring, we all went to lunch at the Good Earth. Brandon, your Dad and I met them in surgical waiting.

Sunday, October 19th, 1980

"During the night another young man arrived... a neighbor of yours -- lived on Simmons Drive and his name is

220

Kenny. He was hit while riding on his motorcycle and is critical with severe head injuries. Your Dad checked his monitor and his cranial pressure was in the 40s. Your top was 11 so we knew he was in bad shape.

Tuesday, October 21, 1980

Again, you are moved up to your own room. This time up on the 3rd floor.

Wednesday, October 1980

"This is the night of the week I usually see Morgan and Kendall and they have been most anxious to see you. The 5 of us go Round the Corner for dinner and then to the hospital in 2 cars! Morgan drives Brandon and Kendall. Kendall is a bit leery of going upstairs (since only 2 at a time anyway) So she and I go to the surgical waiting. As we walk down the hall, a large group of people is standing in a circle. Dale, the Chaplain, is with them and he and I catch up on you! He says, "I see them all and David will make it and will be O.K. He looks different than the others. He tells me that Kenny died 5 minutes before we arrived. Just what Kendall needed. At this point Brandon and Morgan come downstairs to report that you are serious, again. Putting you upstairs just doesn't seem to work well. Your temperature is 105. When Brandon, Morgan and Fred went upstairs, your Mom was there and said they would be moving you. Morgan meets Wendy for the first time. Your Dad comes down and says it will be a while before they can move you back to ICU, so the girls and I leave for Englewood. Brandon is visibly upset at Kenny's death. Later tells your Dad Kenny lived at the end of his paper route and often he used to give Bran a ride on his motorcycle after Bran delivered papers.

Friday, October 24, 1980

"Today you opened your eyes and your mouth is open."

"This is the first 9th grade trip retreat for trip 81. Brandon's trip, so we are away for the weekend; close to Conifer at Beaver Ranch."

Sunday, October 26, 1980

"Your Dad, Brandon and I walk into your room (you are back in a private room, out of ICU, again- this time for good!) And your eyes are open. (Actually your eyes are distressing to Brandon who says, "He looks like he's on drugs.") They lack your usual expression... but they are open. You squeezed my hand until my hand was numb! When I told you to relax, you did. A nurse came in and flicked her fingers toward your eyes--- you blink. She closes your eyes again and repeats the process, saying to us that is a super sign! Brandon shows you the eagle he started embroidering on my shirt. You moved your right leg and foot, which I saw because I was standing at the foot of your bed. Your Dad and Brandon were at your head as your Dad was cleaning out your trach tube.

Monday, October 27, 1980

"Given food in the a.m. and had a bowel movement. As your Dad said, we haven't been excited about your bodily functions since you were a small baby! At 4:00p.m., you leave Boulder Community Hospital (where your life had been saved and kept going to this point) and are moved to room 338 at Boulder Memorial Hospital where intensive therapy of all kinds will begin. They have been coming to Community twice a week to work with you. Your Dad and Brandon visit tonight. Your eyes are closed, but responsive to them via your right hand. You moved your legs when asked and relaxed grip when asked.

Tuesday, October 28th, 1980

"Green soup in your food tube (into your stomach via your nose) to check length of time it is taking to move it through your system.

Wednesday October 29th, 1980

"I fixed dinner for your Dad and Brandon. (I) Ran sweeper, cleaned up their pad. Brought the new bedspread from Englewood. Your Dad wanted, but couldn't get in Boulder. Went to see you at the new hospital. Your Dad and I went in first, then Brandon and Morgan. Your Dad brought in

222

Kendall about 2 minutes later. Billye (the nurse) found all 5 of us in the room and hit the door (ceiling), she insisted that there only be 2 at a time. The three of us said good-bye to you, hugged the Cole men and split! Your room is full of the things that make it your room, ie: pictures, posters, music, and a beautiful kite, etc. Your Dad called me later to report he had talked to Billye about who we all were. (At Community they all knew who I was and trusted us with who we had with us.) Later on Billye and I have a good chat and I find out she is from Arizona. We discussed your 9th grade trip and she knew all the places we'd gone to. She's cool now, now that she knows who we are but still insists only 2 at a time!! Your Dad says the 32 of us will still go in together. Before we left the hospital, I talked to your grandfather Cole when he called. Doms and Toby left today for California. When they return, it will probably be with more clothing. They left in such a hurry and hadn't planned on being here very long.

Everyone assuming that you'd be awake by now.

Thursday, October 30th

"All of your family will be gathering, as the hospital team will be evaluating what you need and where you need to go. Your Dad and Bran felt they didn't learn anything they hadn't already known, however, they were engouraged.

Friday October 31st, 1980

"Halloween night. Your room is darkish when we arrived. You were asleep but looked really rested and lighter I thought. Your Dad and I went to the Gapter Road haunted house. I was impressed with how really professional it was. When we left the hospital your Dad teared/choked up and said, "Barb why is it taking so long?" I did not answer--Because I guess only you know that. What's to say, but to be supportive!

Saturday November 1st, 1980

"Today was spent at the Boulder Unitarian Universalist Church parking lot working on the 9th grade trip Boulder fund raiser: Namely called firewood, (sigh). I contend it's harder than Eco-cycle. I ran the log splitter all day, which is hard on

223

the ears and the gasoline fumes are overwhelming. (In the end, 28 cords were brought down from the mountain, split, delivered and $1000 was earned!!) Every fiber of my body ached--took a soakie bath and because it was so late, we by passed seeing you at the hospital and spent a brief period of time at a part at the most Reverend Forest Whitman's home. When you were critical we hardly missed a day, but now the days are similar without change.

Sunday, November 2nd, 1980

"I drove to Denver in the morning and worked at the first Universalist. Then returned to the log-splitting project with 2 trippers. We worked until dark, but I snuck off to fix dinner for your Dad and Garfield' (my nickname for Brandon after Garfield the cat)-- This fall there was a comic strip where Garfield does fun things with a baseball cap. Then we were off to the hospital. You were tired, but I felt, really responsive to us even though you had on your foam-rubber knuckles. You moved your right arm all the way up to your shoulder. Eyes opened and closed. I showed you my BAMA shirt which I was wearing.

Tuesday, November 4th, 1980

Election Day 1980 and we vote for you. Your Dad had your absentee ballot waiting. He was home sick so went to the hospital in the afternoon and met the daytime crew. OT said you are doing everything she wants to have done.

"One of the nurses, complaining, says you no longer want her to take blood out of your arm.

"I say hurrah-- give 'em a fit David Duck!

Thursday, November 6th 1980

"Family meeting with current evaluation report. Your Dad and Brandon encouraged. Your ? asked finds these sessions depressing. This time she left J.B. and Spring at home.

Sunday, November 9th, 1980

"A red letter day--I was in your room alone when Carole (Roth?), speech pathologist, fed you ice chips for the first time and you swallowed without being retaught. She had a foam rubber thing that looked like a pop sicle to stimulate your lips, but your tongue, as if you were seeing who was there: you checked out my Navaho spider ring. Alan, Barbara, Chris and Scoot Cole were at the hospital to see you. Craig Balsley and Paul (Klemperer?) came to visit while the ice tasting was going on so I left so they could visit with you. 'When they came down, they said you were chewing up a storm, and Carole (Roth?) was very impressed.

Monday, November 10th, 1980

"Tonight is the night the Munch-kins (J.B. and Springs) spend with your Dad and I was included as it was Veterans Day, so had stayed over. I helped Spring with her math in the dining room while J.B. and your Dad worked on names of States and Capitols. Spring had been to the hospital with the Bucks, she said. Today David was eating a vanilla milkshake. Spring had the giggles and the two of us had a fine time. Brandon was not feeling well so went to bed without dinner.

Tuesday, November 11th, 1980

"Another red letter day when we arrived we found that your trach was out! Your right arm is up in the air moving around. You are watching Smokey and the Bandit on TV with your left eye. YOU LOOK GREAT!!

Wednesday, November 12th, 1980

"Today they ran a LPN test on you. About your kidney....

RH (right half), functioning fully; LH, top half fine, the bottom a little cloudy. They ran a dye through you to check functioning. No blood in your urine for the past 24 hours.

Friday, November 14, 1980

"About 25 people associated with the Boulder Unitarian Universalist Church donated blood in your name today.

"When we arrived at the hospital, Bilye said, "David said, "OH!" and now moaning and groaning at them.

Saturday, November 15th 1980

"Tonight it is snowing, large beautiful flakes. We at dinner at Eddies and went to see you. Your bed is in a different direction. Now you are by the window with the noisy pigeons.

Sunday, November 16th 1980

Tonight a game between us started as you tried and succeeded in pulling off my spider ring. When I asked you what you were doing, you pushed it back on and thus a game begun that we would replay often! What a tease you are!

"Valerie Williamson, Brandon and I went to visit you as your Dad was working. Your eyes are open and you seem to hear all. Today Billye said David and I are going to watch Saturday Night Fever.

"On the way to the grocery store Brandon said, "He doesn't like disco." Tonight I was invited to Alan and Barbara's for Thanksgiving dinner.

Monday, November 17th, 1980

"Heard from your Dad at noon. J.B. and Spring to be over for their evening, stop. Said he would call later. Didn't (which is really unlike him), when he doesn't I become concerned, but remain calm.

"Just used up one blue pen on your journal and cracked out a new one.

Tuesday, November 18th, 1980

"Your Dad called at noon. My guts were accurate... Usually are where we are concerned. We are very often on the same wave length. He was feeling bad about the situation.

Down-depressed. Pulled covers up over his head and did not call into work... He felt lonely last night after taking Spring and J.B. home. When he returned, Brandon was already in bed. Tired of saying David is OK when you are not. He said, "I felt so alone." He decided the pace of late has been toooo much. Work getting him down too, back on previous special unresolved problems. He is kicking ass as before not ready answers there either. In closing, he decided on another cup of coffee, read *New Fortune Magazine* and tries to go see you in the daytime. Hoping for more positive signs. We usually come late when you are asleep. Your Dad promised to check in before my school board meeting. "If not," I said "I'll come find you!" He said that things that make him feel good, right now also make him feel bad. I sent him a hug over the phone, which he said helped, but in person is best. Sorry I'm busy tonight, but he felt the need to go/gut these feelings alone."

6:00p.m.

"F.M.C. called and sounded cheery. Spent 3 hours at the hospital watching what they are doing seems to have helped. He fed you applesauce. Oatmeal would be coming on Friday.

Monday, November 24th, 1980

"Tonight you are responsive to our pratter... Especially when we talk via fingers. Your legs are bent on a blue padded cylinder. All tubes are out!!! You are now in large disposable diaper. Read the menu for the day, had puree' everything.

Wednesday, November 26th, 1980

" Your Dad went to the hospital for training on how to do liquids, saw Wendy, she gave you your stuffed toy which you threw down. She gave you your comb and you combed your hair.

"You are in there and do know, what's up. We've felt all along, but it's nice to have reinforcement!

Thursday, November 27th, 1980

"Thanksgiving-You are truly missed at the Cole

gathering. Barbara commented on there having been leftovers since you weren't there. She sent pumpkin pie for you.

Friday, November 28th, 1980

"Today, you were put in the whirlpool. In water at last! Alan, Barbara, Chris and Scott bring your Grandparents by on way to Idaho since you were sleeping (and an eager driver, I didn't drive over) Disregard the scribble, I was falling asleep and don't know what that was all about. We only stayed 10 minutes. You were so relaxed and looked so like yourself. Tonight I brought you your BAMA shirt. Your Dad hung it on the wall-it was just waiting until you are ready to dress-up.

"Today, the first Bill arrived from Community Hospital.

"Total $23,081.00: chest X-Rays, 3 1/2 gallons of blood."

Saturday, November 29th, 1980

"Your Dad, Brandon, Kendall and I went to brunch at Jose Muldoon's (Last night the 4 of us went to see the "Stuntman"--they managed not to sit by us!) Delicious...then to the hospital. You were awake and active--checking out textures: my green terry-cloth shirt and your Dad's red chambry shirt. Hanging on your door were sheets (of paper?) with drawings, writing, numbers and your name. Really exciting. Billye said you talked this morning--said your sooth hurt. When asked to circle yes or no if you wanted a milkshake. You wrote. "I want a milkshake."

Sunday, November 30th, 1980

"Took you your pumpkin pie from Aunt Barbara's. More good work hanging on your door. This time with a felt tip pen. Your BAMA shirt not hanging on the wall, which I had given you. Your Dad found it in the closet, evidently you had worn it to the gym. Your Dad, Brandon, your'struly all have BAMA shirts as does Bev Bradshaw the woman whose home I've lived in when in Englewood. Bev has a friend in Alabama who has gotten them for us. The "fad" started when I wore Bev's shirt while assisting your Dad with the Big Blue drive to Albuquerque last June for Unitarian Universalist general assembly. Your Dad wore it one day to the sessions and was hooked so Bev got Unitarian Universalists each one. At Thanksgiving she was visiting there and got Brandon a cut-off football jersey (which he wears a lot!!) And the one for you, which we pinned on the wall for visual stimulation.

Wednesday, December 3rd, 1980

"When you are in the gym, you take the brake of the wheelchair and push the chair around with the use of your right hand. Thus around in a circle you go!

Thursday, December 4th, 1980

"When working out in the gym you entertain the younger children with your seal: hand-puppet. When you are done, you used your teeth to pull it off your right hand.

Saturday, December 6th 1980

"Today we hopefully did our last Eco-cycle for this year's 9th grade trip. Was grey, cold and as always, hard work. We ended the day in the dark. Your Dad, Brandon and I cleaned up and went to the hospital. We went to Eddies to eat and Brandon went to a movie with the trippers.

PS: More good work hanging on your door. Brandon handed you a comb and you combed your hair. You lifted the left side of your head and combed the side and the back.

Sunday, December 7th, 1980

"I got up and drove to Denver for my last Sunday to be employed as the RE Cordinator at the First Universalist Church. It has been 8 years with many rewards. One special reward has been the Cole men, thus why I'm involved in your life heavily since Oct. 2nd. (I've kept tabs on you through your Dad since'77... Little did I know how involved I would become.)

"After I worked Sunday a.m., I head to the Broadmoor and State school board convention. Such a wonderful place to be, to reflect, to re-group, etc. Only wish your Dad were here to enjoy the splender, but he has been putting in long hours at IBM and can't get away now.

Tuesday December 9th, 1980

"Report via your Dad about you. Your Dad reported that when you had a hold of his right hand, without his ring (on his left hand). You weren't interested in his hand. Your Dad was on your left side. He said let go of Brandon's hand and reach across for my hand, which is on your left side and you did. You scratched your head as if pondering and then did as directed. A large grin from Brandon and your Dad is very pleased!

Friday, December 12th, 1980

"Tonight Brandon, your Dad and I came to visit. Brandon stepped on your Hopi ring. After checking out your Dad's ring and mine, we asked you if you wanted yours. You sign yes! Your Dad put it on you and you appear to 'fuss' with your fingers. Your Dad said, "You can't feel yours like you do mine..." I said, "David, take your right had and reach over and touch your own ring," and you do! All actions no matter how large or small are exciting to us.

Saturday, December 13th, 1980

"Today looks to be a long busy day. While Brandon and I shower, your Dad goes after J.B. and Spring. Tis Christmas shopping time. We separate. Spring usually goes with me. We all shopped up a storm. Couldn't get lost as we all had on our blue work shirts. Spring and I have recent Kachinas Your Dad did during hospital waits. We applicated J.B.'s on a new shirt (since he has grow) and Brandon is sporting his trip shirt. (Because the groups are so large these days, we start (embroidering shirts) on retreats.) I've filled one shirt, as has your Dad. In the afternoon, we attend the IBM Christmas family program. There's a ticket for you! Next year, you will be there... If you so choose!

Sunday, December 14th, 1980

"This is the first Sunday I can sleep in!... Wrong, your Dad and I were RAs (responsible adults?) at the Jefferson Unitarian Universalist Church for a tripper fund raiser luncheon. Tina Buckendah (Traci's sister, from your trip) rode from Boulder with the food and us. A beauful spring-like day. After the luncheon your dad said, "I'd like to go to Idaho Springs." He and Brandon had been up last summer to fish. So Tina said, "OK," and went with us. Besides seeing your Grandparents, we found an extra bonus: Alan, Barbara and the boys too. Your Dad cut a Christmas tree for Gapter, which we delivered on our way home. First time I had seen your Mom for weeks.

Thursday, December 15th, 1980

"This is the day I begin my new job at the Denver Chamber of Commerce. I go to work from Boulder. (Even though the ski slopes need snow, I am grateful for dry roads between Boulder and Englewood.)

Thursday December 18th, 1980

"What a first week I did have. The d---- Saab died and had to be towed in. I find myself standing on the corner in the a.m., dark and returning in the p.m., dark. Tonight I stay up very late packing to go to K.C. MO for Christmas; however, it'll be via Boulder so I can be with your Dad.

Saturday Decmber 20th, 1980

"We went to the hospital to see you before I left for the airport and Kansas City. As we arrive, they are getting you up for the day. They put you in the wheelchair and tell up to take you down the hall while they clean your room. We show you the snow and fog out the large window. As usual, we chatter "at" you. (I wonder if you get weary of the chatter.)

Wednesday December 24th, 1980

"Your Dad went to the candlelight service at the Boulder Unitarian Universalist Church. He took with him, the flaming chalice I have lighted daily, for you and your life,

231

since about October 10th. My chalice, which now lives at Manhattan (when I cleaned out my office, several items ended up here) was taken by your Dad and used, in your name, as the starter light. I feel good about that as it means that I was in Boulder Christmas Eve, at least in spirit!

Thursday December 25th, 1980

"Tonight your Dad calls me (When we aren't together we talk at least twice daily, I've missed the contact!) He puts a small friend, Spring, on the phone. Spring tells me you were able to go home today for about 3 hours. You opened some presents she said becoming very tired in the end. Such good news to hear. Certainly, your Dad was very much pleased/grateful.

"Your Dad is on a very much deserved (and needed) time away from IBM. I feel he has done really well with your accident and the situation at work. He is strong, assertive when he needs to be and feeling good about who he is.

Saturday December 27th, 1980

"I return to Boulder just in time to co-host a Pingle party for: Betty, Walt and Barbie. Your Dad had spent 3 hours with you during the day observing you do good things in the gym... Kelly (Allan?) showed you her digital watch and asked you, "What time is it?" You said, "2:48," which it was! She kissed you good-bye and when she asked you kissed her back. Earlier your Dad took you outside on the hospital grounds in the wheelchair. Many of your friends gathered around to be with you. Finally, the wind and maybe all the input is toooo much.... you withdraw and close your eyes.

Wednesday, December 31st, 1980

"You look so handsome. While I was gone, your hair was cut and styled (by Penny Adaams). Also, your mustache is gone. I'm not sure how I feel about that one since I find mustacheoed Coles a turn on.

"I worked (beginning to cope with 8-5, sigh!) until 4:ish (we got off early but I needed to go to the Abram's and get the typewriter for Brandon) and one of the women bought me a drink at the Denver Press Club (I'm moving in different circles, HAH!) As soon as I arrived in Boulder, we left for the hospital. You are now in the room across the hall from the previous spot! I brought you a colorful water game from K.C. As I held it up your eyes went straight to the bright colors!! As I say it is for you, your arm reaches out for it. It is a clear cylinder with red on both ends. Inside is a blue hippopotamus with colorful little balls that you shoot into the hippo's mouth by using a button. Because of the angle, you were holding it, your Dad was looking at the hippo's back and was explaining to you what is needed to make it work. From where I was standing, I knew you had filled the hippo's mouth and was turning it upside down to pour them out. You were way ahead of us, and gave us all a good laugh. You thumb wrestled with your Dad and won! We say Happy New Years and good-night. The 3 of us had dinner at Eddies-Brandon to a party. We enjoy a quiet, safe evening at home with a fire.

Thursday January 1st, 1981

"Talk about lazy... We didn't even get up for the parade, but did see lots of football!

Friday January 2nd, 1981

"Would you believe, I had to work today? A bright spot, however, your Dad came for lunch, since he's still on vacation.

Saturday January 3rd 1981

"This afternoon we went to the hospital to see you and you were out on a pass to Gapter. That's great, but I felt angry that your Dad had not been told. Because he is Mr. too, he says nothing and we don't talk about a trip for nothing. We did talk about the fact that we had both thought someday this could happen. (Does this mean when you go home to Gapter for good we won't see you for a while?) We tried to see a show tonight, but they were all sold out. We both agreed, a visit to the hospital would be only to view a very tired you after your outing.

Sunday January 4th, 1981

"David, you have no way of knowing, but I must be very honest with you. I had some good notes, but because of more changes in my life (job, holidays and such) this journal was empty from about 10-10-80 until today. I resolved to get current and serious and as of 9:19pm, I have succeeded! I might add, David Duck (stays afloat, no matter what, he'll rise to the surface), I feel that Volume 1 is plenty so wake totally up, so I may turn this hummer over to you. The blank pages do not mean that nothing happened, but that I have no first hand report from your Dad... I've told him if he wants to fill in some pages that is fine by me. It is a lot to remember and record!! At football 1/2 time your Dad asked if I wanted to go to the hospital. I said, "Of course." But not until you call first!

"We arrive at the same time that Jo and Milt Thompson do. It's the first time I meet them, although I've heard lots about them. Jo says, "I've read your name on the sign in sheet, now I have a face too." You've been in the whirlpool and are tired and relaxed. You look spiffy, wearing a new sweater and your painter pants. Your left leg is bent "on your own." Every day you look better and closer to joining the rat race called life!

Thursday January 8th, 1981

"Tonight Morgan, Kendall and I meet your Dad, Brandon and J.B. at McNichols to see the Avalanche indoor soccer game. Today at 2:00 your Dad attended an evaluation meeting. Staff is overjoyed with your progress! You are doing great! Starting to think and do independently. You asked a nurse if you were supposed to be at the hospital. She said, "Yes, this is where you will get what you need." You asked to call your Mom to check this out.

"All signs point in the direction we'd all hoped and have waited for!

Sunday January 11th, 1981

"After we went to church, where I was not recognized by many, we went to visit you. I said to you maybe you didn't recognize me since I'd lost weight and my hair was longer and

234

you replied, "I know who you are, my brain hurts, it may be something in the water." You turned on your side and said you were tired and wanted to go to sleep. We helped you get comfortable and put a pillow under your legs.

Monday January 12th 1981

"Brandon rode his bike over to see you after school. You said, "Hi Brandon" and the two of you had a super chat. "No," you said today, "my brain doesn't hurt." You asked about your bike and said, "I can't wait to ride again after I get out of the hospital."

Wednesday January 14th, 1981

"Tonight we took Morgan and Kendall to visit you. After Morgan left you asked if you knew her and, "how old is she?" Generally, at this hour, we'd have found you ready to call it a day!

Thursday January 15th, 1981

"Tonight, you went over to Rob Picker's house for dinner! How about that?

Saturday January 16th, 1981

"Went between football games. Brandon took his bike to ride it back from the hospital. You were asleep when we got there, so your Dad was writing you a note when you woke up and waved at me, with three fingers and your thumb, and smiled. You pushed all the pillows out from under your head and wanted the bed down to go so sleep. We removed your blue roll cushion... you turned yourself over on your side to go to sleep.

Wednesday January 21st, 1981

"Tonight your Dad stopped by early. You were up, in your chair, and eating an egg salad sandwich. Your whole family got there about the same time. Wendy, Terry, Spring, J.B., Dad, and Brandon, who came earlier and then we all went to JJ McCaabes for dinner. You had called Gapter feeling lonely and wanted company.

Friday July 3rd, 1981

"Dearest David Duck----

"It is time to bring this to an end and place it where it belongs...................... in your hands. My motive and reason for keeping this for you has been accomplished, (e.g.) to fill in the pieces in the beginning. As you read towards the end, where you had some awareness, I lacked knowing that now memory was back to you. Maybe some of these pages (will) explain why everyone who followed your journey becomes so excited and pleased with things you are doing. Things that seem small and not swift enough, not perfect enough to you!!

"Know and remember how many and how much love and energy has gone to assist you in your recovery...........................indeed,

You made it

Congratulations!!

Enjoy!!

Love and Hugs, Barb

Expect the Miraculous

I had simply ignored all the warnings that I should maybe wear a helmet. I had been under the mistaken immortality syndrome. My surviving an earlier car/bicycle collision, sustaining only road-rashes, had "fatally" complicated my infection.

I have tried to structure this book around the storybook model. The following stories initially have been inspired in 1980 and the following 15-16 years of my rehabilitation, and have been documented in written form, starting from the time I was able to get my first typewriter. I hope that these words do not solve any problems. I am just looking to create the chance, an opportunity for the self-actualization. I had learned self-actualization in my Psych 110 lecture hall, sometime in September 1985.

Because discoveries have always moved microcosms of society to new levels of understanding, I was granted the opportunity to have, for all practical affective purposes, died. I have died and been allowed the chance to share with people my experiences.

I don't have any cognition from my unconscious state of affairs. This story focused primarily on how I was able to achieve some semblance of life beyond the ICU. Then how I was able to succeed with that-this life. That is life existing in an enormously unforgiving world. My world didn't much resemble the apocalyptic images presented by any number of the more popular late 20th century movies; however, nor is there much resemblance with the fairy-tale images which society, if only unintentionally, inculcate children with.

I do not want to begin my story without first reaching back into my history to include all those who were there in the beginning to begin this story. For this is not only my story, however, I can claim utmost authority, making me the author. That is not to say that without all the support, the promptings, the chidings we all need in order to remain humble, I would be able to suggest for you, anything.

What is there that stops me trying to hold a place in that fabulously underpaid world of work? It surely has nothing to do with the loss of any intelligence, and I have not developed narcolepsy, e.g., I am quite able to be out of bed with plenty of time to "go to work."

No!

What has been compromised in my head, however, has nothing to do with the mechanical regions of the brain or my human physique. There is nothing wrong with me that man now, or in the conceivable future, will have the ability to "fix!"

I've since been able to return to my old stomping grounds, i.e.: the "weight room" and I've been able to squat-lift 605lbs. I never lost a child's ability to bounce back from injury, e.g., the resiliency to recuperate, heal myself ad nauseum, e.g., I've fallen off my bike, and in the shower, I've separated great regions of muscle and bone; just the other day, I fell down a flight of my stairs and did not, I repeat-knock on wood, I did not break my neck or any other bone what-so-ever. Blood, however? You'd think I'd been giving blood, but I was still able to get to the emergency room!

A lot of superficial lacerations are all and some stitchery.

What I feel has been compromised in terms of my psyche is in no way connected with the mechanical, affective regions of my brain. My physique, in no way lost touch with the directing centers of my brain. There is not now, nor in any perceptible length of time injuries that a man can fix.... or a woman.

.....Humpty Dumpty sat on the wall, and he had a great fall, or he got knocked in the head! All the King's men and all the king's horses couldn't put humpty back together again.

So, if I'm Humpty Dumpty, and the King's men are personified by the paramedics and doctors, that is all the doctors who had ridden up on their great, charging steeds, professing that they had all the required education, and that they had obtained all those necessary documents to understand what was the matter with me, made me be just like every H. Dumpty. But none of them knew ME! I've not found that there was anyone who could have ever predicted that I would "bounce-back," not to the levels of recovery I've since managed, anyway.

None of the doctors who had prognosticated all those dire predictions: of my limited to nil chances of ever walking again, or of my ever having the ability to talk, to think, or to ever become a contributing member of this society again, none of them had even a clue! I think they were calling the glass half empty and had been trying not to set themselves up, or set anyone else up for disappointment. They didn't have that proverbial clue of all the magnificently mystical capacities my/our God had been sure to include with the original blue-prints.

I hope none of this violates the integrity, or offends all those proverbial, recognized, familiar, hackneyed notorious infamous common well versed mindful apprised abreast proficient familiar well-read academician Dr. Presleys, and all the Dr. Scaers out there. They had been and are still inextricably necessary, but not for me. These doctors did a necessarily poignant, a magnificent job in keeping me alive right up until they looked in their crystal ball so muddled with documentation to have predicted how far I would go, to what level my parents and friends could realistically expect my rehabilitation to reach!

Why they did, I'll never know, but by their saving my life, they have quite unwittingly...or maybe even un/intentionally unleashed an energy maybe equal but entirely dissimilar to Einstein's $E=mc^2$. What's even more frightening is that as I age/grow wiser and older, I am in fact getting fatter....e.g., more mass!

I just don't want anyone to have the idea that either having an insurance policy with all the money in the world would or will necessarily guarantee a full and complete recovery, or that being injured having lived all your life in the ghettos will predispose a person to not being able to become healed entirely. What I hope this story will bring to light, is the responsibility of the individual. Life in this world is meant to be taken with that proverbial "grain of salt."

All the Dr. Presleys and all the Dr. Scaers needed to be installed in the works and to have been put in place with absolute perfection. Their abilities have been established in order that the initial procedures, all the ER (Emergency Room) and the Tx (Therapy) activities are to be implemented "flawlessly;" thereby, creating the best possible environment and opportunity for an injured person! And as a human being I cannot and do not claim to be without flaw, without fault(s).

Intuitively, I probably understood all of this, or I must have at least had the wisdom to toe that proverbial line and practice, practice, practice the entire regimen anyways, because practice make perfect, and if I couldn't be perfect, I'd at least want to be human! If this had not been the case, I probably would not have exercised in excess, I probably would not have dedicated much of my professional education to the institution of health.

I don't know how this is coming across to people. Something tells me that a supreme attribute in the course of my recovery has been my general attitude.

It's hard to remember this one but it seems that I was quite upset not being allowed to soak in the hot tub, the whirlpool, naked. I never wore a suit in the hot tub before the injury; it just seemed so out of place to be wearing a swimming suit while sitting in a hot tub.

Another indication as to my general demeanor may have been my creative rehabilitation. It seemed that everyone wanted me to return to the state I'd existed in before October 2nd, 1980; so to help complete this picture, I began to experiment with my sexuality.

Life just isn't going to get any easier, and the older you are, the more time you've had to get a fix on this reality;

therefore, the older you are, the more so able you are to enjoy life. All of us "old fogies" have figured this out and have learned how to adjust our wants, needs and desires to fit...even to match our means.

The older a person gets, the longer their body has had to degenerate. They are less physically able and more so inclined to need assistance and ask for the help they need. Thus the archetypical picture of the old lady walking along with servants at her beck and call.

Why can't I get something...anything going? What is there in the path, along my pike, which falters any progress, and what is there which presents such an impenetrable obstacle?

When I had been hit by that errant automobile, my initial "thinking" surely must've surrounded the pop quiz, which I would probably not have to sit. I was now not expected to even live to get on with my life. Unexplainable, even to the elders, I now found myself stuck living as an adult in a childlike fantasy, even though I was the only adult searching for that illusive connection with the childhood they estranged prematurely.

Actually, none of these exams were so much pop quizzes, as they were quizzes, which were meant to pop the mind out of the typical lethargy and into the more typical action. I went on to interpret the instance, the impact that instant as my denying the need to abandon the miseries associated with maturity. It became my own attempt to deny reality and to continue to dwell in my own childhood of sorts.

Looking back at my last 7 or 8 years, I am reluctant to even accept the fated fact that I am now a Dad. Could all of this be my reluctance to go through the crisis of maturity and remain in the childhood world that was becoming more and more unreal?

I was entirely unwilling to allow my parents in my life, my activities, and my rituals. Instead, I was to sally forth, only to meet with an impediment. Life does not allow you to make a mistake and to grow from that point onward carrying forward all of your moments of life learning's, and return to my former world of youth as far as I could.

In these Americas, little seemed impossible, and even that one was before the advent of the PC. I had after all just begun my measure of post-secondary education; it was my freshman year at a university. After I tried to, at some time, present to Mom and Dad that badge of a job so very well done, a college degree; however, that percussion, that veritable down beat of the "Shuffle" that was to be my starting gun.

Why then was the track on which I would begin my quest, why had it begun to resemble Nevin Platte Junior High's cinder strewn track? And why would all those great puddles of water begin to resemble the obstacles, those great puddles of life? So, why have I come to expect them at the beginning of the 440, the finish of the 220, the middle and remainder of the mile? The engineering fete presented by having a football field surrounded by the traditional quarter mile track both at the foot of quite the very large lake, neither of which has sufficient drainage, was just too good. Was this to become the training course for all the Forest Gump films of the 20th century? The archetypal childhood found its artificial, even though delayed collapse, in me and my "death."

If this was the case in point, why have I been left out? I'm no shrimp fisher, but then, how many actual fishers of shrimp are there? This is a story about having a head. Something most of us, in fact, do have. Since 10.02.80, I've met people all over the world and have yet to meet anyone without one.

Talking about no-brainers, this one is almost too easy to be considered a no-brainer. "I've managed to supersede one of life's most ruthless dreams." (Hesse, *Damian,* 50).

In a way, not so unlike the childhood practice of mimicry, I often resemble Max Damian, but then, he could be a compound personality conjured up in the head of Herman Hesse.

In terms of my recovery, I had once been counseled not to expect the miraculous. Much of the implication had been, not to expect any sort of return to a life so similar to the one I had left there on the Avenue up in the canyon. I don't want it to go on record that I even sympathize, much less support, such a pessimistic, though entirely safe form of bedside manner, of post mortem council. This applies to either the traumatized patient, or the family.

Even though I can't support the idea of establishing a false sense of security or set someone up for a major letdown, it seems to me that if you don't aim for all the strengths you once enjoyed as well as those which you've not even been acquainted with, you don't have a chance of reaching a level of ability higher than the one to which you awake to.

It may be accurate to remind me that I had only wanted to manage a return to everything I had neatly tucked away in the normalcy which I'd had at my control on October 1st, my sense of grandeur, at that time, had been extremely limited. I could only see what the four walls, the ceiling and floor of my hospital room had within them. I has a window opening onto the Flatirons, four of which I had climbed, but they seemed so far away, unattainable. It is true that, initially, I might have only wished a return to the familiar confines of my own comfort zone, but it was the love, the conversations-often only monologues, the human contact, which gave me the courage to keep on keeping on, to shatter that glass ceiling of therapeutic prognosis.

Once I had the chance to get out of my comfort zone, after I was allowed to explore beyond everything, which I had already known, I was able to finagle a return into the university system. It was here that I found my "id" and it was here that I discovered an MO (*modus operendi*) to help me get through this life. Namely, a wife.

No, all joking aside, it was not until after I had successfully negotiated the ivory halls, and walked on the alabaster floors of a university-(actually it was mostly all just concrete and dry-wall), it was not until after I received my diploma, and had a chance to formally become self actualized, to feel that I was worthy of supporting myself and a wife, besides eventually fostering a new generation.

"Where Are Your Shoes?"

"You'd better get some shoes on. You'll step on some glass!" What goes through my head is not the standard protocol of trying to think of where my shoes are nor do I take a cursory glance at my immediate surroundings to assess whether or not I should be taking evasive maneuvers. No, instead, I become a curious specter of inquiring, "Who does this guy think I am? Doesn't he think I have the ability to see and avoid any glass?" I become very defensive; I return an equally or more sizzling comeback "ask Craig what I say," and in trying urgently not to offend the other, we attend to polite, even stimulating small-talk.

But he doesn't have any of those malicious intentions which I've so fallaciously spoken and attached to the scene. He only spoke from his perception of the parking lot, the sidewalk, or the yard. The fact that It hadn't measured against my image of the terrain in no way made it incorrect. "Whatever's right for you is right." Therefore whatever's right for someone else's reality may also be right for yours, and what is right in your reality also stands the chance of being wrong as pictured by another set of eyes.

Now here's an institution society isn't really in need of cultivating, any more aged Victorian levels of politeness! We no longer have time for or room in our lives for observing a predetermined set of social orders. There are people who lack the resources to stand up and be counted. So why do we have to be so careful? What else is there? You just can't turn around, there's something being sold that will protect you from burglars, from dangerous ultraviolet rays, from indigestion! Still, if I go down to the one restaurant in town I can afford to eat at, it's, "be careful about the food, a woman just died of botulism, so be careful about that."

Then, if I get food poisoning, lined up three deep are attorneys and insurance adjusters. I think it still needs a little finer tuning, just a few minor adjustments. And all those doctors, they certainly do need some more practice.

When I usually go out to get the mail, the sun is well on its way to going down, and by 2:00p.m. the air is already beginning to cool down, but still, I can't stand in the sun for too long. Out here, the mail comes in droves. The hotter, the colder, and the wetter the weather the better. He's in the process for the long haul, the more insignificant the complaint the better. He's already 36 and already he's gauging his days until retirement. If I woke up each and every day with the only measure of success being how soon I would be able to get back in bed, I think I would wonder why bother with getting out of bed in the first place. You could kill more than the one bird with only one stone. For "No stone ever thrown hath caused greater damage than the cherry pit!"

If Craig has already been there, I can see him parked in the "shade" of the fence, eating his lunch, or reading a book, counting his stamps, or whatever it is that mailmen do in their spare time when they're not out delivering the mail.

He very infrequently asks the instant I walk up beside his red, white, and blue truck with black tires. They're the only thing apart from the sunburn on his nose-hold it, even these are blue. I guess the tires are the only part of him that isn't red/white and blue in the sun.

By this time, I become quite visibly perturbed! Doesn't he think I have my eyes open when I walk out to see him and get my mail? "Don't you think I have my eyes open when I walk out here? Do you really think I would trust that some/one-thing would steer me away from all the interesting aspects of my life?

"Get a grip Craig," that's his name!

"No, of course not, you're an adult; you make the choices you need to for your own life. I was simply looking out for your best interests."

Boy, did I ever want to scream! Everyone is working so bleeding hard watching out for everyone else's back, it's really a shame that we spend so much time in the bathroom in the morning all washing our faces; they have really become obsolete; <u>they are only as important as they are flawed.</u> And the promise is an institution only participated in when everyone knows every promise is only made in order to have something to break when you become upset at another aspect of your life. I mean think about it! A promise kept is only a matter of the moment for it can always be broken, while a promise that has been broken can never be kept! So what good is there in making promises? INTEGRITY! Isn't this what we really want after all?

Promises are only made to be broken! That's the only way you know how good they were in the first place. And because they are no-good at that point, why does anyone bother to >promise< anything to anyone... why?

The next time you find yourself in a predicament where you're looking for a promise, or a guarantee, don't bother with it. If it wasn't made with quality in the first place, what makes them think they can have it stand for more than it is just by "guaranteeing it from failure?"

Do they guarantee a cut of meat? Was it ever guaranteed that this life would get for you what you'd always wanted; and exactly when had you wanted something different? Like there was ever something in this life that had anything to do with its creation. Wake up and smell that proverbial cup of coffee! Get a grip! There is not one h--- of a lot out there that is any different from what you never expected in the first place!

Do I make an issue with the fact that my life was short-changed at the very beginning? Sometimes I like to think about all the great things that might have been, if...

But there's not a whole hill of beans to fuss over, except I'd say, if those beans are Arabica, or "COKER?" I had gone to the University with the innocent intent that I would emerge from such an academic institution so full of it that I would be lusted after by all those major conglomerate industries. Those had been my intentions, and they were probably none too far off the mark, but that is a question I will

247

never know!

You see, I never got past first base! Ant that I am no longer willing to trust that anyone is there on deck to come to bat behind me if I ever do make it on base, I've basically given up. You see, I've tried a couple times to succeed with this western mentality, but why? Why do I struggle? Why do I need to bother with having to struggle? I don't have to, no more! Now, it's that I'm all alone in this world. I've no one to play ball with. Everyone turns their back and say, "that's all just silly kids stuff." And I missed something; I was "dead" for a major shift in the historical continuum.

For example, I missed Lennon's getting shot! I was entirely unable to have chosen Carter or Reagan in the 1980 election, I'm sorry! The burden of mistake for all of society rests on my shoulders, but I can't help you with your finger pointing, I can't help that there needs to be any blame.

And who can I turn to now? Who is there, out there who can help me make amends with what degree of potential I was blessed with an opportunity to chance?

But would anything have been better? Would anything really have turned out more to my liking? And that is just another one of those questions best asked as a rhetorical question.

That brings me to the state of the globe, of the Earth. What is it that fools us into thinking that we can cause the extinction of a species, but the answer to this is no-good to the makers of facial creams, and other insundry mascares for they'd be entirely without the vast amounts of their advertising subsidized by someone else.

So, tell me, why are you here; why am I here, why is anybody in their right mind ever here? And here we have that quintessential question which has plagued the questioning mind ever since minds could question. Man has already subjected this query to the process of elimination, to the process of scientific examination and is still trying to verify all the discoveries he's already made over and over *ad nauseum*.

Instead of his ever having seen about implementing any changes in how we go about our existence, we just sit back and reveling, reproducing and relying on someone else to see about implementing if any, the changes which need to take place, Instead, we have fallen back on that age old process of propagation; and them, we grow old, and just like our fathers before us we all die?

But do we really? My story, it's not wanting to act as an ontological forum whishes instead to inform everyone who has chosen to listen, a story about how I have superseded these processes.

When a man is born, he is birthed into this hugely beautiful world as a package. A package neither fully assembled, nor complete. There are still the classes which must be taken, so many experiences still to be had. This might just be why we have put in place, the institution we often refer to as childhood; and why the CEOs of this institution have been embodied so strangely, so mystifying is a concept which scream and cry as we might, we seem entirely unable to be rid of the creatures. And this one is probably one of our greatest fortunes.

In speaking to you, I am assuming that by the time you've chosen to read such a boring manuscript, that you have already been indoctrinated with the basics, those rudimentary abilities to be able to develop a cognitively composite picture of what I am actually saying; however, that is also taking for granted the assumption that you are also able to see with Maslow's advanced level of cognition.

However, I am not meaning to imply that only persons with at least a 6th grade level of education are susceptible to injury to the head. Only that it seems that before the age of 17 or 18 a person-albeit a young person is so overly well protected, there is typically little importance for frightening, for exposing a matter of life which can actually be even worse than death.

So, why do I even hope of somehow getting beyond

what anybody's been able to accomplish since the beginning of accomplishments? Why indeed!

To answer this question, you see I've got these little cheat sheets taped to the back of the desk in front of me. I want only to help you GET IT; that this life does not come with anything that even remotely resembles a guarantee!

I was born on the 9th day of the 9th month. At birth, I weighed in at 9lbs. 9 oz. It took me 9 years to complete my college level of undergraduate education, and I did! My continuing the process, even-nah especially after the injury!! I was down, but I wasn't out. I had things to accomplish, and I'll be d---- if I'd let anything so innocuous as being killed get in the way. I had begun my elementary education, early; therefore graduating from high school at age 17. Only I hadn't spent the usual 9 months in gestation. Instead, I spent 10 months so warm and snuggly. Having gotten beyond age 9, I don't expect to live beyond age 99, and that may be 99 years aboard this planet which equates to age 98. I have very little expectations of living to become a centenarian!

This car, a.k.a. this automobile is destined not to get around, to mobilate without the auto! The medical profession is only here as mechanics; they haven't a clue (clue-less in Boulder) how to process that spiritual piece of apparatus the auto. Don't even hope to be able to look to these "professional Ps," these physicians, these psychiatrists, these psychologists, these psychoanalysts, et. al. to "fix" you after you've broken the "auto," or after someone else has thrown that proverbial "Monkey's Wrench" into the gears making your life run.

" Design the manuscript to be very readable by persons with little or no manual dexterity, i.e. a work-book for persons with difficulty managing books. As he straddled his motor bike and revved the engine a couple times, he seemed so innocent, so inviolable. His not wearing a helmet only reinforced this illusion! I said to him, "You know what on that fine bike, you look very strong, an absolute genius my friend, but you know something else? You're not real smart, either!"

On Wetting the Bed

For quite the seemingly long while, I had to find other ways of managing such an unseemly, extraordinarily embarrassing situation, but just like my confrontations with constipation, over time (as my brain became reprogrammed), I was able to sleep over at friends' homes. I found that it may have been a good idea to push that proverbial envelope, e.g.: for me to create artificial reasons to be successful at holding my bladder through the night, (the Davies' home) until I could negotiate my way to a toilet, or found myself spending the night awake: rocking, changing, otherwise soothing my child. By this time, I already had mastered control of my nocturnal seepages. I had set myself up in extremely embarrassing situations, such as, I had gone to the university and was a resident in the college dormitory setting. Hallett Hall at CU for a semester, and then Harrison Hall at UNC for 3 quarters. By the time I was ready to be living solitarily or with a roommate, off campus, in my/our apartment, I was entirely successful in no longer "wetting the bed."

Don't be put off by wetting the bed. What it might sound like, but is not what I'm saying that you need to embrace, to expect, or be ready to tolerate; just that it's an aspect of breaking one's brain which needs to run its course.

An infant child hasn't reached, and should not be punished or subjected to verbal abuse; they're not "potty trained." It's only an "accident." Okay, it's never an accident; it's just a stage of growth the human body goes through. For me, and my badly bruised brain, I just had to reprogram my system. I am glad my mother was ready and able to give me the space, and to wash so many sheets...again.

There I was, an 18-year-old "baby". I was still wetting the bed. For a couple of years beyond my incarceration.... sorry, I just couldn't resist the pun.

The Idiot and the Odd DC

The Idiot and the odd DC. Untrue, you may say; it's all just libelous slander, you may shout, and it's all about me. I am going to try to show you what I was able to accomplish not despite, or in spite, but maybe as well as having been knocked unconscious for longer than 3 or 4 months. I want to give you more than a diary of my injury. I want to illustrate for you the long, the lonesome, the tedious, sometimes even mischievous rebellious undertaking I've involved myself in, in trying to mete up to the expectations of a very unforgiving world.

This is how I have managed to live beyond the nightmare of having first died and then being able more like being forced to continue to survive. Maybe in spite of the trauma that had ended the life of David. Maybe this is why I am the way that I am: Loud, Raukus, Dareing, at times entirely Unconscienable.

I don't know if this is the way life should progress. I don't really seem to care that I am sometimes embarrasing. Others more often than not attribute this behavior to the loss of a sense; however, I don't think so! Maybe the reason everyone is so hung up, so stuck on this has something to do with the fact that everyone is so scared of death. So in their attempts to avoid the unknown-death, they have chosen instead to be barred from life. Well, I haven't!

I've had the opportunity to try out both aspects of existence. I chose to complete the lesson. This may have been a good choice. Maybe my God felt that I had all the necessary fortitude to stick around, maybe even answer a few questions?

It seems to me that I am most able to think when I am talking or writing. I'm a bit too spontaneous if left with neither hand to "think" with. I would probably have chosen a different medium.

I died. For all intents and purposes, I ceased to operate cognitively or physically for 99 days as reported by the nurse's records; 6 months according to the primary attending (physical

253

therapist), and at least 2 years according to my comprehension and appreciation of the records.

Actually, I don't think that I had actually regressed to the fetal stage of existence, so I won't delve into when life begins! But the infantile stage of development for sure. I've decided to share with you, my death, my life, my having the opportunity to witness the process of maturation, with a mind that has already progressed beyond the sensory motor aspects of maturation. I've written this book maybe in hopes that you will not have to experience.... first hand, to empirically know what it means to die and be forced to exist in a world that is neither forgiving or kind.

Ernest Hemmingway is noted for the quote: "This world breaks everyone while there are those who go on stronger at the broken places."

I agree with this proverb. And I am . Yes, I am stronger about the head than I had been for the 18 years leading up to the 1 day my God had chosen to take me aside from everyone else and make me very different.... "odd?" If you'll allow me to coin a phrase from the title, I'd had to try everything again.

The interesting thing about my story is that I am trying to relate, in documented form, what every infant child surely must be trying to tell us with their cry.

Most of the experiences from my first try at life are still there. This may be the single biggest flaw in my attempts to relate to you from the eyes of a child. I can still remember doing any number of events, which everyone who was there would probably tell you I did. I have no recollection of having lost my virginity before my first death; therefore, I died a virgin.

I think I have the factual, the analytical synaptic connections, which contain these memories, still in place. I feel that my having returned to the university when I did made it possible to begin the stimulation of all my neurons, those synaptic clefts, to start the whole process of learning off on the right foot.

"This world breaks everyone while there are those who go on stronger at the broken places." Why was I was stronger about the head? Had this been a simple process of my growing older? Or was the strength in having been able to get myself back on the straight and narrow, to have been successful in my returning to school and getting that elusive college degree?

This I will never know, nor do I think I really care to know. It's like the character who gets to try out his life from a different angle or to see into the future. Hollywood had a blast with these concepts. There was really no way of actually testing their theories in real life; they were safe, but they were designed around a notable human condition, a condition that, from time to time, everyone seems to experience.

I sense that I've been able to reach the levels of recovery which I have in part because of the life style I knew before I corrected some errant driving behaviors. Maybe I lived the way I had in preparation for my God's bigger purpose, is it the chicken or the egg?

In my first go around I may have had everything much too easy, all the experiences I scheduled to have were maybe laid out too neatly in much too straight a line. Or could it be that God (my God) had just had another moment of 'down time?' I know for a fact that he had been working himself over time, trying to keep me on the straight and narrow, while I did not grow up on the straight and narrow. As a matter of fact I think it should have taken far longer for my atonement.

Who is "my God?"

That particular concept, that entity, I believe is different for everyone. For a pastor's daughter, the girl with whom I once had the distinguished pleasure and opportunity to have met, for her having also experienced death tangent with life; her God was probably a beautiful woman who always had a clean, pressed dress waiting in the closet.

Or for the young man I knew through my brother, the late Bill Kerr, his God had probably been the first to throw a raucous in the library, if in fact he had ever thought of going to the library. But my God was a Virgo, and my God really wanted me to become a successful writer. A successful writer of prose and fiction, but first my God had seen it as imperative to give me a full blown shot at life and death,

While I was in high school, immediately prior to having a crash course in vehicular metallurgy, I was unwittingly given the nickname (unknown to me at the time), the nickname HO Cole, an acronym for Hunk of Cole. At the time, however, I was committed to the allegory of the American Dream. I was going to get my education in the usual way. I was going to find that great job in the usual way. I was going to work--days a year, in the usual way, and go on vacation with a wife whom I found, in the usual way. We would have that typical suburban house, and I would father 2.7 children (in probably the usual way.)

However, I didn't want to be so hugely attached to high school, and be so shackled to my past, tethered to my history. Or have a girlfriend back at the high school while I was in the college arena, surrounded by all those "College Babes." I didn't want to be faced with the devastating task of averting my eyes every time I sat next to a girl of the opposite sex, who I would maybe want to have as my girlfriend.

A favorite line, one of a great number of others: Red sky at sunrise do not be chaste, but do be wise (carry an umbrella), Red sky at sunset worry thee not, no need to yet.

The intersection of my universe and the universe belonging to Joe Lynn was never taken for a passive event. More often than not, it would be accompanied by so much celebration. Like a bride and groom acting as icons representing two entirely different tribes of neurons. Man in form as a male is only significant at the instant of consummation. His bravado was present only in order for him to attract a host to gestate his prodigy. History not biology has gone on to assign events to his primary instincts.

Society has since been able to establish any number of

256

other institutions, other capacities in which he is able to participate. I am on a tangential course; my life is meant to sustain the lives of others. I have been put in place not in order that I affect anything, but in order to enable others to carry out their own purposes.

If it would appear easier to you, you in a more western frame of mind that I have no place in this society, I must correct you. I am here as the court-jester, the comedian, a buffoon. I am an Upthemallogist, a philanthropist; I really have no purpose, other than to see that people are able to laugh, if not with themselves, at themselves. Who would want to do anything with a retail hooligan anyway?

The collision was neither Joe Lynn's accident, nor was it in my card to have an accident. It only seems that my universe was on a "collision course" to make me a writer. I had been in preparation for the scene all my life. It just so happens that Joe Lynn had to become involved in the sticky mess, up to his proverbial bootstraps. It's not his fault. He couldn't avoid the scene. There really was no way. He just had to do exactly what he did, and I had to do exactly the things that I had done as well.

Do you think the title is a little self-deprecating? Is it only a martyr's version of infamy?

I have very little attachment to the words, for they're only words. So what if I call myself an idiot in my first life; it doesn't really seem to matter a whole hill of beans, unless of course those beans are leaded. Then they would be best ground up and producing my next pot of coffee. Besides, I would still have to pay taxes for the dinner I ate and maybe every day for all three meals as well. I would still be responsible for buying the gas I use to power my car, and I would still need a restroom when I need to go pee.

"But," you may say, "you look so different, you laugh too much."

I've just had to adapt to these things. If it's always raining outside, most people would probably adapt either to

257

always being wet, or to staying inside, or always carrying a "bumbershoot."

That my events are different from the events that you have adapted to doesn't bother me. Should it be such an issue for you that I talk out of the side of my mouth, or walk with a hitch in my stride?

I'm not proud. I had to learn how to get out of my ego. In order to write this book, I had to get out of my ego to get out of my house, my familiar surroundings. I have befriended so many new, so many different people, because of my destiny. Do I know anything different? Yes, well no, maybe. Have I wanted things differently? Maybe.

The issues you seem so fixated on could just as easily be among my concerns. However, I have no right to be angry. I have no right to be proud. I see the world differently, but I know I shouldn't condemn people for their differences. I am not as dumb as I look!

My growing weary of the stares from so many others should not be construed any differently than people being forced to the back of the city bus because of the color of their skin. Why should I be angry being passed over by an employer seeking to fill a job, they have a need, and I do not fill it, so get a clue! Glimpse the "Other Side of the Wall." Pink Floyyd, The Wall. I thought we were beyond that, but it appears that we are not. We are, after all still so fixated in our own homeostasis.

We all are fixated in our comfort zones. It's not for me to judge where your concerns should be or how you choose to say hello. Heck, if that were the case, there would be very little international travel. We would get there and ask for a glass of water and be pummeled to death. Why? Well because we were in Deutschland and asked for "a glass of water," not *"ein tassse wasser!"* Do you see how silly this all is? A person is not discriminated against because they speak a language other than your own; people with bright red hair are still allowed to vote.

I'm not proud. I have no attachment to the term 'idiot.' I only hope this doesn't get in the way for you either. My having chosen the term 'odd DC' was merely me exercising my poetic license.

Along with the accident taking away my consciousness, I also lost my 'id.' For the next 4 or 5 years, I was just Dave. Then, at the University of Northern Colorado, winter term 1984, while I had been in a psychology course, PSY 110 with an extraordinarily beautiful instructor, a TA, Jerri Chance. I found it taped to the back of the lecture seat in front of me.

I'll never forget Jerri! It has often been said that you never forget your first love, and I guess I never will. She saw right through the facade obscuring me and my intellect. Besides her uncanny ability to see through my facade, she was outrageously beautiful herself! Maybe using the word outrageous slants my appreciation poorly.... just let me say that if I had not been reined back by the teacher-student hands off policy, I might not be single even as I speak. And if she had had similar feelings, she would have been my bride! Sigh... if only? If only, a couple of pretty pathetic words, don't cha think?

What I postulate might have benefited my return to productive life. Vitamin B-Complex! I had been out of the hospital several months and my mental status was still being regulated by the dictums of all those doctors and nurses and therapists. Then I began my own vitamin therapy. I took an almost cost prohibitive number of Vitamin B-complex pills. At first, my body was not used to so many nutrients: my face would turn bright shades of red as blood flowed to the area where the vitamin was needed most. I took these pills, of course without first checking with the hospital. My mental status took on great strides but only after I was "paroled." It was only after I was outside the confines, the politics, the stuck structure of the hospital, that I had the opportunity to experiment with compounds outside the limiting parameters as dictated by that infallible course, of the scientific method. By only doing, what science had already discovered was beneficial, but 3 pioneers, we would still die of strep throat. To trapse along that mysterious path of unknowns. To try *avant-garde* practices that the ADA would very seriously frown upon. If I am as far along in my recovering having discovered the enormous benefits of my having flooded my neurons with vitamin B-complex as far along in the process as I had; I might be interested in seeing what would happen if the vitamin therapy had begun much earlier, diet too.

History has shown, on down through the ages, that when a civilization reaches a plateau, a level of cathartic stagnation, there needs to evolve an almost spontaneous revolution.

We may have been exposed to too many, too frequent, too messy, too loud, too abominable, to study or to simply abandon the energy of a "war."

Has this planet, this distance from the sun, already seen one or several other existences? Is the planet that we call Earth the only satellite ever to have circled what we refer to as a galaxy? Are we the first attempt at the plan to populate the Universe? Are we the last attempt? Indulge me for just a minute. I think I may have just figured out a new continuum. Now let's just take off our already recognizable conceptualization of the Universe. Just suppose the evolution of the dinosaur wasn't just a freak occurrence that nothing we know about is. That very possibly everything has already happened or has been happening for the largest number we have to the power of 10 years? (Our finite conceptualization of forever.)

And what is there that is so special about the basis of our chronology: the year is man, as we know his being to be, has he already been tested? Are we through being tested? Are we able to accurately measure the time of anything?

I realize that it's probably heresy for me to expand on any of these thoughts, these concepts that are much less than accepted.

"The Idiot and the Odd D.C."

"The doors to the dormitory dining hall lock at 7:00 p.m. on the dot! I've got to go!"

Were these the final words I would actually be able to utter? Okay, final four words.

Fall term 1980; Dave Cole, 17 years old, a Freshman Civil Engineering candidate, and already I had seen several weeks of class, and already I learned an incredible distaste for my ROT-C (Reserve Officers Training Corps.) roommate who I am sure jointly harbored a similar animosity for the civilian likes of me. I had occupied, also enjoyed, the idea of conspiring with me to tease the likes of my roommate?

October 2nd, 1980. A Thursday

"Tomorrow is a Friday, and of course I'm not quite as prepared for the examination as I should be.... to enter class wearing my new 'shades,' that would be so cool.

"Hey, give me a break, I was a freshman, and I needed approval!"

Surely, these were my thoughts; I can't be too sure though, the amnesia has made everything so muddy. I had been revisiting the scene of my 18th birthday celebration to retrieve a pair of sunglasses.

I had just turned 18, and now I was an adult, and now I was eligible for the draft; however, I was still just another Dave. There on the campus of life I hadn't found my 'id' yet.

This book is more than a diary, and it must be more than just another travel guide. I do not intend to sully people with the miseries of my Head Injury, however. I do wish to fill the void, for if there had been a book of this nature at the time of my injury, I am really quite certain that my rehabilitation would have benefited enormously.

So why has it taken me 18 years to put this manuscript together, and have I indeed sacrificed my credibility by not

261

having done something at a much earlier time? It has taken me the better part of those 18 years to complete my education, to get married, and to finish my investigation. Another aspect of my *modus operandi* since the injury had been to do everything myself, if only to prove that I could still do it.

I think it is Ernest Hemmingway whom I am quoting when I say, "This world breaks everyone while there are those who continue on stronger at the broken places." I ask, was my world breaking me, and am I now stronger at that broken place, e.g. the head?

The idiot? What Idiot?

Don't you mean the Iliad? And where did you get the 'Odd DC?' Don't you mean the Odyssey?

No, actually, I meant to say the Odd DC, and to use Iliad would have been plagiarism. This is a story, which sees itself acted out and reenacted over, over and over, *ad nauseum*.

This is a story but not really a story. A story being a tale created in the mind of the storyteller. Real life indicating that there are or were facts to back up any of the claims made.

Is this maybe an autobiography? Well, yes, but not really anything of the kind. A biography, yes. However, it was an automobile, which molested me and modeled me to look like a nasty, a ghoulish very bad sort of nightmare! This is not a fable surrounding some magical machine, there was no vehicular inspiration, unless you wish to consider the casual relationship between myself and a car and inspiration.

"What goes around comes around." Almost like a cyclical voyage, don't you think?

This is a story of a cyclical voyage, of a life-my life and a voyage made with numerous marked changes of fortune!

Once upon a time, in a land far away and enchanted there lived and played a prince of a boy. A lad, who in this story was fair of skin. He looked out over his father's wealth through eyes, which were opulently blue. Their peering out over land, which he had so often been the council of his elders to one day be his world, or at least his world might resemble them to the degree of perspiration he would be willing to sweat out.

In his world, he would sport and play; journey and explore. Then as days passed on to days and the year evolved into another year, this young prince, me, matured and grew. So brilliantly stout, and handsome and strong I would soon become. This is how life is supposed to be; rather, this is the way I was always been led to believe it would be.

The actual year this story occurred is really of no consequence. This is just my version of a story, which has been told and retold throughout the history of princes and men, and princesses and women, too of course.

If I may be allowed to go back far enough, I could easily apply the principles to many of the fables and fairy tales and nursery rhymes. Rip Van Winkle comes to mind.

So, good ole Rip was obviously not struck by a car, and no, he did not suffer some industrial trauma. Maybe he was thrown from his horse, or possibly, he slipped on some loose stones, what do you think? Had Mr. Van Winkle been pickled, preserved, by an excessive amount of strong fermentation in his bloodstream? Maybe he fell face forward into a puddle of ice water; this would have caused a surge of blood to his brain. Was there also involved a Cerebral Vascular Accident (a CVA, or a stroke)?

Had his injury, in reality been the cause of a 20-year coma, or has the fable been subjected to liberal poetic licensure? Or had the absence of E.R. personnel and an educated Physical Therapist resulted in the excessively long duration? It seems to me that a combination of the aforementioned possibilities probably extends the excessively long period of down time. Just think about it though. "Humpty Dumpty sat on a wall, Humpty Dumpty had a great fall; all the Kings men and all the Kings horses couldn't put Humpty back together again." From where, do we get such nursery rhymes, fables; where do they find so much inspiration, such clandestine, often morbid, inspiration?

While I never qualified for that all expenses paid trip to the Coroner's Office; for 3-6 months I was unable to contribute to the advancement of the human population, much less the Western variety of our species; therefore, this is why I feel I was deceased. I feel safe in assuming that you may have had such, or similar feelings.

This one is a tale with few if any predecessors. None so articulate anyway (that I have seen). As a matter of fact, it seems uncanny that this prince should be the first to recall, to recount of his having suffered or of even having lived such a life. There are are of course fairy tales told and Halloween stories sold, but never actually having been lived out in the first person by any of the expressed or apparent authors. This, it should be remembered is not a short story. As a matter of fact, it's pretty long, though I doubt very seriously that any publisher shall be willing to print my entire story, so I've eliminated much of the less newsworthy jargon.

I begin my tale, my biography. Almost autobiography in the fine years immediately following the decade, which followed the years just after the world, was at war. The digital enumeration beginning'197... I grew up, my not having to fight, claw or kill, nor did I need to spend my time reading, hearing, or watching others commit any of the atrocities of which I have just spoken, Instead I was more interested in being a kid!

Kennedy was to be assassinated only shortly after the day of my first birthday. H---, I didn't care. As a matter of fact, I couldn't have given a s----, but I probably did. I probably soiled more than one cloth diaper; we didn't have the disposables yet, or was it that my Mother wasn't bent on living her life without struggle.

The education of my early days had been preoccupied generally in a big brick building- a school building. Twelve years later without any due or undue hoopla or fanfare, I successfully maneuvered my way well beyond my first days in preschool. I had begun high school in an institution, which had originally been located only a stones throw away from my childhood home. We'd say, "within spitt'n distance." As it was, I had to travel some seven miles to attend classes at Fairview High School. I very readily tired of riding the conventional school bus to school. It had come by my house about an hour and a half before class would even begin, and because I lived farther along towards the end of the route, I would often get there with a little more than an hour to wait in the building for my first class.

Besides, I had a friend who lived directly across the unpaved, oily, greasy, dirt road named after the state highway director at the time of its establishment, Mr. Gapter. We spent so many long hours of the ever imperceptivity shortening and the lengthening days. And because the days never seemed to get any shorter, or longer, the length of the school year seemed to grow. That is, it had grown until Saturday, June 7th, 1980. When I was given a little red book; and no, it wasn't written by Mao Tse Tung. This little red book has written in it: Having fulfilled the requirements as prescribed by the Board of Education of the Boulder Public Schools, of Boulder County, Colorado, David Fedrick Cole is entitled to this Diploma given this seventh day of June, Nineteen hundred eighty. It failed entirely to mention anything about the with honors part. But I had; I had been successful and graduated with honors, and this was the final something I would complete with honors for the rest of my life! I had now had something to look forward to. I could now enjoy all the freedoms accorded an adult. My birthday was only about three months away, and I would no longer have to be devious in order to get my beer.

It was summer. I was not legally obligated to work yet I had chosen to work. I could see it as being quite possibly my last summer off. My final summer to spend lollygagging about the fields. H---, I just graduated from high school with honors, and being that I was scheduled to begin college in 2 months, I just didn't want to work. But I did work. I always wanted to be a step ahead of tuition. I didn't want to graduate like all my friends.... many thousands of dollars in debt, so I worked a couple of fabulously, low-paying jobs. They were the only jobs I could find available. They were hot; one was inside an un-air-conditioned garage at a car dealership, the other outside tieing re-bars at a concrete form assembly manufacturer. It was okay though; I was 17 years old, an honor graduate just out of high school, I didn't mind acting out the part of a slave, as a matter of fact, I considered it a privilege to be assigned to go get doughnuts for the 9:10 coffee break every morning at 8:30. It was my high school graduation, and I was done. Finally finished with the tedium of scholastic exercise every kid is plagued with for 12 or 13 so years, and I had planned, my life was going to find me with a wonderful job, working for a wonderful company, maybe I would even own such a wonderful enterprise. So, I considered it almost an expected present to have planned a wonderful bicycle excursion that summer, as a graduation present to myself.

So with Jim, I planned. We mapped out all our destinations. We called ahead and secured several maps for our "holiday of a lifetime." We were off to tour the Western edge of the United States by bicycle.

I was sure that we were being set up, set up for something really big. At the time, however, I just wasn't really prepared for the initial political, much less subsequent familial ramifications, for the epitome of perfection as, eventually, it was to become. At its onset, it didn't really look like much; it even felt like a victimization, but I wasn't about to take that laying down, coma or no coma. I was out to make the world, and I wasn't about to let anyone or anything get in the way.

Almost as soon as I "woke-up" from my traumatically induced coma, I began receiving input like, "what a shame it is that you had to be hit by that car." By not having any further input, I adopted this as the way things really were. I was angry. I needed to place blame, but because I was incapable of articulating my anger, I had to act out my anger, very much as every child does. But this time, I had the foundations from which to build. I didn't have to go back and begin at point zero; I had muscles. I had a voice if only dysardhric; I was

266

very fortunate! And like the child growing up with only English, or only German, or only French being spoken, the child learning only one word for every object he witnesses in his surroundings, I didn't have an opportunity to view my "lot in life" with any more than anger . I just want to bare this spot and have it be known by everyone who helped me in the critical, the crisis. The emergency moments may have already been enumerated by my insurance adjusters and myself. I want to say that I am forever in your debt, whatever that may mean to you, and that this is good.

You may be asking yourselves, "I don't get it, David's writing a book in the same genre so many other books have already been written."

This is where I must correct you. I am only writing this as an epic way of trying to reek out the cessation of bicycles being sacrificed by so many errant automobiles. I meant to write a book in which every page held some point you could refer to back to it as; that page where.... But to do that without any preamble would be similar to your saying hello to the next president of the United States without their having even been elected. And you should know, this might very well be the case!

1980

1980, actually, what a very big year. A very big year in the life of the United States, music lovers everywhere, and in the life of a recent high school honor graduate. That's me.

And I'm sorry, but I am entirely without any responsibility for all the calamities which 1980 wrought. I was dead. My heart may have been beating, but for all intent and purposes, I was dead to the world affairs. Maybe, I set this one up. So much has occurred since I began to entrust the Universe with my needs and problems, maybe I set the stage for all this to happen. I graduated from high school and did so with honors, a 3.65 grade point average, and a diploma signifying only that I had "successfully fulfilled the requirements of graduation as prescribed by the Board of Education of the Boulder Valley Public Schools. District number Re 2. Boulder County, Colorado!" Indeed, I was also able to navigate the western most border of the United States, that's highway 101 and 1, by bicycle from Seattle WA. to Santa Barbara CA.

Upon reaching Santa Barbara, ill fate lie in wait, and dashed into traffic before I finished crossing an intersection. Maybe this was meant to be a warning; maybe it should have alerted me not to ride my bicycle in traffic anymore, but it didn't. Instead, it only reinforced my sense of immortality. I was now even more sure that I was invincible. No car could injure me! Nothing could knock me out of circulation; all my years of weightlifting were paying off in immeasurably huge sums.

I don't need more chances, as so many scream for; instead, I need less willfulness to pre judge me just because I don't walk the straight and narrow. Fewer stigmatizations, defamatory remarks, some made publicly others less evident to the unaided eye or ear, but made never the less, metaphysically!

The precursor or secret phase: This is an examination of a person's life before the actual onset of trauma. This is where

I hope to be able to make the greatest difference. I figure, why the h--- spend so much of my waking existence writing anything if it doesn't affect something? Even the checks I write; if they did not affect something, I'd be less inclined to draft them at all, but without writing them post humus, I have been most entirely unable to write many of these words.

The measure of everybody's life; their successes and friction unrealized successes and even their attempts at living a life as a temporarily able bodied human being, (TABED) is quite often reflexively aligned with what I've lived and witnessed in others. And don't be concerned that the measure is skewed because I am only one individual and there are so many other people being afflicted-affected by TBI. Persons for whom their lives were never cut out to take on an active-constructive role in society, and all those who have never had the gumption to relate their experiences to the larger society; and therefore, they've simply gone on to take their place on some accountant's data register and are heard from no more! I am entirely unwilling to concern my writing with these persons, or to fully examine their rationale, reasoning, or guiding modus operandi. However, I am able to grant them this latitude, for I have no respective perception of their lot in life. This may take me out to be the fall guy, that bad cookie, the aberrant author who is so callus, so rude, and socially estranged. If this should be the categorization which you have assigned my personality, then so be it; I cannot hope to refute your sense of integrity, but I can hope to get you off the dole, to get you on your way and to hopefully lessen your susceptibility to becoming just another statistic.

But we need statistics too. We need them, if only as a way of showing others, to impress, digress, and otherwise ingest society with even a single iota more control over their lives. This serves to make them happy, to pacify their need for affecting other, more impacting calamities such as rioting in Los Angeles, or garbage striking in New York.

The discovery chaos phase. I had a clear identity with who I was, what my strengths were. I was on my way to impacting society in a measurably sizable way, but what I was entirely unaware of, was that something could go wrong. I was without an internalization of the processes involved with the metaphor, death. Now, after the fact, my illusions of death, of immortality, are even actually reinforced.

To me, death was reserved for the grandfathers of the world, the men who went to battle, and only then for me. This was only to be after I married, procreated two or more individuals, and sought after an experience everyone needs to undertake at least once in their lives. I was entirely committed to living. Almost pathologically invested in this life; I was serious about making this time a good time, a prosperous time; however, I didn't actually have anything to go on, nothing to judge how things were really going, but then reality is such a nebulous term. There is no baseline, not even one from which to gauge my hunger.

Was I really hungry? Or has all this been somehow incorporated, programmed into my sense of reality, like a computer program in which you've got to set the stage, you've got to make the input understandable, and you are responsible for any mistaken results had by the machine. Because I was shown the possibilities of what life could be like, had I chosen to be birthed into a different culture?

My homeostasis might never have known eating into a sickened state of gluttony. My equilibrium might have been adjusted to always walking upside down. Upside down being as it related to the conventional, this 20th century Western sense of right side up.

We might never have even known what it was to breathe oxygen. Now I seem to be delving off into the metaphysical arena or ontological realms.

As a young adult, not even an adult yet, still a teenager 18 years old, and I was just beginning to expand my parameters of experience. So far, I had 30 days to enjoy life in this new, legally new categorization, though for all other purposes I was still "wet behind the ears." As well as in front of the ears and in the ears too; I was wet all over, except if I wanted to commit a crime, then I would become an issue; I would have been tried and hung as an adult. This is the way it all has seemed to work out. I wreaked some terrible calamity on some poor unsuspecting soul, and now I had to pay for such an infringement.

As it were though, I was to be hung without first being tried; without ever having been found guilty by a jury of my peers. No, they all have would have been at home or in the dormitory or in class. I had fallen between the proverbial cracks in the roadway, but also through the cracks in the medical profession. The abyss into which I had been cast was to hold alterations so profound, I wasn't about to take them on alone. It was a relief to know that emergency medicine had advanced to the levels it had.

After patching (stapling) me up enough so that no more bodily fluids could leak out and stain my shirt, pants and socks, they were able to arrange the pieces in a bed for the next 3-5 months, after which I was to begin the stepped up regimen of bodily re-education.

Before I was scheduled to undertake the long lonesome process of rehabilitation, I first had to master a couple of rudimentary abilities.

Because I wasn't expected to access that infamous next level of recovery *ad nauseum*, I became a freak, an aberration, a disorder of the mind. But none of this with my mind!

I have so much trouble appreciating a woman's problem. It has been made out to seem the result of the accident, but I would rather think that it is because I'm a man. Because women are so h---bent on gaining equality in the world, they are expectedly acknowledging their lowness or place in society. If I am really strong, I don't have any need to go about voicing my strength...

This is all new to me; I'm just learning on my end how I deal with it! Trying to find areas that will help me grow, just like Bittin is an artiste, and that's where she can move toward.

Like she says..... She's not the Bittin she was before. Heck, I'm not the person I was before.... But even after the three years, which have gone by, I wouldn't be the same Cindy anyway; we change, it's just something you never ask for or expect.

Right... when you go down to Hammond, you'll never come back.

Yeah, Pied Piper, huh.

The person you were when you went down can never come back, but the person you are can come back.

No! The physical carriage will be the same; but the personality coming back is entirely different. The person coming back. I like me.... Where would I be if I hadn't been hit by a car?

Right, you were planning to be an engineer.

"This may be my ego speaking louder than my reality, I don't know, but I can envision myself fitting the traditional role of the engineer. Of my getting up every morning many hours before the sun, my rushing off, driving 16-20 miles to work every day, working behind a desk until noon, going out and having a two martini lunch, finishing the day and then going home to my wife and 2.4 children for the rest of my life. And it wouldn't even really be a life, but I'd be living it."

"No, all my life before the accident, I dreamed of being an artist, dreamed of being a writer, that's the only reason I chose to become an engineer. That always appeared the shortest route to having enough money so I could retire early and write. That's all I wanted to do, write. Being an engineer was just the apparent, easiest way to making that dream come true."

So you pursued that until your brain injury?

"Right, because I saw engineering as a short cut to writing, the easiest way to enough money to support my bad habit. This way, I have huge surfeits of stuff to write about, as well as a paycheck. And I'm able to write and it's all just

273

great, it's wonderful. Everything's perfect, I can write!

My days go by in flash. I'm doing just what I want to do, I'm doing what I love; I write! I realize I got the newsletter out just a bit late this month... I have an excuse though."

"That doesn't even matter. I can't keep track of when I'm supposed to be getting a newsletter out. My time and space is kind of screwed up, so the time doesn't matter. The only thing I would really miss is my pay-check. My concept of time isn't real good."

Bittin is an artist and she can do it through graphic art, and you do it through writing.

The awareness polarization phase. The recovery, rebuilding phase.

I just saw what we have to face up to. Everyone has to wake up and smell that proverbial cup of coffee! I, as a TBI, have been accorded the secret, I've been empowered with the same message that is being spoken by all the news programs, and movie scenarios; it is being made out as a sickened monster that is fun to play with. But I've got experiential learning and intellectual understanding so deep and so profound, I no longer fit into any of the puzzles out there. All my life I was told I have the charisma, the character, and the facial qualities I need to get through this life in high style. I was inundated with the message that I was beautiful and would be sought after by members of the opposite sex. I was manipulated into cursors and precursors until I no longer felt the need to struggle.

So where does this get me? The very same spot where so many others are actually are living! Only I can no longer be human! I can no longer ask for assistance; if I do, our society's emergency squadrons are alerted and I am rushed to the hospital. Is this a free service? H--- no! I get transported, by ambulance, complete with paramedics all the way across the county to the hospital. Did I resist? Did I object to the procedures? Funny thing you should ask, why yes, I spoke out; but was I treated as a rational human being? Of course not.

Instead, I was told that another human being had for some reason been assigned with the responsibility for my welfare. "Your resistance is what gives us the right to treat you the way we would treat anyone with sun-stroke!"

"But I don't have sun-stroke or even heat exhaustion! All I asked for was a drink of water!"

"And what was I told at that Point? I was told by the ambulance attendants that there was no water available!"

I mean get a clue people! Taking an ambulance to an outdoor event, on a day as hot as it was without any potable water aboard was exceptionally negligent!"

I had to phone my father, who, of course was only so obliged to rush to my rescue. Because I was transported entirely away from my only means of transportation a bicycle, and because the bike was "impounded" by the police department, I was stuck with no way of getting home.

Fortunately, my father was again obliged to escort me all the way back across town to a volunteer fire station and then took me home.

Shortly after my mailbox begun bulging with bills, hospital bills. Paramedic/ambulance fees, fees to balance the services of more than one radio technologist. So, what was the prognosis/diagnosis of the attending emergency doctor? Get this! Ply the patient with water and other non- alcoholic beverages.

I mean, at the time I was 24 years old, my sister was a mother at the age of 21, and they so disempowered me, but why?

It must have something to do with their training, their medical training? They didn't even have the intuition to let me think for myself. Instead, they deemed the matter as fraught with potential in the need to avoid anything that even remotely smells of lawsuit.

I was in Boulder on summer break from the university; I wasn't stupid! I was just thirsty.

Are they willing to sacrifice us in the name of being human? Do we really want to witness the USA being transformed into a "Marshall state," are we losing touch with what it's like to be human? We are living in a society where the population is rapidly with staccato, becoming an older bunch of individuals. Is there any room to maintain the mask of being anything less than human?

I see there are two or more radically different types of people in our society. There are the "worker ants" they only need to work.

While I was deeply affected, and while I was in a chronic state of affairs at the hospital, I would try and try to fit into the general milieu of society. Whenever I tried to work through my mail, the United States Postal Service was against me. Each postage paid envelope seemed to be made smaller than what I would need them for; if it were to pay a bill, they always seemed just a smidgeon smaller than what I figured was a standard sized check.

Shortly after my stay at the hospital, I was given a journal, and journal writing seemed to be the best outlet for me. It released quite a sizable chunk of angry emotion, which would probably have resulted in several storms of much misdirected energy. I very easily filled at least 3000 empty pages. I would recommend having a journal available. If writing was one of the physical abilities involved in the accident, may I suggest a tape recorder, and if speech was also involved, having a stenographer at hand could fulfill this need. But then I find that the actual physical act of writing is part of the benefit of telling my story.

The following is only a "*Readers Digest*," abridged superficial skimming out of those books. They begin almost a year and three months after my accident, and are included here verbatim. They have come directly out of my journal. There has been no editing or grading for proper English; there has been a good deal of space filled in to make my ramblings seem a little more coherent.

Even More Journal Pages

1/2/82

    I would like to, at this time, tell you what would be a nice reward for surviving a Volvo to the head. Two or three hundred thousand dollars or a new house in Northern Oregon or Southern Washington with a hot tub, eight hundred dollars to spend on a new bike, and a long thank you letter from Joe, for living. Seeing how Joe was only insured to the bare legal minimum, I cannot ask, and expect or hope to receive more than this. But I mean, I am so angry that this amount of money will never repay me and all those near me for all the trouble and heartache which Joe Lynn's instant of juvenile miscalculation has caused me and my family.

1/5/82

    I woke up around 12 or 1 with nature begging me. So I got out my urinal and met nature; however, I didn't put it back on the table after I was tired of nature. Then for some stupid reason my tummy was cold so I rolled over.

    You may well be asking how did you wet the bed after using the urinal. Well do you remember I didn't put the 'P' pot on the table? Well it was still between my legs so that as I rolled over the 'P' pot came with me. Whoops you may well say, well all I said was oh s--- so there I was at 1:00 in the morning, a cold morning if you recall, and there I was, running around with my jackets and warm-ups on "spitting" on myself whenever possible, making my bed in new sheets that I luckily found. That was just the beginning of a miserable morning. I went into the house (My bedroom had been in the garage about 80' behind the main house.) With the 's ----' expecting Gail and Grant to be there at 6:30 and take me to school in time for a class. My brother gave me a ride home so that I have time to write in here and there before din din.

1/7/82

    Well school went O.K. since I got up about two hours earlier than I did on the 6th, but even doing so well with my time. I don't feel like I am being led in the correct path to make my life in the future comfy. I have so much fun doing everything I should be doing. If it weren't for having friends who expect so much I would probably be dragging through life with no care for or about anything, except my physical well being which I need to blame for my being alive at all. To continue with the day I met an old friend who was a year behind me. Her name is Judy Turner and was with a friend whose name was Stace or Steph. And they took me to lunch at 3:00 until 5:00 so I got back with enough time to look up the name of the restaurant I wanted to take Gail and Grant to. I remembered its location and the fact that it had the Roman Numeral II in its name. I was right about the numbers and the location. It was volume II next door to the Village Theatre where they came to pick me up.

1/11/82

To start with the weekend as Bryan's condo was great. The first night we all sat around and chewed the fat and talked, all fourteen of us. "Na" (Naomi) and Jim came up for the evening and the next day of skiing. Without those two there were only nine people at the condominium, this created the perfect number to enjoy the weekend with and I did. The next day, everyone took off for the slopes while I just stayed in and did exercises for four hours and took very short naps in between every set. I decided that a whole group of college age kids drinking and listening to music (no one smokes) or watching TV, this went on for about five hours until I went to bed at 11:00pm, was a wild night doing nothing but playing a bunch of junior highish games such as fortunately/unfortunately, animals which is where there is a circle of people and and MC in the center, or at least close to the center.... Sunday they all went up skiing, everyone except Kelly A and Kathy C. We all walked out to the shuttle and went up to the ski area for lunch. Besides lunch we all read out of a book called *The Silver Wolf*. I did a fairly good job of it seeing how I can't see too well or two of everything that I do see.

1/17/82

I got all my math homework done. That felt good having most of the day with very little to do except exercise. I am going to try and lose my belly button except for the scar. It won't be too easy but I figure, I've got the will power of four twenty emaciating individuals. So it won't be too difficult except, for all the people around me offering pastries and pounds cake. All I know is that it felt really good to have Judy Turner comment on how skinny I looked. On this diet I will be crunching all day but just carrots and apples. For protein I'm afraid the most fattening food of all... cheese. Soon I am going to a separate apartment so that I can get used to living all alone in that big dark dangerous world outside the one I occupy presently.

I think that it had been early in the course of my rehabilitation in which I had the overshadowing notion to prove to the world that, "hey, I'm okay, even though I may have hit... (or been hit by) another one of those life enhancing proverbial walls. Even though my wall had come at me in the form of a 2 ton, plus or minus a half ton, automobile, it would surly take more than knocking me unconscious for 5 going on six months to keep me under wraps.

I had to be mildly belligerent, insisting that even though my viability as a man was now the subject for much questioning, that I was encouraged to enroll in a hugely \rather stepped up version of physical, occupational, and speech therapies.

It was time to be blunt! Now was the time that I adapt my thinking, my time \space physical adjustments to an entirely new position, and I had thought that making the adjustment twice a year as we would either spring forward or fall back an hour to maximize our sunlight time was difficult. I had after-all never been here before.

Would I be up to the challenge? It was actually nothing I could ever have prepared myself for: I was more of the mind that said I didn't want to remain in this new environment: my mind. My mind (even as compromised as it had been) it wasn't ready to adapt to these unexplored, unmapped, and by me, inexperienced events.

My initial motivators must surely have originated from my reluctance to settle in. To accept my frustration, the horror of only having long-term memories of the life I lived before 10/02/80.

So David, if your short term memory was so intensively questioned, severely in question, how do you account for your being aware that you were so unaware of very much?

Repetition, and speed-or the lack there of! I was slow, and not just in my motor activities. I had to say most everything twice, to repeat each of my thought once if not more than that. I look back on these early cognitive therapies as quite possibly many of my most important lessons. (Personally I don't think such therapy was so intentional, as it was done out of frustration in the beginning and as a way of putting a check on my validity... to see if I knew I was talking about as we got more towards the end of my therapy.)

The molasses I was emulating--creating was probably what saved my ass too. I've always had the desire to please and impress. I'd always been a "brown noser." Even before I was able to walk at all, or even to walk at all well. My earliest motivator and what was instrumental in my even being in rehabilitation: I had wanted to ride a bicycle. My earliest affective thoughts had surrounded my being able to get around, my getting back on board a bicycle.

Janice Tomita, my primary physical therapist, was adamantly against the idea of my ever getting back on board a vehicle which had so very darn near killed me. However, and this is a pretty big however, I am walking pretty much and mostly due to several of her pretty much unorthodox methods of rehabilitation. I don't know though, I didn't have any therapy minded education. Maybe they were in fact quite usual.

Discuss Friday May 13th, 1983 and the several weeks

leading up to 5/13/83. It was Monday, or a Tuesday, a Wednesday, or a Thursday, or a Friday, I was living on West Pennsylvania on "The Hill" and a block away from Dick's Bicycle Shop. I would be more than able to ride my bike down off of "The Hill" to Nancy's restaurant and then up to Boulder Memorial Hospital on Mapleton Avenue for outpatient therapy.

By this time, my speech pathology, and occupational therapies had both discharged me. I'd been able to accomplish everything which they had in place for me to accomplish. I was there at the rehab hospital primarily for PT (physical therapy) and TR (Therapeutic Recreation); it seems Janice Tomita just wouldn't give up trying to discourage my dream of riding a bicycle again.

Anyway, it was on this data that I did all of my travel by bicycle so that by the time I was in front of Ms. Tomita, I had ridden at least 10 miles. It was customary for me to "perform" for Janice so that she could make an assessment of my gait. She didn't want to see me aboard a bicycle... ever again; however, today she was also astounded with the smoothness of my walk, the strength in my gait. I don't want to fore guess the professional abilities of PTs all over; however, I can also attribute such remarkable progress to the therapeutic implications of riding my bicycle, of recreation.

I am in favor of everyone having a chance, a choice opportunity, to get out of the way of, or over, or around an experience such as this one in their lives. Preferably an experience just a little less intensive, even though not necessarily an experience even a little more mundane, not a Sunday-morning-meeting sort of experience, or by reading this book. I don't want to dis-employ, neurosurgeons, PTs, OTs, speech pathologists, psychological therapists, Taxi drivers, and the myriad of other professionals out there in order to manage such traumas.

I do not want to eliminate the need for so many other individuals, or even the rest of society, to also have one of these profound, life altering experiences.

"How silly," you may say.

Gena, my wife, had been in the running to be valedictorian of her 1985 high school class; she would have too; however, she came across one of those profound, life altering experiences.

I am not suggesting for everyone to go out and have their ability to walk around profoundly altered. The events to which I refer: getting married, securing the type of employment one could really enjoy, to be graduating from the university of one's choice, or having and/or getting to raise a child.

Parenthood is certainly not one of those issues, which everyone, injured or not, should move forward with. My wife, my partner in crime: similar crime, different date, different MO, she had her license already for almost a year, but had not been the pilot of the car in which she was injured, but was only in 6th grade by 1980 the year of my car-nage. She is now the mothering half of our two entirely intentional conceptions.

Far more gallant than I, she has also witnessed a "stroke," a cerebral vascular accident. This was subsequent-in addition to her preceding trauma, which had already compromised an enormous degree of her ability to readily access her latent potential. In her original witnessing of life behind the veil, of a coma, she also been dealt a hugely compromising situation; half of her vocal chords had been paralyzed.

At this time what I feel a responsibility for affecting isn't necessarily to eradicate highway mortality, or to disemploy trauma physicians around the globe; it is however, now my responsibility to share with the world one man's words of rehabilitation: straight from the horse's mouth. To provide a veritable road map of how I have been able to return to the university, how I have attempted to re-enter that fabulously underpaid world of gainful employment… entirely unsuccessfully. Than to manage a continuation and quite necessarily of my own life.

"Write a book. Document your feelings, witness your

life."

For me, it was my life, my having gotten married, and by the grace of God our having been given the opportunity to raise two children!

I don't want to make you think that I feel like or want to be the Dr. Spock of raising children while living beyond an impacted life. I'm just trying to alleviate all the stresses, all the worry which I felt. Which I sense others may be feeling before embarking on life, necessarily their own, and having also had the chance/ the choice opportunity to see over Pink Floyyd's proverbial Wall, or to go down to The Roches' Hammond. I want to take on a responsibility not too unlike the one Brigham Young managed through his firmly establishing life in a place which few if any thought possible.

The life I wish, I intend to establish, is one not so very unlike the life as witnessed by human beings even since a human began being. However, this is a life compromised by several new conditions, which no one in their right mind would wait in line to register for at the university. This one is a life not entirely graced with that innate resiliency of a child. I was 18 years old, and I didn't have the ability to bounce back, an ability which I'm confident most every child comes endowed with. Endowed with an evolutionary safeguard.

I always felt that I had some responsibility for what was, is and had happened. I think Sigmund Freud had also identified this among his battery of complexes? The "Grandiosity" complex.

Surely not me, I wasn't so bad off. I hadn't lost any irreplaceable bits and pieces of hardware: I could still see and I could still go pee. Shhh, now this one might blanch a few faces, but I felt like I was truly, "on the mend" when I found myself able to attain an erection and even fondle myself ... and ejaculate. That was also about the time I saw myself as in control of everything that was going on.

I would often be found screaming. Screaming at everyone, at everything and usually for no reason at all. For no special reason, and with no real purposeful intent. I just yelled a lot, and not just at those people who had me, "on their schedule." I would scream at everyone in range of my then, not so subtle voice!

I didn't have that studied calm, that classic, at all times politically correct, business toned voice: I'd been to several Rolling Stones concerts, I'd had the experience of conversing while so many other vibrations occupied the airwaves which were also inundated with cigarette and other smokes, water and so many other such vapors.

I'm not saying that I had been prematurely released from my institutional choice for rehabilitation, even though it felt like I had been abandoned. This abandonment came at me not unlike a dream I think that I had had either while still comatose, or very shortly, upon my having emerged.

In the dream: I was in a wheelchair. So it must have been after I had "awoken," or emerged from my extended period of unconsciousness.

There we were, outside, on a hill, and I am in my wheelchair angled across the hill in order that I wouldn't roll down the hill immediately upon being released. Or maybe the brakes had been engaged-there you go, I must have been "awake." Then the nurses. All the people whom had brought me outside, they all just threw up their hands and walked away saying, "Okay buster, we got you this far, the rest of the trip is up to you!"

I didn't walk down the street just in order to find someone to yell at. I was more focused on yelling at those people who loved me, and/or had been hired to love me. And, no, I'm not talking about any ladies of the night, prostitutes or other.

"Don't help me!" I would scream, while violently pulling away from whomever was there, or whatever assistance was being offered.

Even though I was severely injured, I must have sensed, unconsciously, maybe even intuitively, I'd felt the embarrassment, the insult, the effacement felt by so many others, and expressed by the sorrowful inflection in their voices, and by the saddened look in their eyes. Often my choice of words indicates that I felt like I was up on stage, or behind a lectern. I would employ an entire host of ambiguous words, which would keep people at a comfortable distance. Many if not most or all of these words were usually so far out of context and otherwise grammatically incorrect. Maybe it was just my way of insisting that I had still had a brain, that I could still formulate complete sentences. I felt a need to perform, if not miracles, just something a little more entertaining than the animated mess of blubber before you. These thoughts and feelings were, I must have felt, indications that I probably would be moving, advancing and otherwise getting on with my life.

My, "Don't help me!" would then be followed with the strongly put, "Don't help me unless I ask, and you can refuse to help it and when I ever do ask." I must have repeated this announcement several dozen times each day. In the early days of rehab, I don't really think anyone had the nerve, the audacity, the wisdom not to have refused.

My anger must surely have been hidden, maybe not, but palpable even while cloaked behind a mask. I was just as upset by my predicament as everyone else; however, it was easier for me. This aspect of the injury I was in control of. I was holding all the cards. I knew if and when fatigue would enter and indicate my abilities were exhausted, I could feel the myriad of syringes, each syringe filled with an antibiotic, or serum but there was no antibiotic for the "illness" I had.

Now is the time to look at an antidote. Do it now, been down to Hammond. Don't wait until you know what it's like to be injured about the head. Now is the appropriate time to make a measure of, or take a dose of preventive investigation.

Even though of little significance still another indication of the level to which my rehabilitation would take me was when my Mom offered to get me those twirly shoelaces to enable the "pulling on" of my shoe. I surely must have been severely agitated. I'm sure I screamed, "No!" and, "There's no way I want to be seen with those things on my shoes," is probably what I said, all the while in my heart I was probably screaming, "I'm not an old man, I may walk and talk like I should be incarcerated in a retirement home, but I still tie my own shoes!"

I couldn't but this was beside the point. I was still a man, and I had still had a little bit of pride left.

Here is an issue which I am worried about: male nurses are quite necessary, and for me, all 260 pounds of me, they were not only important and necessary; I think I must have lost a great deal of pride, my being bathed by the same male nurse who would bring me my medicines and meals. I was still a boy, a heterosexual boy, I'm sorry, Chip, or whatever you name was, and I could have used fewer sponge baths from you.

A great deal of pride and all of my modesty was surely sacrificed while I was incarcerated. So many nurses; female and male, so many doctors; mostly all male, their undressing me, poking, I got needles in my arms, my butt; I even got a couple needles stuck in the tips of my fingers.

Tying one's shoelaces. Surely a stupid indication of health, but surely one to be experienced while moving through the progressive stages of maturity; both on your initial try as well as any and all subsequent attempts. By way of the guidance from one of my therapists: My OT (occupational therapist), Barb Clause (Maiden name?) was instrumental in my having learned and mastered the one handed tie of a shoelace.

There was only half of each shoe that had laces; it was usually in the right hand column of the shoe. It makes sense though, if you only have one hand, (one correctly coordinated hand) it doesn't serve anybody to expect you to tie a shoe with two laces.

Dianne Young and Holly Meyers who were the 2 Therapeutic Recreation Specialists who came to my rescue, they were also the only therapists willing to help me get back aboard a bicycle. I now realize that they were the therapists in charge of such discipline.

Life's not like that though, if you only have one you're not only expected to use the one you have, you'll also need to find a replacement and another to fill in on the off days, for that one.

Now that I have married, and we have moved out on our own, so far out of town that there is little chance of anyone to notice much less comment, or even to care a rats' ass how a person ties their shoes. While living in my first house away from home, subletting a room from a man who had just won the largest foot race in town, The Bolder Boulder, in 1982. Mark Scrutton was his name, and one morning after I'd moved into his room, I made an awkward comment on the way he laced his shoes. Ever since that notorious morning, however, I have copied the way he laced his shoes. Some people collect shoelaces, I don't care; I collect ways of lacing shoes.

My roommates at the time Niles (?) and Jill (?) were very gracious in their having allowed even encouraged me to live in their midst. I think it may have had economic underpinning: that they needed a roommate on pretty short notice and at a time when the university was not in session. I found this room through Mora Carrigan, a woman whom I had met at one of the many parties across the street from my earlier Boulder address 954 Gapter Road. She was the older sister of the girl (woman) who'd be the class of 1980's Head Girl. Throughout my secondary scholastic life, she had always been Casey; I hadn't realized that it was spelled KC, or that it stood for Kathleen Carrigan.

Looking back, I didn't know then everything that I know now, duh, but I could really have taken more advantage of my friends than I had... except for Betsy Buck. Sorry Betsy, but you're in this story whether you like it, or not, and I thank you. All those trips to Arby's®, and all the Roast Beef! There are several others whom I am unable to resurrect in my mind at this point. I guess Betsy was merely the geographically closest and therefore the first one to have contributed in a very big way towards my rehabilitation, as well as in my self-actualization.

There were Buddhists who sought to convert Europe, a disciple of Tolstoy, who preached nonresistance to evil as well as other sects. We in the inner circle listened but accepted none of these teachings as anything but metaphors. We, who bore the mark, felt no anxiety about the shape the future was to take. All of these faiths and teachings seemed to us already dead and useless. The only duty and destiny we acknowledged was that each one of us should become so completely himself, so utterly faithful to the active seed which Nature planted within him, that in living out its growth he could be surprised by nothing unknown to come.

Although we might not have been able to express it, we all felt distinctly that a new birth amid the collapse of this present world was imminent, already discernable.... But no one is ready when a new ideal, a new and perhaps dangerous and ominous impulse, makes itself felt. The few who will be ready at that time and who will go forth--will be us, that confining idyll into more dangerous reaches. All men who have had an effect on the course of human history, all of them without exception, were capable and effective only because they were ready to accept the inevitable.

I can't be so certain that I had walked around mumbling that I was ready, that I would accept, nay embrace the inevitable, but Herrman Hess was able to have unwittingly documented so many of my feelings. I stood in at 5' 12", I had attained that glorious age of 18, I could now visit that notorious pub on the "Hill," legally, and I think the name was "Herby's Deli?"

Adapted: We can each understand one or another; however, each of us is only able to interpret, correct, and even alter himself for himself and all by himself.

I think that Herr Hesse may have had a sibling/s so injured as I am. His language, his choice of words, the topics he has written about, they speak to me as though he were intimately familiar with traumatic brain injury.

Maybe it is I who must take assessment of my own life as a father, as a husband will remain almost imperceptibly on my fingertips and out of range of my voluntary control. Life, it seems, is very much like a volunteer position in this life. You're expected to make pretty all the piles of shit that arise, but are legally unable to have any-be given any measure of control.

For if it were a case of my volunteering, I would probably have had even a little more control. That is from the moment of impact, my life has been lived, nay existed in a turmoil; however, and I'm certain such a turmoil is no more, no less than the convulsions everyone must embrace as they age even as they get older. We, we who live with such experiences have been given permission. It's a permission to really 'know' what your own death might really be like, and then to be granted another try at this life.

None of the images manage to accompany us on our subsequent mortalities, and just like our previous infancy, it cannot be documented and then replicated. There will only be the opportunity to endow another zygote/gamets juncture with an opportunity to attempt such a document.

Hermann Hesse: Demian, 1965.

WAR: "Yet another one of man's most egalitarian moments completely devoid of prejudice: everyone comes out on the short end of the stick."

Opening line in a journal I was given in 1981.

1/1/82

Good morning, I want to start this book with an introduction. My name is Dave Cole (signed) and I am the by-product of Joe Lynn who was the driver of a Volvo®, the hardest car made. I should know I've been hit by one twice, no not the same one. This book should be filled with words I want to be filled with stories; they are going to be attempted every day so that I am busy every night. School gives me enough homework to keep me out of trouble but this letter to whomever is to be filled with (a) day by night by day account of 1982. 1982 is going to be represented but that is very unlikely so enough of this explanation. I just killed a fly God forgive me. So this booklet is going to be filled with a lot of words about what; I don't know! But I am going to just write in here and here and on another page so you had better get mighty inebriated to enjoy this "diary" or "journal" because I'm not. I'm going to take Gail and Grant to dinner, hopefully am nextes NachtZum where I don't know but I've been there with Barb Lucas. Gail and Grant have not said yes yet so I am going to call them and hopefully they are going to be free on Saturday 1/2/82. Mr. Mann died so Bryan has gone to say good-bye to him at his last party the "funeral." I need to end this day so that I can start to day. So goodbye to you until hopefully tomorrow. My New Years resolution is not to resolve anything.

I am writing in this at 2:30 with the hopes of warm weather. I guess I wasted a line but who cares...do you? I'm going to Denver to see Penny Brewer. I sure want to walk in Stapleton to see how well I do in a crowd. Kenny and Becky are awaiting my call and have nothing to do so I am going to invite them over for a hot tub. Hopefully it will be taken wearing our B-day suits. I would like to explain that I prefer a tub without any clothing on. It is not that I enjoy seeing others naked it is just that I enjoy hot tubs in the nude. I am your typical male. I enjoy seeing the female body so I am hoping Becky will be in the same frame of mind. This summer will be one of a lot of effort seeing how I will be walking cane less or is that spelled cane less or caineless? I will say hi to Penny for you, whatever your name is. I've got a toy mouse named Christmouse and a parakeet named Peete. So what am I going to call you, how about John, (John Journal?)

1/3/82

This is the 3rd of January and not very late, but I am out here in my room and in bed because it is the only warm place except maybe somewhere in South America but not here. I

290

guess my hopes of warm weather got lost somewhere. Today was one of the coldest days I've experienced since the tragedy. I went to church at Bethany Baptist with the Willian because meine Mutter called and said she wouldn't be able to make it in time. To go to church that is. After church, I read the comics and the paper. I then decided it was not a day to be indoors watching F.B. (football).

So I went over to Bryan's house without even considering the idea that they would probably be watching F.B. Today was the last day of the Christmas break so in the morning I must rise and something so that I can go to school looking fairly presentable. I won't be shining because of the day. I am now looking forward to spring break and ultimately to warm weather, the water and Red Zinger Bicycle race and of course no school. I would like to, at this time, tell you what would be a nice reward to surviving a Volvo to the head. Two to three hundred thousand dollars or a house in Northern Oregon or Southern Washington with a hot tub, eight hundred dollars to spend on a new bike, and a long "Thank You form Joe," for living seeing as how Joe was only insured to the bare legal minimum. I cannot ask and expect to receive more than this. But I mean I am so angry that this amount of money will never repay me and those near me for all the trouble Joe Lynn caused me and my family.

Jan 5, 82

...Last night was dreadful but not before it happened, so I figured, you would get bored. But since then a lot has happened. A whole day has slipped away, maybe that explains why I haven't written for a whole day. So let's get started on this entry. Last night was awful. So, you want to know why, well I can't put it off for ever. Last night, I didn't wet the bed while asleep. You may well be wondering why it stinks so badly if I didn't wet it while asleep. Well, it seems obvious to someone who has lived through something as awful as this. Last night around 12: or 1:00 I woke up with nature begging me for some attention. So, I got my urinal and met with nature but... but I didn't put it on the table when I was through. Then for some stupid reason my tummy was cold so I rolled over. You may well wonder why or how I wet the bed after using the urinal; well do you remember how I told you that I put the pot on the table? Well it was still between my legs so that as I rolled over the pot came with me. Whoops you may well say, well all I said was s--- so there I was at 1:00 in the morning, a cold morning if you recall, and there I was, running around with my jacket and my warm-ups on spitting on myself whenever possible making my bed in newssheets that I luckily found. That was just the beginning of a miserable morning. I went into the house with the "s----s" expecting Gail and Grant to be there at 6:30 and take me to school in time for a 7:00 class. If you've noticed I was an hour ahead of time, so today started badly and has gone downhill ever since. My brother gave me a ride home so I have time to write in here and there before Din Din.

1/07/82

Well school went o.k. since I got up about two hours earlier than I did on the 6th, but even with all this doing things with so much goodness and doing so well with my time, I don't feel like I am being led in the correct path to make my life in the future comfy....I have so much fun not doing everything I should be doing. If it weren't for having friends who expect so so much, I would probably be just dragging through life with no care for or about anything. Except my physical well being which I really need to blame for my being alive at all.

To continue with the day, I met up with an old friend who isn't too close. Her name is Judy Turner and she was with a friend named Stace. And they took me to lunch at 3:00 until 5:00 so I got back with enough time to look up the name of the restaurant I wanted to take Gail and Grant to. I remembered its location and the fact that it had Roman numerals II in its name. Well I was right about the numbers and the location. It was Volume II next door to the Village movie theatre. I would like to give my finished drawing of Peete to Mrs. Adams. Hopefully she is back from Mexico, which I very much doubt, so I will finish the picture and hopefully it will be good enough to get me several more haircuts at Crazy Horse.

1/8/82

This is going to be very short entry. This is because I am spending the weekend up in Breckenridge. There won't be any talk of my going skiing because I can just barely walk much less stand while the earth is coming up at me. I hope I can get through with the math homework and all the exercises while they are skiing.

1/11/82

Everyone took off for the slopes while I just stayed in and did exercises for four hours and took very short naps between each set. All fourteen of us. Na and Jim came up for the evening and the day. Without those two, there were only nine people at the condo. This created the perfect number to enjoy the weekend with, and I did. Kelly A(llen), and Cathy C(arfrae), and I, we all walked out to the shuttle and went up to the ski area for lunch. Besides lunch, we read a story each out of a book called *The Silver Wolf.* I did a fairly good job of it seeing how I can't see too well or see two of whatever I do see. We got home (back to the condominium) around twoish and all I did was exercise and play son to the two girls playing moms. Marilyn Davie, Nora, Cathey Kelly, Margeret, Naomi, Kristen, Chris, Jim, Rob, Mark, and I. The one I fell in love with (for the weekend) was Marilyn. She was and is a very nice person; she looks and acts a little like Baki.

1/21/82

I am sick and tired of going to school. I suppose the weather has a lot to do with it. It is cold, freezing cold; meanwhile I have a lot of problems with the circulation on my left side and no exercises for the arm.... I hope to God I am able to run the Bolder Boulder so that I won't have to make up an excuse to use on all the people who think I will be running it this year. My Starvesdale diet did pretty well up until this morning. School has begun again at C.U. So I am wondering how I can see Kelsey and Eileen without them being too bored by my new personality I'(m) ve or at least feel like I am boring.

293

A lot more boring than I was in a coma but none the less boring. My bowels are having a lot of problems; this is because they are clogged and I cannot unclog them without eating anything. I do take a cup of wheat germ every day, but it doesn't seem to do the trick. Writing in this thing (journal) takes up so much of my time that I think when I do finally move out I won't be able to write, as I would like.

1/26/82

Well today was yet another day. Surprising, no? Well, it was, and is a warm one at that. The temperature was all of 70 (degrees). My horoscope said that I was in line for a financial gain. I don't think that it will amount to more than a few thousand dollars at least this time, but I want a few hundred thousand dollars or even a couple of million.

Thu. 1/28/82

I'm not feeling at all well tonight because of all the fighting I have been doing with myself. I mean it is much better to do it with one's self. It, fighting, should not be done with others it should be done with yourself. He consumes so much sugar and then is not hungry for supper. While at the same time, he has been making Pookey bark a years worth of yeps. I wish that (I could get a movie of my feelings so that I would have an explanation for all the things I do.) I get so angry at my Mom for treating me like a totally reliant cripple. I have a saying: Don't help me unless I ask, and you can refuse when I do ask. I have a mind to kill myself so that they will see and believe what it is that I always yell about. She does so many things to help one learn to accept the fact that I was almost killed- David Cole was killed and that leaves the world having to deal with Dave Cole.

That all was before I attended the University of Northern Colorado (UNC). It was here that I found my -id-. It had been taped to the back of a seat in the lecture/recitation theatre in (McKee?). Probably a cheat sheet; also taped up were the ego, and the super ego; it is after all, finals' week. I now prefer to be addressed as DAVID.

Where was I? I think I have griped long enough about the others, so I'll end it with a little thing that Pastor Cassna said: "Why waste all of your energy saying bad things when it is easier just to say bless you all. One more thing that I want to include is that I, just today, was able to sign my name the same or at least as close to the same as before the tragic incident, accident. I didn't (have and accident) F-------Y---, Joe did.

1/29/82

I have thought of something that might be important. My walking is ever so slow. I am able to compensate for any balance losses during the course of the day. I found out just this evening that my gait is a bit awkward and slower when it is late at night like tonight. I have more or less decided to bust my cane over a rock by now. I am using it little or never.

1/13/82

Well I haven't made any entries for quite some time. That's because it has been so f-----g cold. I mean negative days for the entire week. My walking is about bearable. It is ever so slow and pretty shaky. My voice is not coming along too well. I think that I have reached a plateau, but I am going to have to wait until Carol Roth kicks me out to face the world alone.

2/20/82

Carol Roth has "kicked" me out of speech therapy under the condition that I come back in about a month for a follow up check up. And that means that if the follow up check up shows me to be monitoring myself with no mess-ups, then I am going to take her out for a meal to thank her for her treating me; however, I think I have reached the point of giving her therapy. She also gave me a very little bit of help with math. I have progressed beyond her knowledge. My walking has gotten worse since I received and used a new home workout. I think I better go through it once with her (Janice) to be sure I am doing it correctly. I sure miss therapy five days a week. It just gets so boring not getting it R(Thursday), F(Friday), Sat. and Sun. I'm sure glad summer has worked itself around to finally showing up. My (L) hand seems to have given me just a teasing glimpse of getting better/more useable. There is a definite lack of circulation on my left side my (L) hand included. All the letters and cards bring back terrible memories and must be gone through to make sure there wasn't anything said that would be lost. I did find a twenty-dollar bill that someone from Bethany gave me during my time of struggle. I'm giving it back as a donation to the Church.

3/14/82

I have noticed a marked decline in my quality of walking. My Mom says that she sees me supplicating my right foot and thinks that is why I am in constant trouble with my balance. I think she may have picked up on the reason (I am having so much trouble with my balance.) I am also having bad problems with my psyche and the thoughts of my recovery and my age, (18). I am in need of escape from this house and to start my life elsewhere, while at the same time knowing that I am only able to go to the hospital for therapy because I am a dependant as far as insurance goes. So because of that I cannot move the city, much less the state, to try and live alone. What I would like to do is go somewhere on the Northwest coast and buy a house. I know that is absurd, but it is what I would like to do. The I (independent) L(living) C(enter) seems to have me on hold. That will be my first step towards moving out of this expensive rattrap (Boulder). The good part is getting out of the house and living the life of a bachelor for the summer at least. This is due to a good friend of mine: Craig Balsley. He has the possibility of a very good job in Alaska and seeing how he is more or less not being supported by his Mother (his Father died during our senior year).... I don't want to pay $1,505 to the ILC, insurance will pay that, but that makes me feel guilty. I know I am the way that I am because of some fool; and therefore I don't feel obligated towards paying but think Joe should have to pay for everything out of his pocket, but he's a "pauper" so he couldn't pay for everything, anything...

4/22/82

I'm feeling much better about myself. I don't know

quite why but why worry as long as. I'm pissed at my Mother at this moment because she is up at the school (Platt) with J.B., I imagine to practice driving. He's got 3 more years until he's old enough to get a license. I do have my license even though I can't drive. Physically, I am old enough to drive. So, why didn't she take me along to allow me the chance to try? My walk has done nothing but get noticeably better not to me, but to others around me. I feel all the people around me are making the recovery and I am just benefiting from their trust and help. Whereas no one had to suffer through the early recovery, or suffer not being able to play the piano and ride a bike. They have time to put energy into the rest of my recovery. I need to go now and do my exercises.

5/7/82

I will begin with that which caused all of this PAIN and MISERY. I went over the weekend of 1 and 2 May to watch the (marching) band compete in the Blossom Day Festival in Canyon City. Well to make a two-day trip fit onto this one page, it was great, fantastic. The bus ride was rather cramped though, but still more than bearable. So Sunday night, almost Monday morning, we got back and I walked into the house (it was 12:30 Sunday night), and who met me there... Mom. Only because she has some terrible news. Mr. Bunum (my lawyer) had an appointment with the man who killed a very great person who was a great friend of mine. David Cole was killed by some jerk that was in a big hurry only to not make his trip any faster, he drove head on into David Cole. Now this guy killed a man who was a great lady as a girlfriend, enjoyed riding his bike up to Flagstaff twice every weekend, was a great cook, skier, bike rider, photographer, mathematician, song writer, also had plans to get married soon after getting a masters degree in civil engineering, well SHIT JOE LYNN KILLED THIS GUY AND RUINED HIS LIFE ALONG WITH HIS MOM'S DAD'S, SIBLINGS' AND FRIENDS' LIVES, MAEANWHILE giving him total (it's now starting to come back) amnesia of his bicycle trip down the West coast from Seattle (Wa) to Santa Barbara (Ca) following highways 101 and 1. The guy was this great, fantastic, feeling, weight lifting, song-writing friend. These days have been very painful and grueling beyond a normal mans' means of dealing with them. The left over guy who has most of the memories of David Cole but does not have the body to match up to his desires and urges and got rid of Davids' only means of letting go of his anger, pain, hostilities, hatred and love, e.g. : playing the piano, writing songs. Now, the only problem this by-product of David has is with getting rid of all these messed up feelings... (I) can't cry. Writing all of this down releases a lot of the pain but not all of it. That is why he wanted see and give this guy a face. But noooooooooo, my f--------- g lawyer only put me through a living H---. I don't think he has any idea of what he did to me and all of my friends and family. I mean why has it taken 9 f------ months to get as far as we have? I don't want to go through any of these feelings ever again. If I hadn't already wasted nine months with Mike Bynum, I would have him fired so that I wouldn't have to deal with some a------ who takes a man already stripped of just about everything except an urge toeat but none of the activities to burn it off. I mean, I am getting fat. I guess I am going to have to stop eating and screwing around. So why is it I am enrolled in school? Not school, torture chamber. I am so p----- f------ off at Mr. Bynum that there is little chance of my living to a ripe old age. F------ Bynum is hard at work shortening my life span.

      S---!!!!!

I just made plans to spend Thursday night with the lady of my dreams, Gwyn.

(As a reminder: I am leaving all of the expletives in, not as a way of providing shock value, or to increase the marketability of the book; it is just my way of immersing, not necessarily submersing, you as my reader in the experience of being head injured. All of this is what I've found in my journal work, with very little editing.)

Bullfight in the Corpus Coliseum

A Bullfight in the corpus coliseum.

<u>The Idiot and the Odd D.C.</u>

The Idiot and the Odd D.C

You may say, "That's so untrue." Or, you may shout, "That could all be libelous slander," and neither of these thoughts would be so incorrect; however, nor would they be so entirely justified. Sure, they do both describe me at a particular juncture in my life. I am quite assured that they could fit very well when describing anyone. If I could be so brash, I would probably say that could fit in very accordingly with anyone: for Bill Kerr the title would be, "The idiot and the odd BK," or for the current President, they would be, "The idiot and the odd WC." Remember, I'm writing in 1994.

Maybe I should use the President I died under, "The Idiot and the odd JC." But you do get my meaning, don't you?

I thought I would try. I figured that maybe I should make an attempt to show you what I've been through; what I've been able to accomplish after my having been knocked unconscious for a small, but still a rather lengthy period of time, in my life? A period of time which to all those who stood by, on the sidelines had seemed most interminable.

This insignificantly small duration, or so I'm sure it would've been for you. It had lasted longer than 3 or 4 months. And maybe not just because, but maybe in spite of all this, I feel the obligation to share what I've had to do, what I've become.

I am puzzled, how did man, in his infinite wisdom, settle on the need to measure everything so meticulously fine, down to that proverbial "nth" degree? I mean, how is it that so many people have been quite able to survive, and not only survive at the lowest common denominator, but also to have been able to reproduce in spite of there being such a torrent of germs and microscopic entities that can infect us with such

299

catastrophic calamities? Only recently, "Have scientists discovered entire hosts of disease causing parasites in the food we eat."

What causes the disease? Is it so much the scapegoats (sicscapeparasites) that have probably existed in our food for countless years, or is it merely the collective thought consciousness, as is created by our infinitely accessible media, existing in order to create, as almost the exacerbation of another self-fulfilling prophecy?

I, however, want to give you much more than just a diary of my experiences.

However, maybe as a way of introducing you to my injury, I have included them here, although I have included it only as a way of starting you off on the right food.

There have been so many others, and there will be, I am reluctant to say, so many, almost innumerable others to elucidate you in regards to any particular aspect of the experience. I just feel that there is a need to give you more than just a cathartic moment of my own life. I am certain that there are any great numbers of other: equally, if not more so entertaining, inspirational, more finely written examples of the trauma already written, or to be written!

I want to illustrate for you, to involve you in the long, the lonesome, the tedious, sometimes even mischievous undertaking which I've found myself so intricately involved in.

Do I maybe feel some responsibility for trying to meet up to the expectations of a very unforgiving world? If I hadn't been, I'm sure my God would have exploited they opportunity and gotten me out of the picture.

This collection of stories is how I've managed to live beyond the nightmare of having first died and then being able to nay, being forced to continue survive; maybe in spite, despite or just to spite the Satan who would surly have become my next landlord of a trauma which had ended my first life.

Maybe all of this is just an explanation for my being the

way that I am, as if you're probably to stumble across me down on the mall or in the library. I am the way that I am, maybe not proud, but necessarily alive the way that I am: loud, raucous, daring, at times entirely unconscionable.

It isn't for me to say that my life is supposed to follow along in this fashion! I don't know if this is the way life should be. I don't really care that I am sometimes embarrassing, not that I want to be embarrassing, but I just do what I've got to do what any man has got to do. These behaviors are are very often attributed to the loss of a sense by others; however, I don't think so! Maybe the reason everyone is so hung up, so stuck on this has something to do with the fact that everyone is so scared of death. So, in their attempts to avoid the unknown-death, they have chosen to be barred from life. Well, I haven't!

I've had the opportunity to try out both aspects of existence. Maybe I chose to complete the lesson, in this realm? Maybe my God felt that I had all the necessary fortitude to stick around, maybe answer a few questions? So why did I choose the written document as a way of imparting my message?

It seems to me that I am most able to think when I am writing. If I had been left with neither hand to "think" with, I would probably have chosen a different medium. I died, for all intents and purposes ceased to operate cognitively for 99 days as reported by the nurses records; 6 months according to the primary attending physical therapist, and at least 2 years according to my appreciation of records.

It seems to have been anywhere in the course of those 2 years that I was at last able to actually begin contributing to the process of life.

Actually, I don't think that I had actually regressed to the fetal stage of existence, but the infantile stage of development for sure. I've decided to share with you, my death, my life, my having the opportunity to witness the process of maturation, with a mind that has already progressed beyond the sensory motor aspects of maturation. I've written this book maybe in hopes that you will not have to experience...To first hand, empirically know what it means to die and be forced to exist in a world that is neither forgiving nor kind.

Ernest Hemmingway is most noted for the quote: "This world breaks everyone while there are those who go on stronger at the broken places."

I agree with this proverb. And I am. yes, I am stronger about the head than I'd been for the 18 years leading up to the 1 day, my God had chosen to take me aside from everyone else, and make me very different..."odd?' If you'll allow me to coin a phrase from the title. I had to try everything again.

The interesting thing about my story is that I am trying to relate, in documented form, what every infant child must be trying to tell us with his cry. Most of the experiences from my first try at life are still there. This may be the single biggest flaw in my attempts to relate to you from the eyes of a child. I can still remember doing any number of events, which everyone who was there would probably tell you I'd done. I don't remember having lost my virginity before my first death; therefore, I died a virgin.

I have the factual, the analytical synaptic connections containing these memories still in place. I feel that my having returned to the University when I did made it possible to begin the stimulation of all those synaptic clefts, to have started the whole process of learning off on the right foot.

This world breaks everyone while there are those who go on stringer at the broken places. Why was I stronger about the head? Had this been a simple process of my growing older? Or was the strength in my having been able to get myself back on the straight and narrow, to have been successful in my returning and getting that illusive college degree?

This I will never know, nor do I think I really care to know. It's like the character who gets to try out his life from a different angle or to see into the future. Hollywood had a blast with these concepts. There was really no way of actually testing their theories in real life; they were safe, but they were designed around a notable human condition, a condition that form time to time everyone seems to have experienced.

In my recovery, I sense that I've been able to reach the levels of recovery which I have in part because of the life style I'd known before I corrected some errant driving behaviors. But maybe I'd lived the way I had in preparation God's bigger purpose.

In the first go-round, I maybe had everything much too easy, all the experiences I'd been scheduled to have were maybe laid out too neatly in much too straight a line. Or could it be that god (my God) had just had another period of 'down time,' I know he'd been working himself over time trying to keep me on the straight and narrow while I was growing up

Who is "my God?"

That particular concept, that entity, I believe is different for everyone. For the girl whom I once had the distinguished pleasure and opportunity to have met, a pastor's daughter. For her having also experienced death tangent with life, her God was probably a beautiful woman who always had a clean, pressed dress waiting in the closet.

Or for the young man I'd known through my brother, his God had probably been the first to throw a ruckus in the library, if in fact he ever thought of going to the library. But my God was a Virgo, and my God had really wanted me to become a successful writer. A successful writer of prose and fiction, but first my God had seen it as imperative to give me a full-blown shot at life and death.

In high school, I unwittingly had been given the nickname (unknown to me at the time), the nickname HO Cole, an acronym for Hunk of Cole. At the time, however, I had been committed to the illusory American Dream. I was going to get my education, in the usual way. I was going to wrk-- days a year, in the usual way, and go on vacation with my wife whom I'd have found, in the usual way. We'd have that typical suburban house, and I would've fathered 2.7 children, in the usual way.

However, I hadn't wanted to be so hugely attached to high school and be so shackled to my past, tethered to my history. Or have a girlfriend back at the high school while I was in the college arena, surrounded by all those "College Babes." I hadn't wanted to be faced with the task of averting my eyes every time I sat next to someone who I wanted to have as my next girlfriend.

A favorite line, one of a great number of others: Red sky at sunrise; do not be chaste, but do be wise. Red sky at sunset; worry not, no need to yet.

The intersection of my universe and the universe belonging to Joe Lynn had never been taken for a passive event. More often than not, so much celebration, the bride and the groom acting as icons representing two entirely different tribes of neurons' accompany it. Man in form as a male is only significant at the instant of consummation. His bravado was present only in order for him to attract a host to gestate his prodigy.

Society had since been able to establish any number of other institutions, other capacities in which he is able to participate. I am on a tangential course, my life is only meant to sustain the lives of others. I've been put in place not in order that I affect anything, but in order that I enable others to carry out their own purposes.

If it would appear easier to you, you in a more western frame of mind that I have no place in this society, I must correct you. I am here as the court-jester, the comedian, the buffoon. I am an Upthemallogist, a retail philanthropist; I really have no purpose, other than to see that people are able to laugh, if not with themselves, at least at themselves.

The collision was neither Joe Lynn's "accident", nor was it my "accident." It only seems that my universe had been on a "collision course" to make me a writer. I was in preparation for the scene all my life. It just so happened that

304

Joe Lynn became involved in the sticky mess, up to his proverbial bootstraps. It's not his fault. He couldn't avoid the scene. There really was no way. He had to do exactly what he did, and correspondingly I'd had to do exactly the things that I had done as well.

I have very little attachment to the words; they're only words. So what if I call myself an idiot in my first life, that life's in the past, and it is now entirely unreal. It doesn't seem to matter a whole hill of beans, unless of course those beans are leaded. Then they'd be best ground up producing that next pot of coffee, besides, I'd still have to pay tax for the dinner I ate, and would still be responsible for buying the gas I use to power my car, and I'd still need a restroom when I need to go pee. I've adapted to my life!

"But," you may say, "you look so different, you laugh too much."

I've just had to adapt to these things. If it's always raining outside, most people would probably have adapted either to always being wet, or to staying inside, or always carrying a "bumbershoots."

That they are different from the events you've had to adapt to doesn't bother me. Should it be such an issue for you that I talk out of the side of my mouth, or walk with a hitch in my stride?

I'm not proud. I've had to learn how to get out of my ego. In order to write this book, I've had to get out of my ego-to get out of my house! I've had to befriend so many new, so many different people because of my destiny. Do I know anything different, NO!

The issues you seem so fixated on could just as easily be among my concerns. However, I am concerned about being liked. I have no right to be angry. I have no right to be proud. I see the world differently, but I know I shouldn't condemn people for their differences. I am not as dumb as I look.

My growing weary of the stares from so many others should not be construed any differently that people getting up

305

in in eat, being forced to the back of the city bus because of the color of their skin. Why should I be passed over by an employer seeking to fill a job just because I've had the opportunity to glimpse the "Other side of the Wall." I thought we were beyond that, but it appears that we are not. We are after all still so fixated in our homeostasis.

We all are fixated in our comfort zones, it's not for me to judge where your concerns should be or how you choose to say hello. Heck, if that were the case, they'd be very little international travel. We'd get there and ask for a glass of water and pummeled to death. Why? Well because we were in Deutschland and asked for "a glass of water," not *"ein Tassse Wasser!"* Do you see how silly this all is? A person is not discriminated against because they speak a language other than your own; people with bright red hair are still encouraged to vote.

I'm not proud. I have no attachment to the term 'idiot,' I only hope it doesn't get in the way for you either. My having chosen the 'odd DC' was merely my exercising my poetic license, and his odyssey.

Along with the accident's taking away my consciousness, I have also lost my 'id.' For the nest 4 or 5 years, I was just Dave. The, at the University of Northern Colorado, winter term 1984, while I'd been in a psychology course PSY 110. The instructor, the TA, was Jerri Chance.

I'll never forget Jerri! It has often been said that you never forget your first love, and I guess I never will. She saw right through the facade obscuring me and my intellect. She saw the real me. Besides her uncanny ability to see through my facade, she was outrageously beautiful herself! Flower, my using the word outrageous slants my appreciation poorly... just let me say, had I not been reined back by the teacher-student instructor transference/contested hands off policy, I might not be single even as we speak. And if she'd had similar feelings, she'd have been my bride! Sigh.... if only? If only, a couple of pretty pathetic words, don't cha think?

What I postulate might have benefited my return to productive life? Vitamin B- complex! I'd been out of the hospital several months and my mental status was still regulated by the dictums of all those doctors and nurses and therapists. Then I began my own vitamin therapy. I took an almost cost prohibitive number of vitamin B-complex pills. At first, my body was not used to so many nutrients. My face would turn bright shades of red as the blood flowed to where the vitamin was needed most. I took these pills, (of course without first checking with the hospital). My mental status took on a great stride but only after I'd been "paroled." It had only been after I was outside the confines, the politics, the stuck structure of the hospital, that I'd had the opportunity to experiment with compounds outside the limiting parameters of the scientific method. Of only doing what science had already discovered was beneficial. To traipse along that mysterious path of unknowns. To try *avant-garde* practices that the ADA would have seriously frowned upon. If I am as far along in my recovering, having discovered the enormous benefits of my having flooded my neurons with vitamin B-complex as far along in the process as I had, I might be interested in seeing what would happen if the vitamin therapy had begun much earlier.

History has shown, on down through the ages, that when a civilization reaches a plateau, alevel of cathartic stagnation, there needs to evolve an almost spontaneous revolution.

We've maybe been exposed to too many, too frequent, too messy, too loud, and too abominable to study or to simply abandon the energy of a "war."

Has the planet, this distance from the sun maybe already seen on or several other existences? Is the planet that we call Earth the only satellite ever to have circled what we refer to as a solar system? Are we the first attempt at the plan to populate the Universe? Are we to be the last? Indulge me for just a minute, I think I may have just figured out a new space-time continuum. Now let's just take off our already

307

recognizable conceptualization of the Universe. Just suppose, the evolution of the dinosaur wasn't just a freak occurrence that nothing was known about is. And that very possibly everything has already happened or has been happening for the greatest number we have to the power of 10 years?

And what is there that is so special about the basis of our chronology: the year. Is man, as we know his being to be, has he already been tested? Are we through being tested? Are we able to accurately measure the time of anything?

I realize that it's probably heresy for me to expand on any of these thoughts, these concepts, which are much less than accepted.

The Idiot and the Odd D.C. Part 2

The Idiot and the odd DC. Untrue, you may say; it's all just libelous slander, you may shout, and it's all about me. I am going to try and show you what I was able to accomplish as well as having been knocked unconscious for longer than 3 or 4 months, maybe in spite of this. I want to give you more than a diary of my injury. I want to illustrate for you the long, the lonesome, the tedious, sometimes often mischievous undertakings I've involved myself in, in trying to meet up to the expectations of a very unforgiving world.

This story is of how I have managed to live beyond the nightmare of having to first die and then be able-nay- be forced to continue to survive; maybe in spite of the trauma that had ended my life. Maybe this is why I am the way I am.

I don't know if this is the way life should progress. I don't really seem to care that I am sometimes embarrassing. This behavior bothers me and more often than not, it is attributed to the loss of a sense that by others; however, I don't think so! Maybe the reason everyone is sohung up, so stuck on this has something to do with the fact that everyone is so scared of death. So in their attempts to avoid the unknown-death, they have chosen to be barred form the unknown life. Well, I haven't!

I've had the opportunity to try out both aspects of existence. Maybe I chose to complete the lesson, in this realm. Maybe my God felt that I had all the necessary fortitude to stick around, and maybe answer a few questions.

It seems to have been anywhere in the course of the last 2 years that I was at last able to actually begin contributing to the process of life.

This world breaks everyone while there are those who go on stronger at the broken places. Why was I stronger about the head? Had this been the simple process of my growing older? Or was the strength in my having been able to get myself back on the straight and narrow, to have been

309

successful in my returning and getting that illusive college degree?

This I will never know, nor do I think I really care to know. It's like the character who gets to try out his life from a different angle or to see into the future. Hollywood had a blast with these concepts. There was really no way of actually testing their theories in real life; they were safe, but they were designed around a notable human condition, a condition that from time to time everyone seems to have experienced.

Final Journal Notes

ATA II (All That Anger)

5/9/82

Still I think it was just a play to get me in the spotlight so that Joe's Lawyer could see if I really did need that $25,000 dollars. It's not that I need it right now, but in the future there will be a great deal of need for it. And I would like to purchase a real-to-real tape machine. A receiver and a turntable. Riding a bike would be the biggest luxury of them all. I tell you writing songs and playing the piano was my release of emotions and pain; now with that lost I have no practice with crying, in fact I am very adept at not crying.... My walking has seemed to be regressing meanwhile my Left arm is showing it all, it is tightening up. I also think it would be faster it I typed it. And to type it I would like to get an Apple computer with a print out. Well, it is really kind of late for a school night.

5/13/82

I am not about to give up the constant struggle at working to become independent. This feeling seems to be a good release of all the negative feelings that have been chewing me up lately.... Being a resident of Gold Hill, she was snowed in. And was supposed to pick me up. I'm not saying that it is all over, it just won't happen tonight... I have about thirty pages of info. Locked up in my brain, only my hand cannot last the time and energy that is required to do that... O, by the way I came out with about 22/3 verses of a song I don't have the music down but the music is stored in my head (what's left of it).

5/16/82

The only girl, no, a girl that seemed to be beautiful inside and out, and what an outside she had... Not that I will never recover, but never the less made a big scar in my ego. I mean, here I was telling people what a wonderful girl... No electricity, heating or running water. Please don't get the impression that I had a miserable weekend; no, they were extremely nice and supportive.... It's like training for a race on a sea level track and then going to Nepal to run the race.... not saying the weekend was miserable just that I don't have any desire to live that kind of life.

5/17/82

Today my walking seemed to me to be lousy, but to my therapist (Janice), it looked rather smooth. Because of the fact that a good night's sleep does wonders for my physical recovery, I think I will quite... It may just be some dry heaves for the sky but hopefully it won't be just an empty promise.

5/18/82

I got a call from Pam Allen, second in command at Nancy's (Restaurant). They would like me to come back and give it a shot. Maybe not in the position of line cook, but never-the-less cooking. Now this came at the same time as I got my shit together and called the International Rehabilitation Association about their getting going on the prospect of looking for employment, doing something that they think I would like and be able at. But Nancy's called and said there was a need for my coming back to work. EXCELLENT, AUSGEZEICHNETE! This is just what I need to get off of my ass.

5/19/82

I got very perturbed today at a certain John Spekien. He had the audacity today to blame the fact that he didn't get through all that was required on the fact that the school year was ending too soon, because us in the senior class wanted it to end sooner. I don't care though, I've already graduated, and going to school for me now is just a farce.... To talk about my physical self, I am finding it very difficult to walk but I believe that I have (with the help of Janice)... When I shift my weight to my left, I overly shift.

5/20/82

Conversation found itself right around the upcoming "Prom." She mentioned how she didn't mind them too much but would much rather go out and eat a not-so-stuffy dinner with an escort, then she would enjoy getting dressed up to go to a stuffy dance and then go somewhere else with her date... That's perfect for me; I can't dance. I've tried in private but the spasticity in my body makes it impossible to dance. My walking seems to be better since I don't shift my weight overly exaggerated to the left with every step. I don't feel too overly bitter towards Joe, but I am not saying that my life has been looking upwards only recently; rather than existing down in the dumps where I hope Joe is at this moment. Usually when I write something about Joe, I hit something or let out a string of cuss words, but now I just refer to my assailant as the f------ Joe. I don't let the bad negative feelings get in the way of my everyday life. It just seems like if I picked up my speed of writing it would be economical to start writing a book on this. Good Night!

5/21/82

Whenever friends visit and I trip or something, there is an almost loving tournament over who will get to help me first. This is great, but it only puts me in a very dependant position. This is a place I am working to escape.... It's just that they see this poor cripple in a bad position and they all want to receive the brownie points for offering a helping hand. I find it necessary to get mean, just to fend for myself. If it comes to this, I get a lot of "I'm not going to help him, he doesn't need my help-Theeeeeere, seeeee?" It's not that I resent them for any of this overwhelming help, nooooo. I just wish that they could be there for money seeing how's that's what kind of society we live in. Because I've always had a very poor out look on myself, I am again sitting at home on a Friday night. I hate Joe for what he has caused for my body. I am thankful to Joe for giving me a way out of college without "losing face."

5/22/82

I am feeling very good, great even, since my good friend has come home. We talked a little about my getting on a bike again. I am making a date in my own head to be able to ride up to Flagstaff for the fireworks... I guess I am in a place

313

where I can let my lawyer do all the financial aspects of the accident. After it's all done, I would like to meet the grunt that was in such a big hurry… It seems like I may have spread my bed of woes too broad. I mean playing a lot of energy into one branch leaves not much for the other branches, while the other branches are supporting the trunk. Sort of a Catch-22, you need some friends to help with something-x-. While you're doing that -Y- and -Z- are being held at bay, but....

5/25/82

I would like to start this entry with the idea that I love Barb Lucas and get along with the two older siblings, but Danny who is in junior high is more or less like my brother. Barb is rather mature and says that, which is socially acceptable, but is on the side of life which I, since the accident, abhor.

5/26/82

I begin to feel like life was going by me and kicking me out of the way.

5/27/82

I guess I would do better as a hermit. All alone not being helped or hindered by others. The only problem is I enjoy talking to people immensely, so I guess that rules out that.

5/28/82

School was a nice place.. to visit, but I wouldn't want to live there. Just watch all these predictions be contradicted in a totally opposite manner... Riding a bike, that is something that could fill up a lot of time, and Holly my rec therapist is going full tilt at trying to get me on a bike. Not a trike but a bi-(two) cycle- (wheels), on a two-wheeled bike. She has been in the business a bit longer than I have been alive, and she sees me as riding my bike to the hospital. I would love doing that, but between here and the hospital, there are alot of cars with Boulder drivers behind the wheel. That is what has got me scarred... By the way, I just sent Christy off into the world with a rose. To be sort of bighearted about it, she loved it; meanwhile, I enjoyed it. The flower shop is about two blocks away from the bus stop and having made it in between rounds of the bus is rather impressive, to me at least.

I was out riding the bike while she was going through her departure, and I missed seeing her off. To have finished school, ridden a 3-wheel bike, with plans of getting a 2 wheeler soon, seeing Christy off with a rose and not having anything wrong happen. It makes me wonder, am I up for another disaster?

5/29/82

Today was the first day where I didn't have anything to worry about. On the mental side anyway. Oh, I did need to get tickets to the Roches, but it was a Saturday and the select-a-seat was closed....

I am out of school so this summer will be spent working on my physical self... But I put more time and energy into therapy. Not that this isn't my every living moment activity, but I don't have to go to school and struggle with the people there then go to the hospital and struggle with myself... I do have plans of going to work Tuesday, early so I need a ride at a very unlikable hour, 7:30a.m.

I got rid of it in my kneel walking and thusly in my walking. Bryan went hiking with Robert Picker; I can't hike so I didn't go. I wish I could ride a bike, if I could my summer days would be filled with riding my bike. Janice T. doesn't like the idea of my riding a bike....ever. But little does she know (she does know a little) I am already one-step into the idea of riding a bike physically, not just mentally. Well-el, if nothing happens in the way of riding up in the mountains, I can look back on this as a good try. My therapist doesn't like the idea of my ever doing that which killed David Cole and left me, the by-product. I do not want to be able to drive; it's just that I don't want to be totally dependant upon the automobile.

6/1/82

Today was the day I was supposed to start work, and I

315

did. The show last night was great (The Roches). I will work from whenever I get there until 11:30. It is working out great. Work that is. Today I started out by cracking eggs for omelet's, and separating yolks for "bene sauce." After that they set me to work peeling potatoes for hash browns, this is difficult enough for a person. I with one usable hand was slow but persistent. I'm glad they decided that it was a chore not for me.. That took d---- near the rest of the day, (there) being a good 3 dozen in a 10lb. sack. I am so tired that I do not have any intention of doing a good job in therapy tomorrow; I will certainly try, but that doesn't guarantee any success.

6/3/82

Well today was today was today. In other words, it was your basic day. Except for the fact that I visited with Ken Mann, which was a basic pick-up. My visit with Kenny wasn't really all that thrilling. He is very supportive as far as helping me gain independence, but as far as emotional things go, he sort of brought me down. He is graduating though! I've never seen a man with as much perseverance as he has. Taking four and a half years to complete high school is the one biggest example! I can't get the feeling I have in words written down. I am truly very proud if not overjoyed at the thought that I have one good friend (who) gets out in only 3 years with d--- near a 4.0 grade average and to have another friend who goes at it with a desire he needs to get the diploma even if it takes him awhile. While your (you're) stuck in the middle having gotten out with a 3.50 average, then needing to return for a fourth year because of what some jerk on the outside of your world did to you. This is a strange situation, to kill a man and then to have him around on your dying day. Not the entire person but the body, face, legs, and desires of the man you killed. This is why I want to be able to ride again.

6/5/82

Today is the day on which Kenny Mann gets his high school diploma! I love Kenny very much, and if he doesn't trip, he will become a high school graduate. Also graduating will be Alan Thompson, John Mabry, and the love of my life,

Ami Balsley!

6/6/82

I haven't needed to take any chemicals to go s--- for about a month and a half. That is a very big improvement, why did it take so long to happen? My Mother has been very nice lately. She cleaned and vacuumed and left a note telling me how lucky she was having a son like me. I don't really mind it's just that I write some things in you to get them off my chest, and any of those things are convicting of others, and I am sure that many of them are incorrect. They are just the way I see them. Well my walking has sure been fine as far as speed goes. I think that is due to the fact that I am not going to school any more. School is its title but it seemed more like an aggravation to me. (The wind) it is rather brisk at times, yet I am not willing to let anybody walk with their arm holding me. The mere fact that they are there throws my cadence off. I appreciate all the concern, but when it is forced on me, I get very irritated. I have to say in a very stern, aggravated voice, no thanks! The way it usually comes out is, "get your f---- hands off me."

I just wanted to apologize to my Mother. Sorry Mom I just had a feeling of extreme burden and abandonment. It seemed like I was finally stepping out, while I was having that feeling it seemed like I was pushed aside by the entire world, not just you. In reality, I wasn't stepping out on my own, but was using you along with many others as my legs. Only I can tell my legs to do something and if they don't want to do it, I can b---- at them and they cannot resist. Only people aren't legs and they can comprehend and retaliate against me. Once I am on a bike, I will be able to step out for real on my own. The day ended nicely with my apologizing to her and spending the afternoon across the street with Bryan.

Well it seems like life is getting better but, you can never trust it. Bryan Cabral asked me if Janice knew the people of Boulder will jog the 10-Kilometer Bolder Boulder, but those who insist on driving around in the middle of a bike race should be arrested.

I cannot ride a bike because I was "Killed" while riding one. And it irritates me so bad almost to make me want to refuse to get into the thing that killed me. Only they are how this society moves about, and this society is so totally bent on moving around and I live in this society. So I guess I must set myself into the pattern of moving about.

6/15/82

To have something this devastating occur before I was able to start my life as a man seems a bit ludicrous if not devastating. I come into contact with. Rebecca Twigg is one of those people. Before we were even talking on a bevel level, I told her why I was in seeing a chiropractor. She gave me her signature and signed it on her picture, cut out of the paper. She is extremely beautiful, intelligent, and competitive on her bike, fun to talk with, and busy. She is going to go home, in Seattle. I love that area of the world. She gave me her address and phone number just in case I am in town.

6/18/82

She likes the idea of sleeping with me, but is a little hesitant about screwing. She got in the Hot tub-the Tubb with me naked. Nothing happened to me physically, but in the form of having some incredible desires. Not that she is unattractive or anything missing, and she obviously isn't ashamed of her body. It's just that I didn't feel anything towards her in the form of, "She here, she's naked and no one's home, so why not take advantage of the situation?" I would have felt like a real louse had those thoughts even materialized in my head. Not that they weren't there, they just didn't get into the tub to come out of my head. We did talk about that while I gave her a back-rub. After the back-rub, I didn't have to think five times about telling her that it (would) have been uncomfortable doing it on the Tubb. Meanwhile, there we were, sitting on the rim of the Tubb when who drives in? My brother and a friend of his. That was rather embarrassing. So we crawled into the water. Quickly but under control. Later we worked on her bike, but it was too d---- cold for me to do a fairly decent job. Still we didn't get anything accomplished besides tightening her

318

already tight rear derailleur cable, and showing her how to remove and replace her rear tire. She said that she had just recently had a relationship with a guy who was very inconsiderate of her, showing deep emotions, then turning her off, hot then to ice. I took this as her saying that she didn't want to start another relationship for a while. She said that it wasn't anything along those tracks of thought, just that it was a "bulletin" on where she was. This may be the case and I won't turn her off without first checking it out. That didn't come out right. What I wanted to say was that. I don't trust her, but that I won't turn her off like her last love, for a long time. I love this lady not just for her physical features, but more for social being. Today was the day of the Morgul Bismark, only it was raining just a bit too hard. So I didn't go, just sat around in my hot tub with Judy Turner. She's incredible. She says she doesn't want to say that she loves me because she says she doesn't know me. She says, "You don't know me, I may turn out to be a turd." There was this fragrance about her that just turned me on.

6/20/82

While at my Dad's house for Father's Day, I took a little bit of time and went to visit Judy's family and to go with them to look at some shoes for Judy, didn't get anything, neither of us. A wasted trip. But my Dad said he was very happy to spend the day with me. I learned a little about Judy's parents and her grandmother. They are definitely down-to earth people who don't go to extreme lengths to look impressive for their daughter's friend. We had a very relaxing conversation, nothing too overly hostile on either side. I guess I feel that their daughter is suited for a more spectacular, at least, at totally that's the way I see them seeing me. While I was there, it seemed that they were going out of their way to make life as cozy as possible for me. Now they didn't do this in a blatant manner just that I felt them being that way.

6/24/82

She still shows some enjoyment for me, while I told her that I didn't have a gut rendering love for her, but still

319

wanted to see her. Sort-of-like a signature in a yearbook. You don't want to commit yourself, but want to express a lot of feelings, not love, but deep feelings. I feel kind of stupid. Having almost asked her into marriage and telling all my friends about her, and then disposing of it all. Oh, by the way, I met a girl I knew in high school; Kim Perkins is and was her name.

I guess it is all do to the accident, and my ability to organize my f------ life, has got quite a bit to be desired, if not definitely lacking totally in areas of extreme importance. Getting killed has much to be desired, but so does not being killed. Mom uses the "Head injury" as a pair of pliers, to apply pressure whenever I am not performing, or behaving in the proper manner. "Both as an excuse to apply pressure and as an excuse to the folks around me so as not to be totally embarrassed by what I do. Well, if she could only see video tapes of me when I am with "people" while she is not there. I'm not real clear as to whether it is just me in any situation, or if it is only when she is there, that I act in such an immature manner.

6/26/82

I gave it a try but didn't do quite as well as I hoped. The bike itself was just a little bit on the small side. I guess it's a Catch-22. You can't ride, a bike that's big enough for you well enough, and you can't ride a little one at all. I guess if the Lord didn't want me to get back on a bike ever, he made the mistake of "giving me the perseverance that I have." Paul Schultz came over for a Tubb. "It was a nice place to chat; only the chatting wasn't that nice.

"To go back to the bicycling problem. I would like to surprise Bryan Thompson with a great huge graduation present. The trip down the West coast by bike.

"He said he wanted to do it when I could ride a bike again, and he is going to receive his college diploma next spring, so my graduation present to him will be the trip. Also on the trip will be Ken Mann who also graduated, from high school, but still an incredible feat.

While I am getting much better every day, Morgan Richards is *in der Krankenhause* with a kidney infection. It seems funny to be going to visit someone in the Krankenhause after spending so much time there myself. I will go anyway since having visitors when I was in there was wonderful. A different situation, never the less a delicate one. I am currently unattached to a female of the opposite sex, so I am looking at all possibilities. Morgan is a fairly attractive member of the opposite sex, so that makes it all the more important to go to Der Krankenhause to see a very dear friend. Now I don't love her like I love Stephanie, but Steph is attached in a rather disgusting manner, permanently for the time.

6/30/82

Not that I will even go onto heavily traveled roads until I am ever so steady on a bike. And the thought of living somewhere as densely populated as Seattle gives me the willies, it being almost, if not worse, than Denver. My Mother, tonight, told me that she could not even come close to knowing how I feel. Well that is all fine-n-dandy, I can't remember the way I was feeling that I would have the same beliefs, feelings and quite a few other similarities in my personality as I would have, had I not been hit so hard. I (head trauma aside) think that I would have wanted to split this Boulder scene for wetter climate. Either Southern Washington or Northern Oregon would have fit the bill very nicely. Only, I do not want to rent an apartment, I would rather own a house and make payments towards that, not give my hard-earned money to some rich tycoon who is sitting pretty in a house with a lawn and a garden. I don't see it as even remotely possible, but that is what I would like to do during my life. To earn a living, helping people seems incredibly attractive, now what that occupation would entail is out of my grasp. I have no way of knowing whether or not I would make a good showing at being mature (muu-tour). I got a letter from Judy T, and she acts like an incredible martyr, calling herself shy, flustered, and easily embarrassed. While building myself up as an incredible rock to be leaned on without a quiver, not the same as my version of a rock. The rock I was referring to there was on the idea of a "Powerful giant Redwood," whom I was before, transformed into the capabilities of growth that a rock has.

7/1/82

I got a call from the Regency movie theatre. They did, at last, after my pestering them for about three weeks, turn up with my wallett. In it was only a dollar. A dollar, my driver's license, and a $58 check to cover my returning a bicycle helmet, and a lot of sentiment, in the form of ticket stubs to all the concerts I'd been to since the accident. Coach Desmarios had called back to make two appointments. I have finally come to the understanding that the roads of Boulder are made for cars. Cars, cars, and only cars, maybe a motorcycle here and there. So I am looking forward to learning how to drive. I may flunk the first time, but we're all in the same boat. We all flunk the first time. While I am also in the position of getting back on a bike, it seems strange to be relearning how to drive. I may just flunk the first time, so what, everyone's in the same position. Out with Ms. Meyers and a rather shaky training bike. Today Judy and her mutter took me and them up to the lake, and I did go swimming. Not all that far but more than just a little ways. With all this going on, I am going to Heaven. Just because I was destroyed by a car doesn't mean I am going to become totally destroyed. I have the sense that the accident was just an interlude in one of the world's great symphonies.

7/7/82

Only two months and two days left of my childhood. Not that I ever want to go through these fun and trying days again, it's just that I don't feel ready to be an adult, man, yet. The fact that I was killed as a teenager, and have had to do all of my growing up in a short two years. It would be an easier game if I didn't have to go back to toddlerhood. I mean having a 19-year-old body that is not near the potential and capability of you as a normal person is hard to handle. With all of my wisdom and soundness, as a whole. I think if I may be granted this small space of big headedness, that the Lord is, has separated me from the rest of the world to be. Not physically or financially, but socially, or there probably won't be a third try.

7/8/82

Today was the first try, at driving that is. I didn't hit anyone, didn't even come close. The instructor said I did a fair job, and that there were quite a number of things I need to work on. I am going to go tomorrow to look at a bike with specs. So that means I am learning to do what almost killed me, while at the same time learning to do that which I was doing at the time of the incident. I don't necessarily want to live in Seattle, but at this time, I don't want to live in Denver. More like Boulder at the rate that it is growing. I just got a call from Linda Rozek saying the I.L.C. has a room for me. My feelings are that I do want to get out of this house, but I do not want to live with the monthly bill of $1005.00 for room, board, and training in independent living. "Living a day for someone else as opposed to living a day for myself." That is a direct quote from me. I say it when I do not have to live my life for someone else. Applied when it was convenient for me. Now that it is becoming a co scripture rather than a convenience, it is sort of over-bearing. Now, Judy T has been rather frequent in my mind. Now, don't get me wrong that she embarrasses me. It's just that I can't get her out of my mind, not that there is any reason to get her out of mind, just that I get the feelings from her that she isn't infatuated with the appearances I do have. Meanwhile I am stuck with the realization that I am guilty of, sort of but not exactly, asking her for her hand in marriage. I feel rather guilty for she is the first lady to intersect with my plan of desires and likes-and -dislikes. I do want to get her in the family way. I know it's rather cruel to like someone for their person and not just for their person's body. It's just that that is the plain (plane) I am in at this moment. Mom really is hard. She talks about how to fix the bike. With me standing right there. My mind is saying "no," that's wrong but my conscience is saying she's your mother, don't rock the boat. Worse than if I didn't call at all, I just called and she wasn't home. She= Judy Turner.

7/11/82

At work I got a call from Mom saying that Mr. Bynum wanted to confer with the two of us at noon. I then received a call for Holley (Meyers) saying that she needed to move our session up to 1:00. Well, why is it that life can be so boring for an entire year and then become almost too busy? She was willing to run me over to Table Mesa to begin the process of getting a rehab bike. I feel ah so wonderful being able to tell people what they need to do to help me. To put another chapter in on my continuing story of Judy Turner, I am finding her more and more attractive and humorous. The most important thing, she is "fun to be with."

I, d----it, am not going to take the money I am receiving because of a need and give it to someone else who thinks they need it worse than I do. I am finding that the more money you have the greedier you become. But first thing on my list will be a bicycle. I have already begun to purchase a rehab bike, while the one I would like to graduate to will be near $1,000. So, because of this, it needs to have all Campagnollo components, or almost completely equipped with Campy.

7/12/82

Work, after I got there, was great. That one cook who used to talk about movies all day was a bit more mellow. Others gave the mention of the last movie they saw, what movie they will see, and what movie that is showing is the best. Because RTD is on strike, Handi-ride won't give me a ride home. It was a scorcher today upwards into the mid-nineties.

7/13/82

Today is Bran's birthday. Right now Brandon is in Ninilchik, Alaska doing what I would love to be doing (fishing?)

7/15/82

I must have been on the rag. Janice was extremely nice and helpful today. It appears that I am fully prepared socially to move into the I.L.C. I will continue this after I go watch

JB's race, the "Morgul-Bismark." The race was great. It seemed almost masochistic watching all the little kids doing themselves great bodily harm trying to win a race on a trip over the "Hump" and up the "Wall." Judy isn't home so I don't have anyone to call and talk to, or invite over for a tub, hot.

7/16/82

To know that I can go from near death to riding a bike in two years will be simply amazing. Then another thought tells me, "Dave, you've always been a loser, so why trick yourself into ever wanting to ride again, I mean I have taken you this far so don't fool yourself into thinking that there will be another gift just waiting for your taking.

7/17/82

Well, Mike Claus married Holly Meyer. Getting to the wedding was quite an accomplishment. I was able to "work" the car fairly well, a whole lot better than in the recent past. Tomorrow is another day, another experiment. Just watch this be chapter two in "David's Stupid Ideas."

7/18/82

I just got up to catch a butterfly, who has been tattling in my window for several days now. Rather than put him out of my misery and his entrapment, I got him on my finger, and because he trusted me, that gave me time to finish talking to my Mom on the telephone and to take him outside to shake it off my finger, to set it free. I met the rest of Judy's sisters except Connie last night. Betsy, Connie?, Katie, and the finest looking and the only one single is Judy! I also met David, Judy's brother-in-law, also a bicycle fanatic. I'm glad I didn't meet them all at once because they each have a winning personality, but Judy has the appearance to match. I sent my letter off to Twigg. I hope Rebeca reads the letter and not just her hired guard/screener. Instead of my riding my bike, I went out and helped Bryan overhaul his bike. My brain still clicks as far as knowing how to fix a bike but it is still having a hard time swimming downstream to the hands, to tell them what to do. I feel I am setting my goals far too high to be reachable. A

Catch-22 of sorts; too high to be reachable, yet if they aren't fairly high then they will be too easy to reach and life will be along the lines of boring.

7/21/82

Only I was busy all day. It started with a driving lesson, in an automatic. He will take me out for a drive in a clutch-equipped car when there is one at home.

7/22/82

Today was a day, which I'd looked forward to for several months, only to go through it and have it seem like a very cruel treatment. I spent the day at the I.L.C. I don't want to move into a place like the I.L.C., a live in, eight hour a day, 56 hours a week, school for the handicapped. Now for me, a very special, individual case/problem, I cannot see setting myself up for that environment, having come from a place of no handicaps. I just could not see me living beside people who never got a chance to try and succeed in this crazy society.

I mean, I do feel for them, but to set myself up at their level, at their pace, would only give me a crippling environment to try and beat my handicap. It seems like putting a mouse on a cheese free diet, only living in a house made of cheese. It can only be a direct hindrance to the end product (the goal). To try and get me physically well, even strong. It does not seem to be very protaganishing (beneficial, productive) to do it in an environment of people who've never had a glimpse of what it is like to be strong. (It may sound cruel and uncaring, but it can only be run by people who are able to do it. It is just a place where people who have little or no chance of being able to survive in this society . I, on the other hand, have a handicap that is overcome able, at least to a near total recovery. While they (the people at the center), are going too school to find out ways to make life as comfortable as possible...

1 The I.L.C. is a place for them to learn how to deal with the world as it is. (While) it may sound heartless and sadistic, uncaring, it is the only way to look at them, "cripples"

with a considerate (compassionate) eye. To treat them as if they were ABs would be twice even thrice as unfeeling uncaring...

7/23/82

We took advantage of Judy's having gotten her license and went downtown. While we were there, I really blew it. What? About $28 $30... Judy is really one h---- of an incredible lady. The only thing being that I am finding her body to be more and more desirable all the time. I just feel that my, total recovery, will take some thinking and associating with friends who are willing to push, to coerce, and give a strong example to be. A goal. Living with people who have no chance... to live with these types of people would be more harm than help. . I cannot hope to get the correct feedback if I am living with a bunch of people learning alternative methods of fix (fit) themselves in today's society.

The same instrument that I, not I, but David was killed on. I can hear you asking why ride a bike again if you feel the act of riding put David in a spot where he was able to be killed. I guess I need to try and make a difference between David and his by-product, Dave. So Dave has the growth potential and the possibility of a Redwood all locked up in the features and the strength of a rock. My Mom is sort of like the crowds in Yosemite: hurting the real beauty that I contain, but still providing the admiration, which I need. A rock cannot actually grow into a Redwood tree, but to never be able to realize those thoughts is very demoralizing.

7/25/82

I guess it makes me feel rather ridiculous to begin talking to her as a person and find out that person has a body and is of the female type.

7/29/82

My lawyer seems to be doing a pretty good job. The interest rates have hit their peak and will be leveling off soon; to get it now is good. Instead of the earlier quote of $ 1036,53, I can look forward to getting $ 1075.?? per month. A small difference per/ month, which makes a fairly big difference per year. Now, it is still not enough to raise a family on, but with the added income there will probably be very little change in the desire to be a father. Though there are many ways to deal with being handicapped, even crippled, that's a very bad term to use, yet it does accurately describe how "they" are. So I had 18 years to figure out that I wanted to go to CU, so what if I have 1 month to figure out where I'd like to go for a second try. Getting out of it by talking about it. I would like to overcome it, which entails getting to the point of going back to school, getting a good paying job, moving out of the house. My Mom agrees with the part about moving out, but she sure is going about it in an A-B (bassackwards) way. When I said I didn't want to go to the meeting, by her saying that it just showed how "thick headed you are." When I came back with, "That may be the reason I'm even alive." It will occur on a very tight rope. I must put the idea of marriage out of my head.

7/30/82

Mom and I went out to dinner at Karen's Kitchen, and who shows up, but "Mom" and her boyfriend. I think his name was Wally Vonhelms (helmet in German)?

ATA IV (All That Anger)

When I was in school, it was a real struggle not to be "in the groove" with everyone else, it was more you must be uncool to be "cool," in the circles I hung around with. My Mom and I have discussed my future plans. Getting a car, going to college, or just moving to the Northwest...

8/1/82

Tired or not my Mother does not realize it and asks me to drive down and get some charcoal and lighter fluid, "Gulf," not (the) "Safeway" brand. Well just to carry on with my story, I succeeded. The driving was great. Having only received six hours of sleep from 9pm to 3am is not nearly as bad as 6 hours from 3am to 9pm. (You figure?)

8/3/82

just drove up to the lake, couldn't find Paul (Klemperer), drove up to his house, "He's down at the lake, drove back down to the lake, found him, we both stretched out in the sun. We got rather hot and went for a swim. We swam out to the first raft, got out and did a bit of sun worshiping, got rather warm and headed back to shore. It was a bit difficult swimming in water that had only been warmed by the sun's convention. It was cold enough to make you snatch a breath of something into your lungs. It turned out to be 0_2 most of the time, but H_2O once in a while. Now the human body is not built to accept H_2O into the lungs, so I tried to get it out: cough, cough, cough is the procedure I resorted to, to get the H_2O (water) out of my lungs. Well I am telling you about it so I must have succeeded in getting to the shore. Well I've just told you about a couple of things that I've been scared to do since the accident. Swim and Drive. Judy, Judy, Judy. She plans on being gone for another two weeks.

8/3/82

Mom so rudely interrupted. I was going to take my bike over to Larson Engineering and hadn't put it in the bus yet.. Only we adjusted the wheels so that they were on the ground 96% of the time. That made it hard if not impossible to practice riding on only two wheels. We rode down to the end of the Centennial Trail at 55th. Nothing drastic happened. I RODE THE BIKE, with only one difficulty, two difficulties. The seat was too low which didn't allow me even a near full extension not even hyperextension. Because of this, there was no way to go fast also cloneus was aggravated. I do believe I'll be on the bike for the day. Not the day, but the month.

8/4/82

I am plain sick and tired of living here @ 9=5+4 Gapter. Mom and I seem to be at the end of the rope that is between us. The rope between her and Brandon broke; it wasn't a very strong rope. The one between us is incredibly strong, but my trying to get to the end just weaves another chord into it. Rope seems to be beginning to "fray" a bit, which would send me falling. Bran fell many years ago, but Dad was there to catch him. I was let off the chord but found the landing too hard and asked for a pad, so Joe L. hit me very hard, only to hang me back on the chord, spinning now.

8/5/82

I did it, I did it, nobody wanted me to, but I did it anyway. I got up real early, didn't hear there to be too many cars and rode up to Platt. I rode along Gapter to Dimit, turned left, rode up to Cherryvale, waited for there to be no cars and crossed from Dimmit to Baseline. Only had one close call and was able to recover with amazing grace. Ride up to the Nolands and then on to Fairview on Monday the 16th. Come back and stop by the Turners on the 19th (W). Those actions must wait until I can ride without the training wheels, probably just an idle dream, though all the friends and relatives who wanted to know the day I did what I've wanted to do for so long. There is one other lady I need to tell, the woman I went to visit the day I received the fatal blow to the head, Gail Lurie.

8/6/82

I NEED HELP. I mean I am not the way I am because of something I did, and getting back to where I need to be, I need help. It does seem that I will be getting back on a bike. Yeah. That is just one of a very few things I have wanted to do.

8/7/82

I then squoze through the bike opening in the Centennial Trail. Problems began when I tried to cross on the western most bridge. I tried to get up the sharp incline onto the bridge and f----- up; I fell over, on the left side. Just sit back and get yourself better. They even said it looks like I don't even need training wheels, which is exactly how I see it, the only problem being starts and stops. She was the one who made the urgent suggestion that I go see "A Gentleman and a Sailor." What the h---, you only go around in this life once, for me twice, but never mind and might as well make it a lot of fun, enjoyable.

8/8/82

I miss her, not so much for what she gives to me but how she accepts what I can give her. Is "King of Hearts," which is showing at Chautauqua. I rode my bike to Church the topic was marriage and sex. To have comments last sort of showed me that everyone was tired of the preacher. You can't ride down the West Coast 'lest you can ride a bike, and you can't ride a bike 'lest you continue trying'.

8/9/82

Would be a physical impossibility. Just her saying that makes me want to prove her wrong. I feel like a bad person for leaving her at the apex of the biggest hill in my life, and seeing all my fellow class/trip mates, while at the same time I am not greedy, and don't want to keep my accident and recovery from those it would benefit not the most, yet benefit the same. To be an example of strength that very few people (thank God) are given the chance to try and do. I guess I'm just an egomaniac with a very well to be self-esteem. Coming up very soon is all the more depressing 21st birthday of Ms. Carfrae. I don't know what to get her, except something to go along with the fact that she will probably be getting several bottles of "Hard Stuff," Alka Seltzer[®.]

8/10/82

One point of positiveness, I did find all my lyrics, not just the notebook full of them, but also the free pages I used to record the lyrics when I didn't have the book with me. To try and move the piano is unlogical.

To sell it would be unwise. I see no way of solving it, but I don't want to give up a comfortable life.

8/11/82

I guess I do want to be able to come when making love with Judy. I would also like to get her in a frenzied state of self-being. I do not want to have intercourse with her, at least not now. All it will take is a car and a bike and the ability to

331

ride it. Once I am at a place with these things, I won't be content. I am glad the settlement was not for a lump sum and a couple hundred dollars each month. That is, if the annuity company doesn't decide to close up. I am set with an O-K wage for all that I have been going through. I know that I really harp on my Mother's problems, but if she wasn't around, I wouldn't be. Friday it is tentatively planned to go up to Platt, and attempt to ride with no T-wheels. This evening, I drove JB and myself up to R.V.P., no sweat, it was a dream come true. I did miss the turn to get to R.V.P. but that only tested my ability to think fast and get us there. We made it and there was a happy ending complimented with a 1/2 ham, 1/2 green pepper pizza.

8/12/82

The day I am going to initially ride a bike- no- T-wheels is Friday, the 13th. A bad luck day for everyone who believes in that stuff. Do I? Naa, never. Just you watch it turn out to be a true-life occurrence. I think that I am going to go look for a car, a Volkswagen Rabbit. Was to the doctors (Wee) I got a tetanus shot that will last me 10 years, almost wished they need to withdraw some blood to check for mono; JB and Spring have it presently. What I need to do is get more active physically. Well tomorrow is the big day, or has the potential of being a great day. Tomorrow I am going to attempt an initial try at riding with no, repeat no, T-Wheels. I need to get my rest so that I will perform to my expectations.

8/13/82

Bad luck. That's what today's date is supposed to represent. I don't think so! I received another card from my love, Judy. Well to the surprise and total pleasing of myself, Holly and Dianne, I did it. I f------- pulled it off. Or should I say pulled it out of a hat full of tricks. I just rode my bike with no training wheels. Dad's not home from work yet, neither is Bryan; my Mom is still at work, Brans in Alaska, and Judy's in Wyoming. Feeling about my being able to get back on a bike. Well I was really rather doubtful towards the possibility of ever mounting a bike again. I would like Judy to get home so that I can tell her the great news. Now that I rode today the question is, was today a fluke Friday the 13th or was it a ekulf bing it yadirf eht hteetriiht? If the second is the case, I should or shall be able to peddle tomorrow and show Bryan and anyone else who is there to witness the spectacle.

8/14/82

I am taking Kends R. and we are not being driven to or from the theatre. I, Dave Cole, am driving, just you watch, because I told you ahead of time, I will f-----up. I seem to have worked myself into a corner. With my personality, it's probably the corner in a round room. I miss Judy very much; Kends could see this and kept bringing her up. A real trooper that Kendall is. If I do go up to Seattle with Cathy, it will be on September 2nd. If this turns out to be the case, I will have to talk to Mr. Bynum about the fact that I will be receiving the $1975.?? each month starting in September and confirm with Gail Lurie that the first check will be invested in money market certificates, and I don't want to think about them any more. My going to school and repaying Bynum needs to happen soon. I owe Mike $6000. School will hopefully be covered by vocational rehabilitation. The one thing I am having troubles with, my bowels. Now, they are extremely full which is rather uncomfortable. I drank nearly 5000 ml of water. Once again, I am finding that I miss Judy very much. I also need to practice getting the bike going without sitting on it. If I don't go to the bathroom tomorrow, I will resort to chemical means.

8/16/82

What major I am going to study? I now, at this instant, want to be a writer. The only problem being I don't have a heart set desire to go to CU again. You realize, I haven't ejaculated for many weeks; it must be because I haven't contacted Judy for closing in on a month. While at the Carfrae's for Kathy's Geburtstag, I spoke with her about the trip, of the vacation. It won't be all expenses paid trip to the torture chamber; it will take extra funds, but all in all a nice gift for what I am going through.

8/17/82

Judy gets home and ends my vigil. To have conversed and set up times to see the two people is a sure sign that I am getting back into the swing of life. Laurie wasn't there today so I didn't get to kiss her. That's right; Judy is supposed to be back tonight. I don't know what time, but my countdown has gotten down to 400 minutes. By God, I do miss her. By "her," I mean her person, not just the physical attractiveness. She doesn't get carried away when I'm heavy petting mit her. But the few times it has happened, I was in total self-denial, even enough to tell Steph that we must not do anything we would regret. She is now the wearer of a facade of being a Mormon. She is presently in a relationship with Shawn Williams. Her brothers do not expect it to last beyond her association with Mr. Williams. I hope not, and not for my sake but for her's. I did the unexpected; I swam out to the raft in a very fading light to the point of being dark. Besides my having not been visible very well. The water was colder than a witch's tit.

8/18/82

I went to therapy and got a rash of compliments. Compliments flowing from everyone who knew. Janice didn't know. Janice didn't know and was extremely displeased. We had a very heated conversation. Not to take that, I said that I had worked too long and too hard to not ride. Meanwhile she came back with, "It's up to you, either you walk well, or ride, but not both."

8/19/82

Now that I have the chance of getting beyond where Janice had been wanting me to go, she doesn't want me to go. I'm having a hard time trying to figure out whether it is time to move on, or whether I should listen to her pleas. Maybe if I just increase the amount of exercises I do, it won't have regressive effects if I ride. I took Judy to "A Gentleman and a Sailor."

8/20/82

D----it, I f------- wet the bed last night. Well, I

vinegared my bed and wrapped my wedding present, not for me, but for Stinky, "Smelly" to go back. I was walking slow but to the point; I am now walking rather rapid but not to the point.

8/21/82

I really think that I have found someone who I used to pity but now pity myself for having not "met" Judy Turner when I was in high school. Going out with Steph my junior year and playing with Editorial my senior year.

8/24/82

This morning I went over to Rich Sommer's house for Frustuck. *Es War gut, sehr gut*! I also went down to CU to talk to a counselor about getting back into the swing of things. I was very discouraged by his attitude (Richard Klein). I guess I would like to go to CSU to be in school with Judy.

8/26/82

Judy is really helping me keep my senses. I want to go to bed with Judy, no not f---- her; I am still a virgin.

8/27/82

Well I shan't count the minutes until Judy leaves for school, for the minutes 'till I leave for Seattle. 1120 hours until I leave for Seattle, that's 2880 minutes for Judy and 7200 minutes for myself.

8/28/82

What she needs is what I have, the ability to listen, make a few comments, let the other release feelings that don't need to be stored and walk away with the knowledge that you have just helped someone. To help others, not to hurt yourself in the process of such. Well, Judy and I went for a picnic up Sunshine Canyon. We were involved with the lunch from 11:00 until 1:45, then we went about some extracurricular activity I need to hit my sack of H^2O.

8/29/82

Had a very heavy oration with Judy. Almost to the point of crying, but no, I have lost that ability. Judy, on the other hand, no, both sleeves did cry. The hymn was one that I did know, "Morning Has Broken," was the tune. I did have past memories of singing it. Judy came out and scolded her Mom for allowing such people as myself up on the patio! (I'm pretty sure all was in jest.) When I get to Tacoma, I am to give him (Uncle Bailey) a call and if his landlord was gone by the time I get there. Or I can stay with Penny, or or, (I had innumerable opportunities.) It sounds like I am going to be away for a spell. Not to worry, you're coming too.

8/30/82

A certain Johnathon Hopkins came over just as I was getting ready to retire. John continually harps upon the idea that he doesn't sell the Lord, just that he should be the one who is responsible for telling all around him that it is the only way to gain righteousness. I like him as a total person, but his "holier than thou" sort of friendship is not where I enjoy dwelling. Or even more disgusting, that she was in the hospital or mortuary. She just called and she's alive "just leaving Fort Collins, late."

9/1/82

Of all the good things to happen today, Janice, (my PT) was very positive about my walking. To be leaving at such a peak in my life seems almost too good to be true.

9/2/82

I haven't yet been asked to drive and because of how late it is getting I don't want to drive. I am feeling like I am just along as a very definite burden, granted I did pay for gas this stop, still I haven't done my fair share of piloting "Herbie." He either figured that we were unwise, or that there really were "Jack-a-Lopes." Maybe I am just a bit too senseless and unfeeling, so bad that what turned everyone on, really was disgusting to myself. Maybe the "Head Injury" is what makes me so closed to the rest of society. I should really lead the life

336

of a hermit, isolated from a good majority of the world. Closed off from society, society except Judy. And I seem to have the identical feelings towards many of my meetings with society. Well, we continued our trip to Burley Idaho. Once we got there we were fed once again.

9/7/82

Today we are going to the "bumper shoot, "(a festivity endemic to Seattle.) At the Davies, I listened to the radio. It wasn't Rock-n-Roll, wasn't Disco, wasn't really anything, just the Wall Street Journal over-n-over-n-over again.

9/9/82

This morning at 4am, I wet the bed. (As things have been turning out, it was also for the last time.)

"I've got to go!

"They lock the doors to get in line for diner promptly at 6:30."

Don't quote me, but I think these were my final words as I boarded my Univega for my trip back to the dormitory?

That was back in 1980, and for less than a month, I had been 18; however, I had only "logged-in" for recognition as an adult that is in the eyes of the court and the insurance adjusters for less than a month. My birthday, September 9th had been only 27 days earlier; and that is less than a month. That one may have been a little in my favor. I could still be expected to "bounce back."

I was the statistician's favorite friend. Or he was mine. The odds that I would emerge from my traumatically induced coma weren't listed among a coroner's prerequisites.

Dave Cole, the Idiot
Known now as David Cole.

From the experience that I have had with David, he has come a long way from the accident. He has a family that depends on him. He laughs at the world and what happens around him. Nothing seems to get him down. I love going to his house to see what crazy things he has done. One day, I went there and David and Gena were laughing over something he had done. They laughed so hard it took them awhile to tell me. David wanted to make some mashed potatoes and had grabbed the wrong bag. It ended up being oatmeal. He just thought there was something wrong with the potatoes! Instead of getting upset like most of us would, he laughed about it. They are one in a million to be around. Life is hard for them, but they don't let it get them down.

"Aunt Francis" Ritts
Gena's PCP
(Personal Care Provider)

Forgiveness for Joe

October 2, 1980! Wow, what an afternoon that was! So much twisted bicycle, so much broken headlight and shattered windshield, so much loss! That now, that was only the beginning. What did I lose? I lost my life; I lost my personality; I lost my future; I lost my strength; I lost the ability to feed myself, go to the bathroom, and speak. I lost more than I can ever write down. I lost my considerable potential as a boyfriend, a companion, a spouse.

What did you lose, Joe?

Did you lose your confidence? Did you lose the use of your driver's license? Did you lose your drive to live? Did you lose your future? How did you explain all this to people? What did you say? What did you do for transportation? How did you spend your Halloween, your Thanksgiving, your Christmas? Did you vote that November? Did you turn on the television and learn of John Lennon's murder first hand, or did you have to learn of it months later as you were coming out of a coma, unable to think, speak, or move?

What a contrast in our lives. Your thoughtless act peeled my future away from me like an onionskin. What happened to you because of it? Do you ever think of me? I have never heard from you, and I am curious.

Guess what? My own speed, my own velocity would need to have been nearly 200 M.P.H., or I would need to have weighed more than 800 pounds if I wanted to weigh -or to have been in the same weight class - as you, my adversary!

Now, I know why I was riding a bicycle. I've been told why I was where I was at that instant. I am not drafting another "Dear John" letter; it isn't just another letter to your "average Joe" out there on the streets, either.

Well, Joseph, and you know who you are, I don't have the appropriate credentials, I'm sure, to hear your confession, but I need to let you know something. I will not hold you accountable for your grievous error. I can only forgive you your instant of miscalculation!

I am that child of God who was christened with the pristine opportunity to conduct a symphony of sirens as syncopated by a single percussive downbeat, between those thousands of static pounds of errant automobile! That's you, and your actual weight, your dynamic mass at passing speeds against 40 pounds of bicycle, dynamic and already late for dinner.

I wasn't static, nor were you! Why you chose me to become involved in such a sticky mess, such an accidental, even incidental instant, that "nano" second of breadth, I'll never know! But the situation was handed to me without my consult or consent. I was faced with only one choice – to live or die – and I chose life.

That choice has culminated in far more than just this manuscript! In reworking my brain so that it could think, articulate and control my body, I began anew to build the man I was to become, but under new rules of engagement. I was given the opportunity to rework my social life, my spiritual life, and my intellectual life. I began to see the inner workings of society from the impoverished side, impoverished not by a loss of income, but by the loss of human connectedness and approval. I became a misfit due to the many circumstances forced upon me by the collision. However, Joe, I did not stop at that juncture. I kept making choices to live. To accomplish. To achieve. Every day has been a struggle to make it, but make it I have. I have a career, a wife, three children and a mortgage!

One moment of time nearly took my life. In the next moments of time, many people crowded around to save me. I owe so much to the first responders to my accident. They saved my life without pausing to inquire if it was something I wanted them to do. They just did it. I want my life to show them how glad I am that they were there. Not at first, of course. I was not conscious. And then, when I "woke up" and realized that who I was was gone, I got a little cranky. Then for months afterwards, much of therapy was a grind, with such slow progress that I forgot to be grateful. But from the time I could climb back on a bike, I have been ever so grateful for all of them

So, Joe, I would never have agreed to meet you like I did, but God has drawn from this disaster much good. I would never have met my beautiful wife, we would never have made so much love, and she would have never birthed Aberdine Gena-C, Malachi David, and Sariah Rose!

For this I am in debt to you!